101 BIGGEST MISTAKES

Nonprofits Make and
How You Can Avoid Them

101 BIGGEST MISTAKES

Nonprofits Make and How You Can Avoid Them

ANDREW OLSEN

Newport One Press

101 Biggest Mistakes
Nonprofits Make and How You Can Avoid Them

Published by Newport One Press

Copyright © 2019 by Andrew Olsen

ISBN (paperback): 9781642375695
eISBN: 9781642375701

Printed in the United States of America

"Failure isn't fatal, but failure to change might be."
—*John Wooden*

Introduction

NONPROFITS ARE SOME of the scrappiest organizations you'll ever experience. In many respects, they resemble start-ups. Think about it. Small groups (generally) of highly dedicated, focused believers coming together to achieve something greater than they could ever achieve on their own. They're often cash-strapped, moving faster than their infrastructures can keep up with, and frequently learning and adapting as quickly as they can. The majority of nonprofit staff are able to do so much good with so few resources. The general public has come to expect nonprofits to behave this way. But one thing I've noticed is that unlike the corporate sector, there is little in the way of generally accepted "best practices" across the nonprofit sector. This results in organizations that serially make mistakes—often resulting in detrimental impacts to their staff, their donors, their revenue, and ultimately to the achievement of their mission.

In *101 Biggest Mistakes Nonprofits Make and How You Can Avoid Them*, you'll hear directly from industry veterans who have over 300 years of combined experience inside nonprofit organizations and inside leading consulting firms serving nonprofits. They are experts in strategic planning, government relations, leadership, finance and administration, program development, marketing, and philanthropy.

Contrary to what the title might suggest, this book is NOT an admonishment of the nonprofit sector and those who make their career within it. Far from it. I know that one of the least-funded areas in the nonprofit sector is staff training and development. That is at the core of what brought me to envision this book, to assemble this group of expert contributors, and to bring this work to market. Everyone makes mistakes, whether you work in the nonprofit sector, the commercial sector, or anywhere in between. In the corporate sector there are entire industries designed to provide coaching and teaching at all levels of an organization, even customized to market niches. These industries help teach leaders how to improve and do their jobs at the highest possible levels. There are also plenty of works outlining best practices in strategy, design, staffing, leadership, management, finance, etc. Roadmaps, if you will, to help corporate executives, leaders, and individual contributors avoid costly mistakes and maximize impact for their customers and businesses. The same can't yet be said for the nonprofit sector.

In this book I've compiled the 101 biggest mistakes that cost nonprofits the most, and given you expert recommendations to help you avoid making these mistakes yourself.

101 Biggest Mistakes is a topic I began thinking about back in 2008 when I went to work inside a nonprofit and quickly realized that there were some foundational mistakes that the organization was making simply because we didn't know any better. It wasn't that we were actively trying to sabotage the organization or our own success—we just didn't know what we didn't know. We were a group of dedicated, well-intentioned people who, left to our own devices, screwed a lot of things up.

As I think back on that experience, what strikes me is that

this wasn't a small organization. Nor was it a cash-strapped charity. We were a large regional organization with an annual budget of more than $160 million, but we didn't budget for staff development or outside training. That just wasn't something we focused on. There was entrenched policy that we followed because "it had always been that way." After leaving this organization and spending the next 10 years consulting with over 500 other organizations, I came to realize that the same mistakes I had experienced in 2008 are made to one degree or another in a majority of nonprofit organizations.

My goal is not to suggest that you shouldn't make mistakes. Mistakes are a normal part of life, and from time to time we'll all make them. Rather, my goal in writing this is to help you proactively identify some of the costliest mistakes made in our sector, and to give you the insights and the tools you need so you don't make these same mistakes. Go make other mistakes, for sure. Learn from those and improve. Don't waste your time and energy repeating mistakes that you can avoid by reading this.

Each chapter will address specific mistakes, nonprofit best practices, and other industry tips from across our sector. You'll get real-world examples of how I and my other contributors have made our own share of these mistakes, mistakes we've observed others in the industry make, what we've learned from them, and what we'd do differently today. More importantly, we share what YOU can do differently today to avoid making the same mistakes we did. Even addressing 101 mistakes we've seen in the nonprofit sector, I hope this book is received not as an exhaustive list, but as a continuation of dialogue that perhaps you yourself are having about how the nonprofit space can be most effective. To that end, I'd welcome the chance to hear your feedback on how these mistakes resonate with you, other mistakes you regularly see, and especially, more ideas for how nonprofit practitioners like you and I can collectively continue improving.

And if you find your organization repeating one or more of these mistakes, and are looking for help, I hope you'll reach out to me. I'd love to help you get connected with some of the people who've most helped me.

Don't hesitate to share your thoughts on this topic with your own community on social media. You can add your voice to the conversation by using the hashtag **#101NonprofitMistakes**.

Thank you for your work in making the nonprofit sector the best it can be!

Sincerely,

Andrew Olsen, CFRE
aolsen@newportone.com
www.linkedin.com/in/andrewolsen
www.andrewolsen.net

Acknowledgments

THIS BOOK IS a compilation of insights and perspectives from more than two dozen industry leaders and experts, many of whom have served inside nonprofits and as consultants to nonprofits. Together, we have more than 300 years of combined of experience in nonprofit leadership and development.

I am so grateful for this tribe and every individual in it. This group of amazing friends who are thoughtful, selfless, and committed industry experts. You can learn more about each contributor by reading their biographies at the end of the book.

It's also important to acknowledge a few other key contributors to this effort. I specifically want to thank:

Natalie Parker, our good friend, business partner, and the talented Creative Director who designed the cover art and all other marketing materials for this book.

Jill Lopez, our skilled editor who helped make my first book, *Rainmaking: The Fundraiser's Guide to Landing Big Gifts*, an incredibly successful manual for major gift fundraising—and who jumped at the chance to help us improve this book as well.

Special Acknowledgments

To Deborah: Thank you for always believing in me, for being a great partner and mom to our three girls. And thanks for putting up with the late nights and weekends of writing and editing. Love you!

To Isabelle, Elisabeth, and Eilidh: You three are my inspiration. I do this work and write books like this to help others create a more just and hopeful world for all of you.

Contents

STRATEGY & PLANNING

CONSTITUENT ENGAGEMENT

SPECIAL BONUS CONTENT

ORGANIZATIONAL LEADERSHIP & MANAGEMENT

"Leading people is the most challenging and, therefore, the most gratifying undertaking of all human endeavors."

—*Jocko Willink*

"Failing organizations are usually over-managed and under-led."

—*Warren Bennis*

A S A NONPROFIT consultant I am often called upon by Executive Directors or Board Members to help improve their organization's fundraising results. Usually the conversation begins with a call from an ED or Board Member and a discussion about their fundraising trends over the last few years. They tell me that they're trying "a lot of different things" but that their results just aren't the same as they used to be. They might have an idea of where the declines are coming from, or they might just have a gut feeling about the problem.

In a majority of these consultations, what I (and others in the field) tend to find is that fundraising results are a symptom of a different problem. They're not the real problem. Often, the actual problem is a breakdown in leadership. When leaders are willing to be self-reflective and to change things in the way that they lead and engage with their people, we can often successfully help them improve fundraising results. However, when a leader is unwilling to change, usually no amount of new fundraising strategy can help improve an organization. This is why I want to first focus on mistakes in leadership rather than strategy or fundraising techniques.

MISTAKE #1

Not Valuing Excellence

By Andrew Olsen, CFRE

A better way to say this might be that you accept mediocrity. And this mindset is closely related to embracing a poverty mindset, I believe. In fact, I suspect they both stem from a belief that you or your organization are not truly deserving of greatness.

I don't believe that's true. And let me tell you why it's a dangerous belief.

When this mindset takes hold of a leader, it begins to permeate every level of an organization and becomes part of the organization's DNA. It leads to people putting out only minimum effort, and regularly accepting average results, outcomes, and effort.

If you accept mediocrity it impacts who and how your organization hires staff, how you set goals and strategic plans (in fact, if you don't value excellence, you're significantly more likely to skip this step and not actually develop strategic plans for your organization or team), regularly deliver work behind schedule, show up late to meetings, and disregard both program and fundraising failures.

I once worked with an organization that didn't value excellence. It became clear when we looked at their fundraising results and saw that for each of the three previous years they had set high fundraising goals and not reached them in any of the three years. I asked what their leadership team thought about that, and how it might impact them and their organization. The response I got was shocking. The Director of Development said, "Nothing really happens. They just take money out of reserves to close the gap, and then we move on to next year."

Here are two ways you can begin to overcome this dangerous mistake:

1. **Increase organizational accountability:** Begin to set clear expectations and hold people accountable for meeting them. Start with yourself and your senior leadership team, and speak publicly to your organization about this. The more transparent you are, the more your organization will feel that it's safe to talk about failure in a way that helps everyone learn and improve. When someone misses a target, don't seek to punish them, but to understand why they missed it, how they respond, and what they plan to do to correct and move forward.

2. **Focus on more and better training:** Training is so often overlooked in our industry, and it is critical to overcoming this mistake. This starts with your onboarding process. "Trial by fire" doesn't work well. If you onboard well and provide training early and often that includes helping your team understand organizational expectations around failure and

resilience, and around personal accountability for performance, you'll help create a culture that values excellence over mediocrity.

MISTAKES #2-#9

Not Being Candidate-Centric in Your Recruitment & Talent Management

By Jeff Rothman

The long-term success of the nonprofit sector depends heavily on its ability to attract and retain first-class talent. According to the Society for Human Resource Management, nearly 60 % of human resource professionals over the next decade see their greatest challenge to be in recruiting, retaining, and training the next generation of organizational leadership.

Outstanding talent is a limited commodity, especially in today's economic environment. Nonprofits are competing directly with the private sector for top talent. The data shows that for-profit enterprises are more likely to invest in achieving success in talent acquisition and talent management. Nonprofits that fail to improve their talent practices face the following unfavorable outcomes:

- Increased recruiting and recruiting costs
- Lost productivity
- Lost fundraising revenue while a frontline fundraising position is vacant

- Lower morale
- Increased turnover
- Decreased collaboration and teamwork
- Inability to scale up to meet increased fundraising needs
- Higher premiums for unemployment compensation

A nonprofit cannot achieve overall sustainability until it first achieves talent sustainability.

It's easier to appreciate the importance of talent acquisition and talent management to the long-term success of your organization if you consider how the dynamics of today's talent market impact your approach to them.

The Talent Market

The market for top talent is always competitive, but today's historically low rate of unemployment makes it even more so. As of September 2018, our country's unemployment rate had fallen to 3.6%. Drill down a little deeper and you'll find that it's only 2% among the professional and managerial sector![1]

Companies and nonprofits of all shapes and sizes are finding it more difficult to attract and retain high-impact talent. Unfortunately, not many are adapting their hiring and talent management practices in response to the challenge. They continue to utilize a talent surplus strategy when a talent surplus doesn't exist.

Don't make the mistake of thinking that the talent shortage is only temporary. Demographic data clearly points to an ongoing challenge. Addressing this reality may require a fundamental rethinking of your approach to talent acquisition and talent management. It would be a mistake to pretend you can get by without making changes. Do you really want to take that risk with your organization's long-term sustainability? It's vital that your talent practices are aligned to these market forces.

Candidate-Centric Talent Practices

The talent shortage requires that you adopt a candidate-centric approach to your talent practices. This means increasing your focus on the value proposition you present to prospective and current employees. It means that what you can do to advance their career interests and aspirations should be a foundational element of your talent practices, and in the rest of this chapter, you'll get some tips on how to get there.

If you've already adopted a donor-centric approach to fundraising, this shouldn't be an unfamiliar concept. You appreciate the importance of connecting with your donors on an emotional level and creating meaningful relationships with them. You can take the same approach with your talent practices by putting as much effort into acquiring and retaining high-impact talent as you do with high-value donors.

Yet most nonprofits are not responding to this challenge. Here are a some of the ways in which they're getting left behind.

MISTAKE #2

Relying Too Heavily on Active Job Seekers

It's useful to think of the talent pool as containing two basic kinds of candidates: active job seekers and passive job seekers. Active job seekers are the ones who are scouring job boards, fielding calls from recruiters, and sharing their résumé with anyone willing to take a look. Some might be looking for good reasons—perhaps they are underperforming and in danger of losing their jobs. Most studies show that they comprise a minority of the overall talent pool but are the easiest to attract. You shouldn't rely on them as your primary source of candidates.

Passive job seekers are the people who are not actively looking but are open to making a change if someone taps them on the shoulder with the right opportunity. Most experts agree they represent a majority of the talent pool and are more likely to be solid performers who are progressing well in their careers and are relatively happy where they are. With unemployment at historic lows and more job openings than highly qualified, active job seekers, passive candidates can be costly to ignore. Recruiting them requires a fundamentally different approach than you'd use with active job seekers.

Here are three suggestions on how to address that challenge:

- Network, network, network: Join professional organizations and become active in them. Attend meetings, speak at conferences, and get to know your colleagues. Ask around to see if they know any rising stars who might just be ready to take their next step, even when you don't have an opening.

- Get active on social media: As we'll cover in the next item, don't rely too much on job postings. While they can be effective with active job seekers, they don't work as well with passive candidates. Leverage social media! Promote your openings on Facebook and Twitter, in your LinkedIn news feed, on your blog, etc. Send messages to people in your network promoting the opportunity and asking for referrals.

If you have in-house social media expertise in your organization, get their help!

- Consider engaging a headhunter: Attracting passive job seekers requires a unique set of skills that are usually outside the expertise of your in-house HR team. This kind of recruiting requires selling skills, and that's where engaging a professional, experienced recruiter who specializes in your industry can be a good investment. Make sure you find one who will proactively reach out to the right candidates and effectively represent your value proposition. They'll increase the size and quality of your talent pipeline for mission-critical positions.

Takeaway: With a multi-prong approach to recruiting, you'll enhance the size and quality of your talent pool and increase your chance of making a better-quality hire.

MISTAKE #3

Absence of a Compelling Employer Brand

A nonprofit's brand describes your value proposition with stakeholders and the public. Your employer brand describes your reputation as a place to work. It encompasses your organization's mission, values, culture, and personality. Most importantly, it's what makes your organization a great place to work. A clearly defined, compelling employer brand will make your organization a magnet for top talent and should permeate your entire hiring process. Everyone involved in the interviewing process must understand the brand, embrace it, and be able to showcase it with candidates. It'll also pay for itself—there's a LinkedIn study showing that companies with strong employer brands have half the cost per hire and a quarter less turnover than companies with poor or no employer brands.[2]

A strong employer brand:

- Makes a clear statement of your organization's values, the importance of your mission, and your commitment to the development and well-being of your team.

- Avoids hyperbole or overly generalized phrases like "our employees are our most important asset."

- Demonstrates a clear commitment to professional development (top performers are attracted to organizations that are sincerely commitment to their long-term career growth).

- Lets them know you recognize that the employee/employer relationship is a two-way street.

Takeaway: Failing to invest in the creation of a strong employer brand will make it harder to attract and retain outstanding talent. If you look at it as an essential investment in your organization's future, you'll be better positioned to attract the best and the brightest at a lower cost for years to come!

MISTAKE #4

You Confuse Job Postings with Job Descriptions

Let's make one thing clear right up front: job descriptions are NOT the same as job postings. They are NOT interchangeable. Here's why.

Job descriptions are internal documents that capture the responsibilities, authority, complexity, judgment, and working conditions associated with a job. They are not intended to create excitement and motivate high-quality talent to apply or learn more. They represent what you, the employer, need from the person in that role. They are exceptionally boring and definitely not candidate-centric.

Job postings are advertisements meant to attract qualified job applicants. They are candidate-centric because they:

- Connect with your audience by answering the question: "What's in it for me?"
- Convey excitement about your organization and the impact they'll make
- Create interest and attract better talent
- Address how you will help the candidate advance professionally and make a difference in your organization's success

How to Make your Job Ads Candidate-Centric

Not surprisingly, candidate-centric job ads incorporate many of the same principles as donor-centric fundraising. For example, it's important to:

- **Know your audience:** Put yourself in the shoes of the people you want to attract, and understand what might motivate them to work for your organization. Be able to help them answer the question: "What's in it for me?"

- **Be purpose driven:** For a purpose-driven candidate, doing work that's meaningful is at least as—if not more—important than money or advancement. Make sure they know what impact their success will have on your organization.

- **Create compelling copy:** Give the same attention to writing job ads as you would fundraising copy. Make sure they grab the reader's attention, inspire them about your mission, and convey how your culture makes your organization a great place to work. Repurposing a position description as a job ad does little to create a sense of excitement. Avoid doing it at all costs.

- **Focus on professional advancement:** Be prepared to talk about how working for you in this role will be a benefit to them professionally.

Here's an example of a compelling candidate-centric job ad with strong brand identity:

Director of Integrated Direct Response Fundraising

Work. Serve. Thrive.
Imagine a place where your talent can make a meaningful difference in people's lives. Working at xxxxxxxx is a uniquely rewarding experience in which our employees

work together as vital parts of a much larger mission. We are innovative, mission-focused, diverse, collaborative, values-driven, and focused on results.

We are a national nonprofit organization and the nation's leading xxxxxxx charity. Located in the heart of downtown xxxxxx, our mission is to xxxxxxxxx through a nationwide network of xxxxxxxxxx, and engage our country in the fight to xxxxxxxx.

What You'll Do

We need an experienced direct response fundraiser to lead a team of eager, talented, up-and-coming fundraising professionals who want to learn and grow, and keep your crack team focused and humming along.

Here are a few examples of the things you'll be doing on any given day:

- Oversee the many details involved in developing and launching integrated, multi-channel campaigns.

- Distill direct mail, email, web, advertising, and social campaign results into the important lessons that could change how a campaign performs.

- Draft the best fundraising and advocacy direct mail, email, social, and web copy in the business.

- Manage your teams up and down to make sure they perform at a high level and have opportunities to continually develop their skills.

- Come up with about 14 new ideas for petitions, quizzes, fundraising, ads, video, implanted chips, Google Glass, or some other new technology or strategy that's rolling around your giant brain.

- *Do your part to help us run smoothly and pitch in wherever you can to advance our mission.*

And then there's you . . .

- *You've benched your share of online advocacy and fundraising programs for nonprofits.*
- *Have 5+ years of fundraising experience under your belt.*
- *Want to be the best. You thrive in a fast-paced environment with tight deadlines, and are always thinking two steps ahead of everyone else.*
- *Not afraid to speak your mind—you continually suggest new ideas or ways to improve on old ideas or processes.*
- *Detail oriented! There are a lot of details. You are the person who finds the typo no one else sees.*
- *Wildly curious about what's next in the world-changing business, and game to help us get there.*
- *A true believer. You want to change the world. You are hopeful and helpful and ready to keep your boots on the ground and eye on the prize.*

Of course . . .

We are an equal opportunity employer and all applicants will be considered. We are committed to a diverse and inclusive workplace where we learn and work together to change the world. We are strengthened by our staff's diversity, including race and ethnicity, social class, national origin, culture, sexual orientation, gender identity and expression, language, and so much more. We strongly *encourage folks from underrepresented backgrounds to apply. We love, respect, and welcome you!*

Takeaway: When you write job ads, think like a fundraiser. Create a sense of excitement and accurately convey a sense of your employer brand. You'll not only attract better candidates, but in the long run you'll also improve your employer brand and continue to attract higher-quality candidates.

MISTAKE #5

Falling Victim to Rockstar Syndrome

You can't complain about "talent shortages" when you stubbornly wait for the perfect candidate. Are all of the items on your long list of "essential requirements" really essential? Rockstars are in high demand and the market for them is highly competitive. They know they're a scarce commodity and can afford to be pickier about who they work for; they also tend to hold out for more money. Once you hire them, they want to be constantly challenged and learning, and if they aren't, they'll soon be looking for their next job (which they'll find quickly) and leaving you in the lurch.

Rockstars are not essential for every position, so why do some hiring managers seem fixated on them? The primary reason is risk avoidance—a concern that a poor hire will reflect poorly on them. Recruiting is an art and a science. It's impossible to expect every hire to turn into a rockstar, and probably not necessary. Realistically evaluate where they're essential and worth waiting for. Otherwise, focus on hiring people who have the potential to achieve rockstar status, and invest in their professional development. You'll fill positions more quickly, at a lower cost, and be able to invest more time providing the leadership and mentoring your team needs to contribute at a high level.

Takeaway: Rigidly holding out for rockstars will lengthen your recruiting process and cost you money. Be open to people who don't match up with every "requirement," but have the smarts and pluck to outperform that rockstar you think you can't do without. If you're realistic, you'll find your next rockstar, who—with a little bit of training and a reasonable amount of support—will exceed expectations.

MISTAKE #6

Providing a Poor Candidate Experience

Candidate experience has to do with how job seekers perceive and react to the interactions they have with you at every stage of your hiring process. Poor candidate experience will frustrate job seekers and negatively impact their interest in your organization, no matter how passionate they are about your mission. People who are more anxious to find a new job (active job seekers) might show more patience with your disfunction in this area, but those who can afford to be more selective will go elsewhere.

To improve candidate experience, take a hard look at your hiring process and try to avoid the following pitfalls:

- Long and redundant application process: After uploading their résumé, do you ask applicants to manually enter the same info on another form?

- Being inconsiderate of their time: Treat candidates like any other valued visitor to your office. Don't schedule their interview at 9 am, make them fight rush hour traffic to get there on time, then make them wait for 30 minutes before ushering them into your office.

- Asking irrelevant questions: The best candidates will expect you to ask insightful questions that demonstrate a clear vision for their role and what you'll be expecting them to accomplish. Otherwise, they'll assume you didn't put much time into preparing for the interview.

- Leaving them hanging: Failing to follow up within 48 hours after an interview, then regularly at a good cadence, sends a message about your organization's culture that can be damaging.

- Low-balling an offer: Candidates will think you don't fairly value their skills and experience. Even if they accept, you'll be starting off on the wrong foot and make it more likely they'll leave as soon as someone offers them more money.

Takeaway: Outstanding talent is tough to find. Poor candidate experience will cause the best candidates to question how well-managed your organization really is, and make it more likely they'll withdraw from your hiring process, leaving you with fewer, less-desirable choices.

MISTAKE #7
An Inefficient Hiring Process

This might be one of the most overlooked, least understood, and most problematic recruiting challenges. As with rockstar syndrome, it's symptomatic of an imbalance between how you view the risk of a bad hire versus the potential cost of losing outstanding talent. Putting too much emphasis on avoiding mistakes can lead to a hiring process that involves too many steps, too many people, and drags on incessantly. There are many reasons why this can be extremely problematic:

- The best talent will drop out, causing a decline in the quality of the people you hire: A slow, methodical interviewing process won't necessarily result in better hires—it may actually do the opposite. When a highly qualified passive job seeker decides to interview for your opening, it's likely they're also looking at other opportunities. Someone will snap them up quickly, thereby diminishing the quality of your talent pool.

- Vacancies remain open for longer than necessary: The economic damage caused by having a fundraising position vacant longer than necessary results in lost revenue and productivity that will be difficult to recover.

- Salary costs will increase: Top performers are likely to receive multiple offers, especially in a tight labor market. If you offer them a position before other organizations have had a chance to bid on them, you're more likely to hire them with little or no haggling.

- You'll become known as a slow decision-maker: Your hiring process provides a window into your corporate culture. If it drags on for weeks, you will appear indecisive, bureaucratic, and risk-averse. Top performers tend to be fast and accurate decision-makers and are more likely to gravitate toward companies that demonstrate the same.

- Candidates will lose interest: Keeping candidates engaged and excited about your opportunity is vital to your recruiting success because their level of interest will inevitably decrease as your hiring process drags on, making it more likely they'll wind up working elsewhere. It also increases the possibility that they'll receive a promotion, raise, or counteroffer from their current employer and withdraw their candidacy.

Takeaway: A slow and cumbersome hiring process is costly. It'll turn off top talent, cause them to withdraw from your interviewing process, and result in you repeatedly starting searches over from scratch.

MISTAKE #8

Failing to Address Compensation Early in the Process

Have you ever had a candidate turn down your offer because the salary was way less than they expected? Wouldn't it have been better to avoid wasting time and resources on someone who probably wasn't going to accept your offer in the first place?

Don't wait until the end of the interviewing process to have a frank discussion about money. The first time to have that conversation is at the completion of your initial qualifying interview, prior to deciding whether you want to move the candidate to the next step. Don't be bashful about reconfirming your understanding of their compensation needs at each stage of the interviewing process.

Here's an example of how to open that dialog:

> "Before we go any further, let's make sure we're at least in the right ballpark with money. If we decide this is the right job for you, what do you think is a fair salary?

If the amount they give you is outside your range, you don't have to accept it at face value. The candidate may not have an accurate feel for their market value and/or doesn't want to make the mistake of asking for too little and leave money on the table. Here's how you can follow up:

> "So, if we make it all the way to the offer stage and you are confident this is the right opportunity for you, are you saying you won't accept any offer below that amount?"

Perhaps the candidate will show some flexibility. If not, it's time to move on. But if the two of you are close, it may be worth going to the next step.

And don't forget about benefits. You may be able to compensate for a less-attractive salary by offering more generous benefits (lower out-of-pocket costs for medical insurance, higher retirement plan match, more paid time off, free parking, etc.). Make sure you get candidates to evaluate your offer based on the total compensation package, not just salary.

MISTAKE #9

Avoiding a Discussion About Counteroffers

You've finally found the perfect candidate and offered them the position. Then, even though they've confidently told you they love your opportunity and are committed to leaving the other organization, they decide to turn you down and stay put. While it's impossible to completely avoid this situation, it's important to start assessing the risk during the first interview.

First, make sure you clearly understand why the candidate wants to make a change. If money is high on their list, proceed with caution. In those situations, the easiest way for an employer to keep someone from leaving is by increasing their salary. If they mention lack of advancement opportunities, a poor relationship with their boss, or dissatisfaction with the organizational culture, you're in a much stronger position because those issues are more difficult to fix quickly, and candidates will be less likely to react positively to a counteroffer. Listen carefully for any indication that they may not be serious about making a change. As with compensation, address this during the first interview and revisit it at each stage of the interviewing process.

Here are a few suggestions on how to initiate the conversation:

"Have you talked with your boss about those issues? Have they been addressed to your satisfaction?" (If the candidate hasn't discussed their concerns with a supervisor, it could be a red flag. Consider suggesting that they have that conversation before you go any further.)

"Besides more money, is there anything they can do to keep you from leaving?"

"What if they offer you more money? How much would it take?"

"Have you given any thought to how your boss might react when you tell them you're resigning?"

"Have you thought about how you'd react to a counter-offer?"

Takeaway: Don't wait until late in the interviewing process to assess the risk of a counteroffer. Do it early and often. You'll minimize the risk of investing valuable time with candidates who will ultimately disappoint, putting you in the position of starting your search over from scratch.

TALENT MANAGEMENT /TALENT SUSTAINABILITY

What is Talent Management and Why Does it Matter?

Talent management is an ongoing, organizational process that optimizes a nonprofit's ability to attract, develop, and retain its most important employees. An effective talent management strategy protects your investment in key employees, makes it easier to recruit new ones, reduces turnover, will make you more effective at competing with the private sector for skilled, in-demand talent, and enables you to scale more easily. In short, it is vital to your long-term success and sustainability.

High-achieving employees are always challenging to recruit and retain, but even more so in today's competitive talent market. The demand for talent in the private sector will make it increasingly difficult for nonprofits to hold onto their best employees—top performers are always in demand and often have multiple career options available to them.

Most nonprofits aren't investing in developing a retention strategy.[3] The longer you wait, the more expensive it'll be to fix and the longer it'll take. Furthermore, doing nothing will inevitably impact retention, morale, individual performance, recruiting costs, and your ability to develop future leaders. While these may not appear as a line item on your 990, they'll eventually impact your long-term financial health.

Putting talent management front-and-center will require the full commitment of everyone in your organization, from senior leadership and your board down to front-line managers.

Here's a list of 6 steps you can take to build an effective talent management infrastructure and create a more sustainable and stable workforce. If you're doing some of them already, even on an ad-hoc basis, you're off to a good start. Keep adding more pieces and look for ways to turn them into standardized, organization-wide policies and procedures. If you're behind the curve, start small. Pick the most attainable, impactful items and start building momentum.

6 Ways to Improve Your Talent Management Practices

1. Onboard More Effectively

A comprehensive onboarding program offers a way for new hires to become fully immersed in your culture and creates a sense of belonging. It enables new hires to become productive more quickly, reduces retention, increases performance, and improves your employer brand.

Onboarding is much more than new hire orientation. It's a deliberate strategy that accelerate a new hire's understanding of high-level strategies, current projects, and organizational culture. It also helps them start off on the right foot with developing effective working relationships with their colleagues. Onboarding doesn't have to be time- or resource-intensive, but it's important to make it a priority that doesn't get crowded out by other activities or daily crises.

Have a plan for making sure new employees get the tools they need to hit the ground running. Introduce them to their colleagues, make sure the technology they need is ready to go on day one, and begin assimilating them into your organizational climate and culture right away.

You can find great onboarding roadmaps and checklists on Glassdoor.com.

2. Create a Performance-Driven Culture

Embracing and nurturing a performance-based culture has been shown to be a powerful driver of success. It will benefit both your organization and its employees, and from a talent management standpoint, help you attract and retain your most effective employees—the ones who strive to be at the top of their profession. Here are a some steps you can take to get started:

- Clearly define organizational and individual goals: Let your team know what you expect from them and make sure they understand what it'll take to get there.

- Identify productive behaviors: Spell out what behaviors get rewarded, which are unacceptable, and provide positive reinforcement whenever possible.

- Connect to the big picture: Make sure your team knows how their performance is tied to the overall success of your organization.

- Discourage micro-management: Your team will perform at a higher level when managers set clear, challenging goals, give them the freedom to decide and act, and treat mistakes as learning opportunities instead of failures.

- Celebrate success: Find meaningful ways to acknowledge your team's hard work. It'll boost morale and keep them motivated.

3. Pay Competitively

The belief that nonprofits can hire highly talented people at a discount because of their affinity with your mission isn't a viable, long-term strategy. To compete effectively with the private sector for the best talent, your employees need to be compensated competitively and know that a medical emergency will not bankrupt them, that their children can see a doctor when they need to, and are able to save for retirement through a competitive 401(k)/403(b) matching program. Even if you can't pay private sector salaries, top-notch benefits have a monetary value and can level the playing field.

4. Give Consistent and Constructive Feedback

A former mentor of mine used to say that feedback is the breakfast of champions. Top performers will make mistakes, and when they do, they like specific, constructive feedback that enables them to improve. If delivered effectively—not as criticism, but as a genuine attempt to help improve performance—they will respond favorably, be motivated to make sure they don't make the same mistake again, and reward you with higher levels of performance.

5. Make Professional Development a High Priority

Professional development is one of the most important benefits you can offer. Make it a top priority to work collaboratively with each member of your team to create a meaningful personal development plan. Your team will be happier, more motivated, and perform at a higher level if you demonstrate a strong committed to supporting their career progression. They'll see that working for your organization can be a career builder, not a career detour. You'll have higher rates of retention and increase your capacity for attracting high-impact talent.

It shouldn't be surprising that the most ambitious, talented people will be more interested in working for your organization if you provide them a realistic career path. Ensure that employees at all levels understand what it takes to get to their next step, and demonstrate that promoting from within is an organizational priority.

6. Offer Flexible Work Arrangements

Flexible work arrangements (FWAs), especially the ability to work remotely, have become increasingly common across all sectors of the economy. Studies show that they encourage work/life balance, resulting in higher productivity, greater employee engagement, and increased retention.[4] FWAs are particularly important to millennials, on par with financial rewards.[5] If you haven't developed at least an informal FWA policy, don't hesitate to get started.

The primary reason FWAs fail is due to lack of communication. People who work off-site should feel like they're no different from someone in an office down the hall. It's vital that you set clear expectations on this for everyone in your organization. Supervisors should schedule regular calls with their off-site employees and make it clear to their team that they'll be expected to do the same. Under no circumstances should anyone ever let other priorities crowd out those important communications. If your organization's leadership doesn't make it an important, non-negotiable priority, nobody else will either.

Video conferencing can be a particularly effective tool for this. Encourage its use and make sure everyone in your organization is trained to use it effectively. Lastly, recognize and reward those who communicate effectively with people who work off-site.

For more information on dealing with remote employees, The National Council of Nonprofits has published a white paper and other resources that might be helpful to you.

A Last Word

Happy, challenged employees who feel like they are making a purposeful contribution to the success of your organization and are appreciated for their contributions will be happier, more productive, less motivated to test the market and see what another organization can offer them, and will engender the kind of positive culture you need to thrive.

For more information on the state of talent practices in the nonprofit sector, the consulting firm Nonprofit HR publishes their Annual Employment Practices Survey which you'll find at www.nonprofithr.com.

[1] Bureau of Labor Statistics, Labor Force Statistics from the Current Population Survey, October 5, 2018; https://www.bls.gov/web/empsit/cpseea30.htm

2 The Ultimate List of Employer Brand Statistics, LinkedIn Talent
   Solutions;   https://business.linkedin.com/content/dam/business/
   talent-solutions/global/en_us/c/pdfs/ultimate-list-of-employer-
   brand-stats.pdf

3 Nonprofit HR 2017 Nonprofit Employment Practices Survey

4 Gaskell, A. (2016, January 15). Why A Flexible Worker Is A Happy
   And Productive Worker. Forbes.

5 Millennials at Work; Reshaping the Workforce. A study by Price
   Waterhouse Coopers, 2011.

MISTAKE #10

Recruiting to Minimize Cost instead of Maximize Talent

By Andrew Olsen, CFRE

Have you ever been in a conversation with a nonprofit executive and heard something like this? "We're considering two candidates right now. One has all of the qualifications we're looking for. She'd be a great addition to our team, and we're excited she's interested in us. But the other is so much cheaper—I think we can get him for $20,000 less. He's not ideal, but we can save money. We're going to make him an offer."

Our sector has an addiction to anything that is free, discounted, or cheap. Sometimes free, cheap, and discounted are valuable. But when it comes to hiring and finding the right talent, there's so much risk in hiring to minimize cost instead of maximize talent.

The old adage *you get what you pay for* is still true today—and it is painfully accurate when it comes to staffing.

I'm not suggesting you should always look to pay a premium for every staff position you hire. BUT . . . in critical roles like major gifts, prospect research, and program management, you shouldn't be as focused on saving money on your hire as you are on getting the candidate who can be most effective and successful for your organization.

When you recruit to meet an expense goal, it's likely that the person you hire will never live up to your list of wants and wishes. You'll be unhappy. Your board might be unhappy. And your new employee will be unhappy because she'll feel the tension of not living up to some unrealistic expectations you have—while at the same time feeling like those expectations may be well beyond what is realistic for the compensation she's receiving. This will lead to quick turnover in your organization, and you'll ultimately end up paying significantly more in additional recruitment, training, and lost opportunity.

MISTAKE #11

Creating Unrealistic Candidate Profiles

By Andrew Olsen, CFRE

We've all seen nonprofits post incredibly unrealistic candidate profiles before. They look something like this:

Development Associate Wanted: XYZ Nonprofit is in search of a great Development Associate to support our *critical mission. The ideal candidate will have 3+ years of progressive experience inside a similar nonprofit, strong Raiser's Edge experience, experience managing special events and successfully securing corporate and foundation grants. Candidate should also have verifiable track record of securing major gifts. CFRE preferred. Salary range is $38,000-$45,000.*

This organization might as well be searching for a purple unicorn!

There's so much wrong with a candidate profile like this. Unfortunately, profiles like this are so common in the nonprofit sector. You're looking for a Development Associate. By definition, this is a JUNIOR-level position. Yet you expect that in three years of work experience, this person will have amassed all this experience and expertise, AND that with all that experience and expertise, this person is still looking for a job that pays an entry-level wage. That's an incredibly unrealistic set of expectations.

In reality, what you actually want and need (likely) is a junior-level Director of Development. But because you're afraid of taking on the expense of a more senior role, you structure the position as an associate role because there's less financial risk for your organization. Unfortunately, while you changed the compensation of the position, you haven't changed your experience expectations of the role. This leads to a misalignment between your expectations and the candidates from which you're selecting. And this creates a friction that most organizations and employees can't overcome—even if you find a candidate you think is great and he accepts your offer.

Before you set out to recruit for a new position, carefully consider the essential experience needed, then do your research on what the appropriate title and compensation are for the role. This way, you're much more likely to attract the right talent at the right level and pay grade, and not start out the organizational relationship on the wrong foot.

MISTAKE #12

Not Investing to Develop Your Talent

By Andrew Olsen, CFRE

It saddens me to see the lack of talent development in the nonprofit sector. In fact, Bridgespan Group has studied this at length over multiple years and their findings are sobering. Their research consistently concludes that "Succession planning is the No. 1 organizational concern of US nonprofits, but they are failing to develop their most promising pool of talent: homegrown leaders."[1]

This unfortunately often begins during the hiring process when goals for the position are established. So often one of the top goals for nonprofit hiring managers is "getting a great deal" on the new employee. That is, finding a candidate who will agree to work for peanuts so that you can keep your salary cost line as low as possible. After all, headcount impacts cost ratios, and cost ratios impact charity watchdog ratings. It's a vicious circle, and a terrible approach to hiring. It results in more unnecessary costs to nonprofits than any other single decision that a nonprofit leader can make.

Think about it. You set about to hire the cheapest candidate possible. You invest to train that person, then turn them loose in your organization. If they aren't entirely unqualified for the role you've put them in, they're likely only halfway focused on your goals because they're spending the other 50% of their time looking for a job that pays more! This is likely one of the key reasons that the average tenure of a nonprofit development employee is less than two years.

At many nonprofits, once staff are hired there are few—if any—ongoing investments made in training or other talent development efforts. I met with one Development Officer who nearly broke down in tears when I asked about her ongoing professional development. Through her teary eyes she remarked, "I don't get any training. If I want to go to a conference or workshop to learn how to do my job better I have to pay for it myself."

Here are 5 ways to be sure you're investing in the talent in your organization (and <u>most</u> **of them will cost nothing but your time):**

1. Create an individual contributor development plan for each of your employees that specifically identifies their greatest strengths and how to maximize them, as well as key learning and development opportunities for the employee, and your plan to help them grow in those areas.

2. Make personal development a regular conversation topic with your entire staff, not just your few direct reports.

3. Prioritize staff training and development by setting aside both time and money for each individual on your team to support their training and learning needs.

4. Show your team that you value continued learning by investing in it yourself and sharing what you learn (and how it can apply to them) with your entire team.

5. Coach your people in the moment so they can quickly identify and correct any problems.

[1] Landles-Cobb, L.Landles-Cobb, L., Kramer, K., & Smith Milway, K. (2015, October 22). The Nonprofit Leadership Development Deficit. Retrieved from https://ssir.org/articles/entry/the_non profit_leadership_development_deficit

MISTAKE #13

Not Investing in Leaders

By Adam Morgan

Have you ever seen an organization with a great mission, something that should have all the support in the world, but they never get the chance to live up to their aspirations? Or even worse, they must close their doors after only a few short years without having accomplished much? Conversely, have you ever seen an organization with a mediocre message and programs but is all over the news and is raising more and more money every year? *The difference is leadership.*

Often, in the former case, the organization's leadership lacks either the ability or the willingness to look critically at what the organization needs and to make change when necessary. Sometimes it's their volunteer leadership that struggles, sometimes it's their paid leadership, and sometimes it's both.

So much of the success of an organization revolves around its leadership. Three of the most important qualities of truly great leaders are: knowing their own limitations, developing their emotional IQ, and understanding the importance and effectiveness of positive reinforcement.

To know one's limitations means to know your own strengths and weaknesses. It also means understanding that there will be times when you may not have all the answers, or all the knowledge needed to make a decision, and that is ok. You are a leader to figure those things out, so it's ok to say to someone, "You know what, that's a great question and I don't have all the information to give you the best answer right now. Let me think on it and do some research and get back to you." People appreciate that there are complex answers even to seemingly simple questions. Leaders who don't do this risk pushing people away and developing a reputation as someone who is unapproachable or unwilling to share information.

I once worked with an Executive Director who, while well-meaning, would not admit to not knowing something. It was to the point that he would make up answers and then blame others for screw-ups that would happen based on his mis-information. In a four-year period this organization saw a 50% reduction in staff size, due partially to declining revenue, but also because people just didn't want to work in an environment like this.

Developing your emotional intelligence, or EQ, is critical for effective leadership. The concept of emotional intelligence isn't new to the business world, but it has gained much more popularity and discussion since the turn of the century. Even so, many of us may not fully understand the importance of developing a high EQ. unlike your IQ, your EQ can be earned and increased through practice. To put it in perspective, according to Dr. Travis Bradberry and Dr. Jean Greaves in their book, *Emotional Intelligence 2.0*, only 36% of people, out of a 500,000-person study, were able to accurately identify their emotions as they happened (Bradberry, pg. 13). Why is this important? From the same book, they found that 90% of high-performing workers also had a high EQ, while only 20% of low-performers had a high EQ (Bradberry, pg 21).[1]

A leader with high EQ has the skills to know what his or her team needs and to help provide that. At times this may mean listening to personal issues, as an outlet or sounding board. A good leader will play the roles of coach, counselor, therapist, friend, motivator, and mentor.

Understanding the value of positive reinforcement is also key to effective leadership. It's easy to notice that people work harder and better if they are happy and feel like they are successfully contributing to the organization's mission. Fostering a work environment that provides these things can only be a benefit to any leader or organization. Encouraging and recognizing good work and effort can go a long way towards building organizational morale. For smaller nonprofits, even seemingly small or simple acts of recognition make an impact. Consider taking the team to lunch, recognizing the group's administrative or support person, giving flextime so team members can work from home, showing that you value and acknowledge everyone at different points in time, or asking for and then implementing the feedback that you receive from your team. Small, consistent efforts go a long way in fostering positive attitudes and work habits.

Leaders of small and large organizations experience different types of struggles. Small, founder-led organizations often struggle because while the founder may have had the original idea and vision, they aren't always the best person to lead the fundraising and day-to-day operations of the organization. There is often a failure to separate themselves from what is best for the organization as it grows, and to find someone more capable or qualified to lead.

In larger organizations subordinate leaders—or subordinates in general—often are not given the support they need to manage or operate effectively. This can come from micromanagement, but also from non-management. Leaders must strike the balance between giving those under them the space to do the work assigned to them, or to lead their individual teams, while keeping a pulse on the overall organization and keeping everyone accountable.

Leaders should take an active part in the fundraising efforts of the organization. They must set an example to the staff and board members that fundraising is a priority, and a team effort. Have you ever heard the saying "everyone is a fundraiser"? Well, it's doubly true for the leadership of the organization. If they aren't comfortable talking to, thanking, and acknowledging your largest or most loyal donors and supporters, then they need to re-think why they are in a nonprofit leadership role. They should be meeting regularly with the entire development team to offer their support and—when it makes sense—lend their help in achieving the fundraising goals. Leadership should know of any issues or roadblocks that might keep the team from hitting their goals, so they can work together to overcome them.

Effective leaders need to have a succession plan in place.

Properly planning for succession within the organization can be a way to avoid setbacks and downturns if a key employee or volunteer must move on from the organization. Yet, this is one of those things that often gets pushed aside or overlooked due to the many demands on a leader's time. Leaders, this is a critical factor in the long-term success and stability of your organization. When you reach the senior management and C-Suite level of an organization, the loss of an experienced person in those roles can set the organization back by months—if not longer. You have to address what would happen if the CEO/CFO/CDO one day decided to move on, or in some cases if they have to be replaced. In many situations, that work might fall to your board of directors to ensure that a viable succession plan is in place and up to date. I once studied a case where a long-time Director of Development left without much notice, and when the Executive Director pulled out the succession plan it was so outdated it had the old ED's name, a past board chair who was no longer involved, and was written for systems and a database that they no longer used! Turnover in the nonprofit industry, especially among fundraisers, is very high. It is critical to have a plan to handle it.

This is equally true for advisory boards. As more and more organizations are trying to recruit younger members to their boards, they must be prepared for them to serve abbreviated terms as they go through different phases of their life and career. At a minimum, the Executive Director and Board President should each have a succession plan for the other, so the organization is not left without the leadership of one of those two positions if something unexpected happens.

What can you do to invest in your leaders?

Thankfully, the answers to some of these questions are not difficult. You can invest in your leadership and in their subordinate leaders so that they have the tools and resources to handle every situation that arises. Thanks to the increase in local conferences, webinars, and affordable nonprofit management programs, you can provide high-quality training and professional development opportunities for a fraction of the price compared to a decade ago. You can invest in your staff so that you are helping them grow professionally and personally, and understand the value in staff retention vs. rehiring and retraining new staff members every few months. You can adapt best practices for developing a positive organizational culture, and you can create an environment in which teams thrive rather than simply exist.

[1] Bradberry, Travis, and Jean Greaves. *Emotional Intelligence 2.0.* Talentsmart, 2009. pp 13-21.

MISTAKE #14

Moving Your Best Frontline Fundraisers Into Management

By Suzanne Battit, MBA

When is the right time to move one of your best frontline fundraisers to management? The fact of the matter is that it may never be the right time. Your best fundraisers may not be your best managers, and vice versa. From universities and colleges to global health organizations to social service organizations, almost all nonprofits wrestle with this dilemma. I have seen it and experienced it within all three of these nonprofit sectors. We want to recognize, promote, and retain our best fundraisers and give them more responsibility, yet we often feel that the only way to do this is to move them into a management position. This could be a mistake on many levels, and there are other options to consider.

In the Harvard Business Review's article, *The Best Performers Aren't The Best Bosses,* researchers examined performance data for more than 53,000 sales reps and managers across more than 200 companies across multiple industries.

I know what you're thinking . . . sales . . . it's not the same as fundraising. You're right—sort of. The thing is, the traits that make someone a great, strategic sales pro are quite similar to those that make someone a phenomenal frontline fundraiser. Those are traits like high emotional intelligence, low ego, and being a great listener.

Back to the HBR study . . . The researchers found that "success as a [sales] rep was indeed predictive of promotion: Each increase in sales rank (equal to a doubling of sales) raised a rep's chances of becoming a manager by about 15%. Second, sales performance was negatively associated with managerial success: Each increase in sales rank correlated with a 7.5% decline in the performance of each of the new manager's subordinates."[1]

It's with this lens into the relative success and challenges had by so many professional sales reps—along with my own personal experience during my career in philanthropy—that I share these insights with you.

Why Fundraisers may not be Good Managers and Managers may not be the Best Fundraisers

Frontline fundraising requires a certain set of skills and talents, as does management. Frontline fundraising requires one to be with donors and prospects most of the time. Fundraisers must constantly be thinking about ways to engage and connect their donors and prospects to the organization. They must be thinking about ways to identify new prospects and grow the pipeline, and they must always have their revenue goal top of mind. All of these tasks keep the fundraiser focused on what they need to achieve (and a good fundraiser will want to stay focused on these activities). Hence, there is little time available to focus on what others need to achieve and help subordinates achieve their goals—the primary responsibilities of a manager.

When a fundraiser moves into a management role, many things change. On the one hand, the fundraiser may feel rewarded and that their career is advancing. Additionally, time is now available for planning and longer-term goals. And, in a perfect world, the team they oversee is being managed well. On the other hand, donor relationships have been disrupted as the manager can no longer carry the same-sized portfolio they once could. Also, there is a risk of less focus on revenue if there isn't someone to backfill the new manager's prior role.

Unfortunately, in most nonprofits there is little to no formal leadership development training taking place. Most managers are left to fend for themselves in developing the skills, tools, and experiences necessary to become great leaders.

Invariably, one of three things happens: either the new manager gets so bogged down in day-to-day management responsibilities that they aren't able to spend nearly enough time fundraising; the new manager does not take to the new set of responsibilities and the different skill set required, and continues to be a great fundraiser but isn't managing; or the new manager embraces all aspects of their new role but doesn't really enjoy it because deep down they are a fundraiser and not a manager. Typically, people excel at one or the other—it is truly rare to find someone who excels at both fundraising and management AND enjoys both.

So how should one address this challenge? In my close to 20 years of overseeing different fundraising operations, I've learned a few lessons. Here are some of the most important:

1. **If your strongest fundraiser loves fundraising,** keep them in a frontline fundraising position—rather than a senior management position—and provide recognition and promotion through other efforts (some options below).

2. **If your strong fundraiser expresses interest in management,** before making the change, be sure that they possess the skills necessary for management and understand what management requires. So often, the new expectations are not fully understood, particularly around success now being tied to the entire team achieving something rather than on the success of one individual. Additionally, a fundraiser moving to management needs to be prepared to transfer the relationships with most of their donors to other fundraisers, keeping only a small portfolio to manage.

3. **If you do move a frontline fundraiser into management,** be sure not to disrupt critical relationships—and be sure to have a backup plan in the event it doesn't work out.

4. **When moving a frontline fundraiser into management,** be sure the support structure is in place such

that donor relationships can be transferred smoothly to others and the new manager has the time to both manage and fundraise from a small portfolio of donors. And if someone is new to management, providing training around goal setting, performance management, and team leadership is critical.

5. **Be sure the new manager still has revenue responsibility** to help ensure it remains a primary focus for them and their team.

6. **Spend some time developing viable career paths** for great frontline fundraisers who either don't want to go into management, or whom you know wouldn't be successful in a management role. Be willing to be creative with different paths.

7. **Be willing and prepared to reverse course, without losing your best talent.** If you promote your best fundraiser into management and it turns out he or she is better suited in a frontline fundraising role, don't hesitate to find a way to move them back into a frontline fundraising role. This can be complicated by budget restrictions, etc., but you're better off finding a way to re-integrate your best fundraiser rather than losing them because you made a mistake in promoting them.

Recognition and Promotion Alternatives to Management Positions

When you have a strong-performing frontline fundraiser and key leader ready for a promotion or added responsibility, yet management may not be the right path, consider the following options:

1. Mentorship

One of the best decisions I made a few years ago was to hire a very seasoned frontline fundraiser to continue doing just that, without day-to-day management getting in the way. That said, I knew she had a lot to offer the team, and I wanted to take advantage of that in a way that would be rewarding to her, recognize her contribution, and be beneficial to the team—but also keep her focused on fundraising 100% of the time. We established an informal mentoring relationship between her and the frontline fundraisers. The arrangement engaged her and her years of experience in donor strategy discussions and donor visits with team members when appropriate. It was the perfect solution to provide her with enhanced engagement with the team that didn't require day-to-day management, while allowing the team to take advantage of her fundraising talent.

2. Title Change and More Complex Relationships

Of course, one of the easiest ways to recognize your best frontline fundraisers is to give them a more senior frontline fundraising title, as well as an opportunity to work with larger donors and prospects. The title makes them feel valued and rewarded, and the added challenge of new donors keeps them engaged and eager to build these new relationships. This may sound like a very obvious alternative, however, it always amazes me how often it isn't done.

3. Limited Management Responsibility

Should you have a strong fundraiser who expresses interest in management and possesses the skills needed, consider recognizing them with limited management responsibility at first—perhaps oversight of one or two team members and a commensurate compensation increase. This not only provides your fundraiser with added responsibility and recognition, but also allows you to make sure it's the right fit without having to go too far down the path initially. Should it prove to be the right role, it is easy enough to give them management responsibility for additional team members. And if it doesn't work out, it is a lot easier to adjust the reporting of one team member rather than a full team.

As I stated at the beginning of the chapter, many nonprofit organizations consider moving frontline fundraisers into full management roles. If you have been tempted by this, fear not, for you are not alone! If you have actually made a decision to do so, you aren't alone, either. Hopefully it was the right decision, and if not, I hope you now have a bit more insight for future decisions around the fundraiser and manager roles, and aligning talent accordingly.

[1] Benson, A., Li, D., & Shue, K. (2016, November 27). Promotions and the Peter Principle. Retrieved from https://pdfs.semanticscholar.org/a2ee/72253f99e98f828abd5949af70fe8da1aa38.pdf

MISTAKE #15

Not Holding Staff Accountable for Performance

By Andrew Olsen, CFRE

A few years ago I was working with a major national organization—one that has branch offices in cities throughout the

US and Canada. One of the branch directors told me about the challenges his office was having financially. They were about $750,000 behind their goal for that year, and it was the second or third year they'd run a deficit like this.

I asked him what the consequences of missing their revenue target by such a wide margin for multiple years would be for him and his team, and I was astonished by his response. He turned to me and said, "Nothing significant will happen. Our home office will write off the lost revenue and we'll go about our business." Initially I assumed he was joking. But he quickly confirmed this was truly the case, and that it had been the case for multiple years, with zero consequences. And yet, the organization wondered why they struggled.

Simply put, you can't reward mediocrity and expect it to evolve into excellence.

Nearly a decade ago, I worked with another organization that had similar revenue challenges. This organization—a hospital—raised roughly $8 million each year. Unfortunately, between their staff costs and their other operating costs (direct-response fundraising company, major gift consultant, capital campaign consultant, printing costs, awareness and public relations costs, etc.), they ended up spending $8 million each year. This organization's mission is to provide critical medical care to children with disabilities. Donors sacrificially gave $8 million to help the children served by this organization, yet the foundation was so inefficient with their internal operations that at the end of a given year their net return was $0.00. That's ZERO.

This is bad. It's the kind of bad that should get leaders fired. But it gets worse. Not only did the organization's leadership not get fired, they got REWARDED for this level of performance! I watched as one Vice President at the organization—a guy who hadn't hit his goals for two straight years—was rewarded with a bonus that was nearly $40,000!

What's more, the board of this organization didn't even have a mechanism to hold this person accountable, because relationship touchpoints and revenue were NOT measured as part of this person's goals and priorities for the year. According to his annual review, he looked quite successful. His goals were instead related to staffing, managing expenses, and managing "market awareness."

To help you hold yourself and members of your team accountable for their performance:

1. *Set clear expectations up front.* Ask your staff to repeat your expectations back, in their own words, so that you can be sure you communicated them clearly and they were understood.

2. *Keep your word.* Follow up when you said you would, and in the way you said you would.

3. *Clarify.* Outcomes should be non-negotiable, but the process to achieve them should allow for creativity.

4. *Be consistent.* Help your employees know what to expect from you.

5. *Be present.* Provide ongoing coaching in the moment, and corrective direction each time someone falls short. Do this as soon as possible after an issue is discovered.

6. *Be decisive.* If someone consistently misses the mark and falls short of expectations even after coaching and correction, you owe it to them and others in your organization to part ways with them.

MISTAKE #16

Instilling Fear of Failure in Your People

By Andrew Olsen, CFRE

A few years ago I consulted with a faith-based social services organization. They were going through some difficult changes, and I was there to help them focus their development efforts. Within 10 minutes of the start of our meeting, I could tell that their only problem wasn't just the fact that their efforts were scattered. Their real problem was much bigger.

As I interviewed each person on the development staff—from the part-time person who processed gifts during periods of heavy response all the way up to their Chief Development Officer—what I found was a palpable fear across the organization. They were terrified of their CEO. He was an aggressive bully who needed to be right about everything. If something wasn't his idea it was doomed to fail—others' ideas met with so much resistance from the CEO that they could never get off the ground. If you were on staff and you tried something new or different, it had better work. If not, you were chastised publicly and told that you were wasting precious organizational resources. This resulted in an atmosphere of fear and hesitation. Nobody took risks. The organization and the people in it weren't growing. Everyone hesitated to act until the CEO had given direction. This was a daily occurrence.

Creating or allowing a culture of fear to persist in an organization will do significant damage. Think about the last time you interacted with someone and it truly made you fearful. You probably froze initially, unsure how to respond. Maybe you even thought about the interaction the rest of that day. If you're honest, you'll likely say that you went about your day, but that interaction kept coming back to you throughout the day, distracting you from other priorities. If it was significant enough, maybe it permeated your evening or weekend as well.

Now think about experiencing that every day when you go to work.

Here are 5 reasons to cultivate a culture of risk-taking in your organization:

1. It helps your people overcome the fear of failure

2. You cultivate creative thinking across your team

3. It allows you to surface and test previously unseen opportunities

4. Your people become more confident in their own thinking, skills, and abilities

5. The team learns new skills by testing, trying, failing, and revising

To create a culture where people aren't afraid to fail, the first step is to communicate the organization's tolerance for this type of smart risk-taking. Next, and more importantly, that tolerance for failure and risk-taking must be demonstrated. When employees try a new idea and aren't instantly successful, commend the initiative, praise what went well and help them pivot to the next smart idea based on what they've learned.

MISTAKE #17

Allowing Toxic Staff to Remain in Place

By Andrew Olsen, CFRE

I worked in a nonprofit back nearly a decade ago. One of the key reasons I left the organization was because the Vice President of our organization allowed a horribly toxic employee to remain in place. She was a technical specialist at the organization and everyone knew it would be difficult and expensive to replace her. But her attitude was toxic to the organization.

This person was manipulative, conniving, argumentative, and only looked out for herself. She would routinely misrepresent the true nature of a situation to make herself look better, would blatantly disregard direction that I and several other managers and directors gave her, and would lie about it when confronted by our Vice President.

But the worst thing about this employee was her temper. Without warning, she'd fly off the handle and scream at people. One evening she and I were working late, and we had a disagreement about strategy. She stood at the door to my cubicle for what seemed like 20 minutes (I'm sure it was less than 90 seconds, but it felt like an eternity!) and screamed. I mean *screamed*. To the point that she was shaking, her face was bright red, and if there was anyone else in the entire building they could have heard her. All because I held a point of view on donor segmentation that she didn't share. It was impossible to confront her about this kind of behavior because that only made it worse.

When I brought this up to our Vice President the following day, he dismissed it out of hand. His perspective was that she was an important part of the team, and that addressing her behavior might cause her to quit or not to work as hard as she was.

But her toxicity started to permeate the department. People took note of the fact that she behaved poorly and nothing was done about it. They started to question the organization's leadership. And what this meant for me personally was that I made a decision. The day that my VP brushed the issue under the rug instead of supporting me and helping me deal with the situation, I decided it was time to leave.

More recently, I consulted with another nonprofit organization that, on the surface, appeared to be healthy and well-aligned. However, they had a Director of Development who was incredibly toxic. During executive meetings she'd nod in agreement with everything the President said, expressing publicly her alignment with the stated direction of the organization. But after key meetings she'd convene her own private follow-up meeting, where she'd lead complaint sessions about the President and the direction he was taking the organization. It was her way of exerting her own power and keeping the President from accomplishing his agenda for the future of their organization.

As a result, there was a large amount of confusion throughout the ranks of the organization—with some staff members supporting the organization's formal agenda and goals, and others maintaining an underlying concern and disregard. Ultimately, the only way to resolve this problem was for the President to terminate this Director of Development and remove several other people who had aligned with her. This cost the organization significantly in lost talent, disconnected donor relationships, and in dollars spent on recruiting, hiring, and training replacement staff.

When you don't deal with toxic employees in your organization, it sends the wrong message to the rest of your staff. It communicates that you tolerate bad behavior, and that you don't care about how this negative behavior impacts the rest of your people or the organization. You might think that keeping that one toxic employee is important, but in reality you are likely driving away your best people by not dealing with the problems they create.

Here are the four biggest pitfalls of not dealing with toxic employees:

1. If an employee is behaving inappropriately and you do nothing about it, you're reinforcing that inappropriate behavior—you're normalizing it.

2. Not dealing with toxic employees tells your best people that you are a meek leader, and your best people will walk because of this.

3. It creates confusion at all levels about what behaviors are ok and not ok, and this will cause friction across your staff.

4. Toxic behaviors and attitudes spread like a virus. If you allow one person in the organization to behave inappropriately, soon you'll see that their behavior has spread to more and more of your employees.

If you have a toxic employee, you need to take action before your whole staff—and your organization—suffers. Clearly communicate how the employee's performance deviates from your expectations, work with them to change their behavior and if they can't or won't change given sufficient opportunity to do so, remove them from the organization. Difficult as it may be, your non-toxic employees' well-being (and retention!) depends on you taking action.

MISTAKE #18

Not Clearly Defining Staff Roles and Responsibilities

By Andrew Olsen, CFRE

Have you ever heard someone who works in a nonprofit say something like, "I wear a lot of hats," or "Oh, I do a little of everything here"? Maybe you've even said something like that yourself? Nonprofits, by their nature, are scrappy organizations. In many instances you're strapped for cash, don't have robust budgets for additional (heck, some might even say adequate!) staffing, and the like. That often results in your staff members each doing two, three, sometimes even four jobs! This is one of the big reasons that so many in the nonprofit sector feel ineffective. When I advise organizations on major gift development it's one of the key roadblocks I see to success in this area. I once met a woman who was a full-time Major Gift Officer, was responsible for planning and executing all events for the organization, and was also responsible for writing 10-12 grant requests each year. And her boss couldn't figure out why she wasn't hitting her goals!

One person likely could never deliver on all of those expectations—nor should they even try. If you hire someone to focus on major gifts, they need to have the ability to focus on the tasks that result in major gifts. The same goes for someone you hire as an event planner. If you give that person a dozen other tasks, you shouldn't be surprised if they don't complete those additional tasks—OR they simply fail at the official event-planning tasks. This idea that you can pile on "other tasks as assigned" simply because you need them done and can't afford or don't want to hire another staff member is dangerous. It will result in people not knowing what tasks are most important to the organization, or most critical to their success and yours. This will result in people doing what is easy, not what is necessary—and that won't bring you, your employee, or your organization success.

MISTAKE #19

Embracing a Poverty Mindset

By Andrew Olsen, CFRE

I suspect you know exactly what I mean by "embracing a poverty mindset." It's one of the most frustrating and most damaging mistakes that nonprofit leaders make. It's also unfortunately a very frequent problem.

When you buy into a nonprofit poverty mindset, you think small. Leaders who embrace a poverty mindset are content to run as much of their organization with volunteer labor, even when those volunteers don't have the skills necessary to help the organization thrive. Embracing a poverty mindset leads to nonprofit CEOs and Executive Directors imposing unsustainably low wage limitations on their organization under the guise that people who work for a particular cause should be so "bought in" that they work work for free—or nearly free. It leads to organizations accepting whatever free or low cost goods and services from the community that they can get their hands on, even if they aren't what the organization needs in order to deliver value to those they serve.

The poverty mindset shuts down creative thinking by stopping every new and unique idea with the phrase, "we could never afford that." It embraces fear, forces you to live within a "this is how we've always done it" mentality, and robs those who need you most of the critical support you could otherwise provide to them.

What can you do to reverse this negative mindset?

1. Instead of meeting every new idea with a "we could never afford to do that" response, pivot that response to the question, "what would we need to change or do differently in order to afford this?"

2. You must begin to bring more transparency and more honesty to the true cost of running your programs and entire organization. Funders and individual donors need to understand the true cost of delivering your programs. Under-reporting your administrative costs or trying to shade the real cost of service delivery only reinforces the dangerous and unrealistic expectations that watchdog orgs, many funders and individual donors unfortunately believe about nonprofit overhead.

3. Speak clearly and regularly about the amazing outcomes your organization is delivering, and talk frankly about how those outcomes would be impossible without a stable and significant operational infrastructure.

MISTAKE #20

Hiring Unproven Major Gift Officers

By Andrew Olsen, CFRE

Unproven major gift officers. They're prevalent in our industry—and they can do a lot of damage.

These people are what my good friend and co-author of *Rainmaking: The Fundraiser's Guide to Landing Big Gifts*, Roy C. Jones, CFRE refers to as "butterflies and bumblebees." This is because they flutter around an organization not accomplishing anything, then once they leave you feel the sting of them not having produced any major gifts for your organization. And he's right!

I once met a gentleman who came highly recommended as a major gift officer, but as it turned out, he couldn't produce any gifts. I later found he had moved from organization to organization, making lots of friends and conducting lots of meetings, but he never actually generating revenue for the nonprofits where he worked. He'd take credit for gifts that came in from people who were assigned to his portfolio, but unless you really looked under the hood you wouldn't know that he hadn't done anything to generate those gifts. He went through three or four organizations, costing those nonprofits hundreds of thousands of dollars, before landing in one where someone finally called him on his lack of effort and ability to produce gifts. But by that time he'd cost that organization at least $100,000 in salary, not to mention the potential millions of dollars in lost opportunity.

There was another organization I consulted with for several years that had a similar problem. In fact, I was part of a team of people who helped this organization define and document a highly effective major gift program. We were initially brought in to help the nonprofit's Senior Major Gift Officer develop a plan and structure that would allow the organization to increase their major gift revenue by 3-5 times.

Unfortunately, we quickly discovered that the infrastructure and program weren't the problem. The problem was the Senior Major Gift Officer. Over a 12-month consulting process, we were never able to identify a single gift he had successfully solicited and closed. He was never able or willing to produce a specific list of donors he had developed a personal relationship with, or a single individual donor plan that he had created for any of the donors in his portfolio. He did, however, happily take credit for any direct mail or online gift that was given by anyone who was in his assigned portfolio—even though he didn't lift a finger to help generate those gifts. What's worse is, the organization had no process in place to hold him accountable. They had no performance scorecard. No set of annual performance expectations. And when he didn't meet the revenue target for the year, it was often blamed on "the economy" or "the donors" rather than his lack of engagement and follow-through. To my knowledge, this person is still employed by this organization now, nearly a decade after our engagement. That's a decade of lost opportunity for this critically important nonprofit.

Stories like this are unfortunately not rare. I hear them every day from nonprofit leaders and development staff—and in every case, bad major gift hires cost organizations significantly. **In my opinion, this is one of the most costly mistakes any organization could ever make.** That's why it's so important to hire major gift officers who have proven track records, and the right mix of experience and traits for success.

Here are seven qualities of top-producing major gift officers:

1. They are focused, active listeners.
2. They care deeply about people, and value the art of building deep relationships.
3. They are passionate about their organization's mission and values.
4. They are highly self-aware and self-disciplined.
5. They are results-driven.
6. They are resilient.
7. They are persistent, but not pestering.

Major gift work is simply too mission-critical to allow for unproven performers. Make sure candidates and staff can actually quantify their impact, or you'll be left questioning whether all your major gift 'activity' actually produces any results.

MISTAKE #21

Hiring a For-Profit Executive to Run Your Nonprofit (Even When They Aren't the Most Qualified for the Job)

by Jessi Marsh

When I was a 22-year-old Journalism/Advertising major at Ohio University, I was packing my bag to take New York City by storm. I knew that most of my friends who had done this ended up in basement studio apartments in terrible neighborhoods, and that the only activities they could afford were going to free comedy shows and occasionally walking to the corner store for a Snapple. To share with three people. But I had some promising interviews and just enough overconfidence to assume my story would fast forward through the tough part.

As I walked across the stage to receive my diploma, I never could have guessed where my career would take me. First to a homeless shelter about ½ mile from where I accepted that not-my-actual diploma from someone I'm sure I should have recognized. I had agreed to meet with the executive director there, who I assumed just wanted to wish me luck with my next adventure, but who actually offered me a job and challenged me to give a year of my life to serving the poor. I ended up giving two years of my life at that organization and have never looked back.

I apparently fell in love with being underpaid and spent the subsequent 17 years occupying most every spot on your average nonprofit organizational chart, about halfway through landing pretty squarely in the Development arena, where most of us are slightly less underpaid. Now, as a consultant, (that's what fundraisers do when they die—they become consultants) I see this mistake play out again and again: **hiring someone with a successful for-profit business background to run a nonprofit.**

It's not that it can't be done. I have seen it done well a few times. But here is what usually happens: A nonprofit has an opening for a leadership position, and the board or search committee members start thinking that the organization has an opportunity and should use it to shape up. Maybe foundation revenue is down. The brand of the organization needs to be strengthened. Buildings need to be updated. Maybe the board doesn't understand why so much money is spent on fundraising . . .

And in walks a Caucasian man, mid-50s, in a suit with a fresh haircut and a firm handshake, and hallelujah, we are in business now! There is something about this guy, who lives in one of the nice suburbs and makes self-deprecating jokes about his golf swing, that makes this search committee act like teenagers at a Taylor Swift meet-and-greet. They can trust this guy to turn things around. They may think, "He's one of us and he's used to deadlines and profit margins and project management. That means he'll trim the fat and make sure everyone around here is more productive. We can put an end to the warm and fuzzy, hippie-dippy kumbaya and really get to work."

Now, it should be noted that this could just as easily be a woman. But, in my experience, in most cases, it is a man. Perhaps because the most powerful board members are often men, especially in these more traditional, long-standing nonprofit organizations.

So, who is this guy? Well, he ran or worked for a successful business in one of the big shiny buildings in town for a company with a name like AlphaCom. He knows a lot of people, has been generous to several charities. He reaches a point, pondering his achievement, as he comes to the conclusion of his career that making money is not the critical endeavor for him that it once was, and he realizes he wants to have more impact. To do something more meaningful. To have a more noble purpose. He begins quietly making inquiries, often via a mutual friend of a board member, and next thing you know, he's the top candidate for a nonprofit leadership position, never having actually applied for the job.

Why does this committee seem so convinced that the for-profit CEO is who the organization needs to get things moving in the right direction? I believe it is because there is often a fundamental misunderstanding about nonprofits at the board level. While some (lucky) boards have strong representation of veteran nonprofit leaders, most don't.

So the guy from AlphaCom goes through some back channels, and next thing you know, he's well on his way to being the new CEO. The perception is: if this guy could handle Alpha-Com, this will be a breeze to him. However, the reality is that the odds are stacked against him because of his background. *If he succeeds in any way, it will be in spite of that background, not because of it.*

When the new CEO actually takes the reins and is introduced to the staff, often a longtime, dedicated upper-management staffer is crushed because he or she has been overlooked, or possibly wasn't even informed that the search had started. When the new CEO's background is mentioned, there may an astounding number of wide-eyed looks, heads shaking, and maybe the fear of the unexpected starts to set in. People are afraid and they know change is coming. Everyone in the room is thinking about how this impacts their team, their job and their family. And most are not optimistic that the change will be good.

As the new CEO is introduced and greets the staff, he typically makes an effort to instill confidence—both about himself and to reassure the staff. He may talk in very general terms about how the staff members are important and valuable, and say that he looks forward to getting to know them. The staff claps politely and smiles bravely. But skepticism and fear abound.

As the new CEO starts, he might rely on cultural ideas from his for-profit background that vulnerability is weakness and confidence is king. So he ignores any feeling of uncertainty and dives right in. He quickly decides who to trust and who to ignore, demote or remove. Numbers are reviewed. A restructure is inevitable. Nonprofit musical chairs begins and people who vaguely seem more "professional" or "business-minded" are retained or promoted. Positive attitudes are highly valued at this stage. The CEO is looking for support within the organization, so the person with the most convincing smile and willingness to go along with just about anything will become indispensable to the CEO.

No matter how much the organization and its new leader purport to value honesty and authenticity, the lines are pretty clear. You're either with him or against him—this creates more fear and anxiety. People fear for their livelihoods, and also become anxious that their calling and passion, how they share their gifts and strengths with the community, could all be at stake. There are certainly times to part ways with an individual who is not meeting the demands of their role, and some nonprofits do need to become more courageous about releasing an underperforming employee to their next adventure. **But the vague fear of job loss in the face of a new numbers-focused CEO will cause a kind of quiet, low-level panic that leads people to conduct themselves in ineffective ways.** This erodes what positive culture was in place and pits people against one another.

As the CEO understands operations more, suggestions are made to increase productivity or overcome persistent challenges. The CEO walks around wondering why there isn't better follow-through, why things don't happen faster, why we don't have more graduates, why the waiting list is so long. These are good questions, but the answers are usually rather complicated. Seeking to solve problems and trained to achieve results, the new CEO may opt to make some suggestions or give some directives without seeking to first understand these complexities. As a result, the proposed solutions can reflect a lack of understanding of what it *really* takes to work with the populations the organization serves—these populations are complex, bring about so many unique situations, and are incredibly challenging to help.

While fresh eyes can be helpful, a cursory glance at a complicated matrix of issues and a simple solution that starts with "Why don't we just . . ." are usually not only an ineffective way to improve services or outcomes, but are often rather insulting to the front line professionals who understand the needs of their clients to the core.

The CEO sees that he hasn't reduced expenditures as much as he thought he might be able to, so he starts wondering how much could be done with volunteers instead of paid staff. Unfortunately, it doesn't always work out to take a position historically held by a paid staffer, figure out a way to get rid of that person in an ethical manner, and then fill the position with a volunteer. Occasionally you find a diamond in the rough—that special, passionate, helpful, reliable, organized volunteer who shows up consistently, doesn't mind the dirty work, can take constructive criticism, and is always appropriate and friendly. Unfortunately, the world is not full of these people to begin with, and it is really not full of people who fit that description when they aren't even getting paid.

The CEO might drive forward anyways, realizing that something he can really deliver on is those numbers—reducing costs, first and foremost. Budgets are examined and cut, and when people leave, their positions are not filled. As staff positions are not filled, other staff members have to fill in to get the work done. Because nonprofits are filled with people who care about their organizations, people will work hard to make up for deficits. But burnout and bitterness are inevitable.

The culture becomes more political, with people seeking power and influence—back room meetings in the hopes of keeping their jobs and keeping things as much the same as possible. Assumptions are made about this new CEO's motives. Guards are up, trust is down. The CEO is forced to either 1. ignore it, 2. get rid of key staff and bring in people he feels more comfortable working with, or 3. pause, acknowledge that it's not working, and invite significant input from his team. The third is the best scenario and is cause for hope. The first two will end badly. Eventually the CEO himself or the board will realize this is not the organization or role for him.

Let's remember, this person who underestimated the challenge of running a nonprofit organization is not a bad guy. In fact, he's probably a great guy. He's just on the wrong seat on the bus. What should have happened when we first encountered this person is that we should have considered that he might make a great board member with proper orientation and onboarding. We could have invited him to be on a committee. We could have asked him to volunteer in one of our programs to see how he interacts with clients. We could have honored him (if appropriate) with an award at our annual gala. We could have asked him to give us a large gift. We could have gotten to know him before we put him in charge. **We could have, likely, found a role for him where his experience and knowledge could be leveraged in such a way that the organization was made better as a result.** Not one that constantly confounded and frustrated him.

How to avoid this scenario:

Challenge the assumption that nonprofits are not business-like enough. Do many organizations need to up their game to stay relevant? Of course. But this does not mean they need to look more like large for-profit corporations. They probably need to look more like a very well-run nonprofit organization, of which there are many examples. There are great articles and books written about improving nonprofits—you're reading one right now! There are master's degrees and PhDs to be completed on the subject. There are experts you can hire as staff or as consultants to help you raise the bar when it comes to improving the organization in any number of ways. For example, often the board needs some guidance on what it means to be a high-performing board. Typically, help is needed in the fundraising arena. Staff structure can be a challenge. Branding and communications need constant upgrades. Organizational culture is always an area that can be explored and, often, improved. A seasoned business person with sales, supply-chain, management, finance, legal or marketing experience is usually not the best person suited to lead the efforts in addressing these areas. Nonprofits can and should get better if they want to remain competitive and relevant. But there are many creative, experienced, sharp minds already at work in the sector who have a wealth of knowledge to share.

Consider the realities of lowering overhead costs. Many people from the for-profit sector have great concerns about how a nonprofit is spending their donated dollars. Certainly, if annual trips to Tahiti for the staff of a small, locally focused nonprofit in Iowa are a major expense, this activity must be addressed. But when overhead costs such as staff salaries are scrutinized, some assumptions are being made. Some overhead costs are for activities that are literally carrying out the mission. If you have an organization that provides counseling and case management, so much of the cost of that organization is going to be put toward salaries and benefits for staff. Those staff, and their relationships with their clients, dramatically influence how well outcomes are achieved. Even some costs that are not directly client-focused are critical. If you spend $25,000 on a newsletter that goes into the hands of 50,000 supporters, and you raise $105,000 from that mailing, you are doing great—communicating with donors, strengthening your brand, and bringing in a nice, respectable ROI. Often when a CEO comes to the organization from another sector, these are the areas they start to circle in red pen on the budget. A wise Director of Development or Operations Director knows that he or she needs to be prepared to explain why these expenditures are necessary.

Pay the CEO a fair salary for the size of the organization and scope of the role. An experienced, skilled nonprofit leader should be compensated well. They have a tough job to do, likely have plenty of education and experience that has prepared them for the work, and if you don't pay them well, they will probably find a place that will. If you reduce the salary below the market, you'll certainly get someone who will do the job. But not the best person you can get. And they may not do the job to the level that you want or need—because they won't be as qualified as you'd hoped, or as motivated to exceed expectations.

Look within the nonprofit sector for a seasoned leader. This leader might be a CEO of a smaller organization ready to take on a larger organization, or a longtime Director of Programs or Development or Operations. What this person needs is a history of being at the decision-making table of a nonprofit organization that grew during their time there. This person is valuable because either they helped make that growth happen, or they had a front row seat in watching it happen. If they have held a significant leadership position at a growing nonprofit for 6+ years, that demonstrates that they have been around long enough to stick it out when things get difficult (financially, culturally, legally.) The larger your organization, the more years someone needs to have had behind them in the field.

Consider the talent within your own organization. Don't overlook someone who can hit the ground running just because there is an appeal to hitting the refresh button. Can a new face bring new energy, new donors, a brave new chapter in the organization's history? Sure. But sometimes, minimizing the change the organization has to endure has great value. You can always test-drive an internal candidate as an interim CEO and evaluate their performance in 6 months. This buys time to find the perfect hire if things don't go well. But beware, the interim may be extremely disappointed to not get the official appointment, and may have a loyal following.

Allow key staff to weigh in on the hire.

If you look to the left and to the right and you don't see any viable candidates within the organization, an executive search is in order. A firm can be hired to handle this search, or it can be done with a committee from the board. One way to achieve greater buy-in is to invite staff to have input in the hiring process. It can be a small number of influential staff members that participate in interviews, or it could be the entire staff who have the opportunity to give their input through a survey. They can be asked to weigh in at the beginning—about what they'd like to see in the next leader of the organization. Or at the end, more appropriately with a small number, helping to decide between two final candidates. Trust is built by opening up the process. Additionally, key staff may have much to offer in articulating what the organization needs and does not need.

Create a step in the interview process that accounts for cultural fit. One interview dedicated to assessing a candidate's fit with the organization can reveal a lot about a candidate. But this first requires an understanding of the organization's culture. The culture must be deeply understood in order for the right CEO to be hired to fit into it and drive it forward. If the culture is not understood, or if it has been shifting significantly, a process must take place to understand and accurately define the culture and strengthen and solidify it. Otherwise, a CEO will be hired who will either ignore culture (which creates its own kind of culture, and not a good one) or choose and attempt to push a culture of his or her own choosing. Installing a new culture is nearly impossible, and usually fails, especially if it is introduced by a brand new leader.

Once the CEO is hired, dedicate time to a cultural onboarding process that greatly exceeds the process for the average staff person. The HR staff should be experts in the organization's culture and can lead the process. Other staff who are steeped in and supportive of the culture can participate too, provided they can adeptly discuss the culture in a way that others can easily understand. This is only possible if cultural training and continual, purposeful reinforcement of the culture has already been happening. The point is that a healthy organization has a well-defined culture, and a new CEO must be introduced to the culture in a deliberate way. A seasoned nonprofit professional with successes at other organizations behind them will understand the need for them to understand the organization's culture and be a driving force behind it.

If your organization hires a formerly for-profit executive CEO, here are some ways to minimize the negative impact:

Make every effort to introduce culture effectively. This person will probably not have a lot of patience for this piece of your orientation. They will likely not see the value at first, or maybe ever. But you are doing this new leader a giant favor by ignoring their impatience giving them your very best communicator and culture expert to thoroughly but succinctly explain who this organization is and how it works, as well as challenging some assumptions they might make. Assumptions probably made by the new CEO might include:

- *This is a nice place where nice people work*
- *There is probably very little conflict here*
- *This job will be easier than my last job—less pressure, fewer hours*
- *People who work here care but they aren't tough*
- *The talent in this organization is probably subpar*
- *People work at nonprofits because they aren't capable of more*

So, the person doing the orientation has the very important opportunity to take some time to identify and, if appropriate, challenge any assumptions, politely of course. Some ideas that might be good to consider communicating are:

- *We accomplished A, B, and C in the past year, which was part of our 3-year strategic plan.*
- *X% of our staff have advanced degrees in the field*
- *X number of staff have been here for over 20 years*
- *Staffer Christy H. is nationally recognized as an expert in _____.*

Reduce fear by adjusting the termination process so it disallows the CEO to fire people carte blanche. There are many ways to do this, but with the CEO's agreement, some policies or procedures that can be installed include a process that requires the supervisor to demonstrate that they have given the staff member adequate time to improve and been given a specific, measurable action plan, an agreement between all C-level leadership that terminations be brought to the Executive board prior to termination. In addition to preventing the CEO from firing people prematurely, it also creates goodwill. A CEO willingly gives up the power to fire anyone he or she wants to for any reason is showing that they want to try to fit with the culture and understand it. This can go a long way with staff.

If YOU are the CEO who finds yourself inside a nonprofit organization, and you realize you are in over your head—first of all—Hi. Sorry I said that negative stuff about you. Can we get past my generalizations and assumptions long enough to make some headway? Great. So . . . you think you can run a nonprofit with a business background? Guess what—you probably CAN.

Here are some tips to help you be more successful as a new CEO:

Number one—do NOT make any changes at first. Your job is to LISTEN. Learn. Pay attention. How does this organization work? Who are the leaders? Who are the influencers? Who is flexible and teachable? (One of them had better be YOU.) Find these magical unicorns and ask them to lunch and ASK FOR THEIR HELP. Understand what this organization is all about by doing these things:

Acknowledge that nonprofits and for-profit companies are different. Acknowledge you have plenty to learn, and that you understand that the staff can teach you.

1. Find the magical unicorns (teachable, smart, flexible, influential people) and make them your allies. You cannot do this without their partnership.

2. Remember—"Culture eats strategy for breakfast."— Peter Drucker. The culture is the result of every interaction, over time. Pay attention to the culture.

3. Read every single page of the web site. Understand what every program does. Internalize the language of this organization by marinating in it. Use the words the staff uses.

4. Learn the names of the staff. Even the part-time overnight janitor. Especially the part-time overnight janitor.

5. Make it your business to understand fundraising. It is not the same as sales. And make it your business to make sure you have strong talent in your fundraising department. Consider bringing in reputable consultants to analyze the current situation and make recommendations for optimal staffing and strategies.

6. When discussing any potential changes for improvement, ask for staff input and listen deeply. Repeat back what they are saying so you are sure you understand and they believe that you do. Explain to them your goals (reducing costs, getting better results, serving more clients) and ask them to help you solve your problem and meet your goal. Consider the impact the change will have on staff and acknowledge when it creates a hardship.

Nonprofit organizations are sacred. They fill the gaps where our government and churches and families fall short. They fight enemies. They care for people. Their existence is so inspiring that people have dedicated their careers and lives to their sustainability. Anyone leading one should embark upon that adventure with a great sense of responsibility.

MISTAKE #22

Thinking Program Staff are the Enemy—and YOU are the most important person in the office

By Jayson Matthews

In 14 years of service in the nonprofit sector, I have lost count of how many times I have heard about the many divisions between the development office and the program office. At times, the root of all miscommunication within nonprofits is a failure for these critical sectors to put aside their differences and egos, and sit down and talk.

This division is bigger than what can be solved by doing a couple of trust falls at a communications seminar at work. The root of the problem is righteousness. Program staff think they are solving the world's problems (they are), and fundraising staff are bringing in the needed revenue to solve the world's problems (they are, too). Yet when these critical divisions fail to get out of their silos and work with one another, the work and our donors suffer.

Let's put it another way. Everyone is busy, right?! Everyone has the most important job, correct?! **Yet, from the perspective of the donor and the client—you all work for the same company.**

In returning home from a fundraising conference, my Executive Director asked me what I thought of the time spent. I replied with a general summary of: "It was a conference where most people were complaining that they were the least-appreciated people in their organizations, that no one understood the stress they go through on a daily basis, and that they should be running the organization because they were the only one who understood the board." My supervisor, without missing a beat, replied "So, a normal fundraising conference?"

Unfortunately, fundraisers are considered "magic workers" when they excel at bringing in needed revenue from the public. They are overworked and under-appreciated. Then, they are asked to do it again—plus 10%. Unless you have held a job as a nonprofit fundraiser, you don't understand the stress that comes with the job. I would argue that the only group in the nonprofit sector that *does* relate to fundraisers is—that's right—the program staff.

Working with clients and the public who are using the services of a nonprofit is hard work. Plus, program staff are tasked with program design, managing budgets, managing people, collecting data (including those great stories everyone wants), and evaluation. Like excellent fundraisers, the very best program designers are never satisfied with their impact and are always looking for bigger change.

When these important groups fail to work with one another, the damage caused by this lack of teamwork has both internal and external impacts. Internally, it shows up in three ways. First, there is a general lack of communication between the teams. The Development Team is focused on their revenue goals, and the Program Team is focused on their impact goals. Second, a sense of mistrust is formed as each team thinks that the other doesn't care about the other's work. Third, impact work is only shared via the lens of development staff, which forms walls between the donor and the work itself.

Externally, donors see a fragmented organization with no sense of teamwork. Donors know that money raised will be spent eventually, and if they see that program staff don't respect the development office—then why should they give a gift?

Furthermore, I have heard from plenty of program people that they LOVE the mission and LOVE the work, but they HATE the fundraisers. An indicator of this point can be seen by the percentage of staff who are also donors to the organization.

Why does this happen? The "overhead myth" put a critical eye on all non-programmatic staff in organizations. There have been plenty of times as a development officer that I have wanted to start "I'm overhead" campaigns that humanize the people behind the expense. In other words, I think development staff feel beat up. Furthermore, I have seen program staff outwardly dismiss fundraising work as "sales." This "us vs. them" mentality doesn't help.

On the flip side, I have seen fundraising staff put program staff on a pedestal with lots of self-defeating comments, like "You do the REAL work around here." There is also something to be said about specialization. More and more staff members are coming into jobs with degrees in nonprofit management or fundraising. While not a perfect system, there is a beauty in the model from the 1970s and 1980s when nonprofits were run by a small team of workers who had a personal connection to the mission.

How can we heal the divisions between program staff and fundraisers? Peace, love, and understanding? In all seriousness, all employees of a nonprofit need to understand what everyone else does. I recommend internal "follow the money" education efforts within organizations. Program staff must learn how to sell the mission and speak with donors. Then as the gift comes in, development staff must see the dollar at work and be able to explain why it is working. Then together, the team can explain why more investment is needed to continue the impact. Orientations, shadowing, and "lunch and learn" opportunities are great ways to build cross-team understanding. Plus, I am also a fan of management making it easy for staff to volunteer for the organization. This helps keep the big picture in mind.

What happens when we do nothing? Internally, staff will leave and spread their hatred of the other to another organization. While program staff do not change jobs as often as development staff, it does happen. I think the biggest impact is from the donor's perspective. Donors observe a lot of things, and when a team isn't working well with one another—that image burns bright.

What to consider when tackling this issue? Here are three things:

1. **Start with the controllables: Your attitude and your labor.** If you are a Development Officer, ask yourself, "Could I explain every aspect of our program as well as our program staff?" Ask yourself, "Can I share a personal story of when I interacted with one of our clients?" Ask yourself, "Do I have a good enough relationship with the program staff to where I could hand over my top donor and have them go off on a tour by themselves?" (The answers should be "yes, yes, and yes" by the way.) Frankly, you have the ability to control the time you spend at work and the attitude you bring into the office. If there has not been a culture of partnership in the office, then START ONE. Bring in coffee or pizza. Ask lots of questions. Ask program staff why they have dedicated their time to this mission. Talking shouldn't be a problem.

2. **Practice being a coach.** This is one of my best leadership tips. Coaches know the game enough to teach and challenge others. They train, they motivate,

and then they watch the players play. A common factor for all nonprofit staff is that they all have to serve as a teacher to one population or another. Development staff can teach donors. Program staff can teach clients. If you want to lead an organization, become the best coach you can be.

3. **My final tip, know that this is HARD and may take a LONG TIME.** It would be easier if we could hit the pause button, train everyone, then get back to work. Oh, if I had a pause button . . . Yet, if you feel like you are ready to learn more about programs (and the entire organization), you will make this a priority and act.

MISTAKE #23

Not Celebrating Your Staff's Wins

By Andrew Olsen, CFRE

This is something I'm personally guilty of, so I share this with you because I learned the hard way just how detrimental it is to a team.

Here's the scenario: You're a leader in your organization. Whether you lead an entire organization, a large team, or a small group of staff—you're a leader. And those on your team look to you for guidance. They look to you for the benchmark of how to behave in the workplace. And they look to you for confirmation that the work they're doing is important and valuable.

But you're busy. You have your own work to focus on, and the care and leading of your staff to manage. Your stress level is high because you've been handed unrealistic goals, you might not have the support you need from your Executive Director or board either. I get it. It's tough to lead well.

The mistake I made—and what I want to caution you against—was that I didn't take time to celebrate my team's wins. Instead, when someone on my team accomplished something, I would certainly say something like "Great work" or "Good job." But that was it. It was temporary and fleeting. By the time I said it, I was already focused on the next goal. On keeping us on track toward achieving whatever the next big thing was. That's how I'm personally wired. **I don't stop to celebrate my own wins along the way, so it never even crossed my mind that I needed to do that for my team.**

This caused the people on my team to believe that I didn't care about them or the work they were doing. At the very points when they should have been most excited about the impact they were making, my lack of enthusiasm actually caused them to fear that they were failing, or that they were doing things that weren't important to me or our organization. It was devastating to the morale of individual members of the team, and eventually to the overall team dynamic.

Finally, one of the younger and more courageous members of the team approached me privately and shared this direct feedback with me. It hit me like a ton of bricks. She was right. I had failed my staff and the team, and in the process I had caused them to question their value.

So take a breath. When your team accomplishes something (even small wins), take a moment to celebrate them. Help your individual team members savor the victory by showing them that you're proud of their contribution and the impact they made. You'll be amazed at the effect such a small gesture on your part can have on your people.

MISTAKE #24

Emphasizing Process over Outcomes

By Andrew Olsen, CFRE

Last year I encountered a Chief Development Officer who, to hear her tell it, managed a group of fundraisers who couldn't do anything right. The thing is, her team was hitting—and surpassing—their goals each month. They were raising more money month-over-month than the organization had raised in any of the last few years. They were meeting with donors more frequently than the organization had ever done in the past, and donors were responding positively.

So why did this CDO think so poorly of her staff? She finally shared with me what the real problem was. She had a specific view of how every engagement with a donor should go, and what the average day for a Development Officer should look like. Her people weren't following her prescribed plan in the way she thought they should. And because of that, she discounted their successes and instead focused on their procedural failures.

In reality, her people were doing exactly what they needed to do to engage donors in the organization's mission and motivate them to give. And it was working. The problem wasn't with her team. It was with her inability to see that outcomes determine success, not whether you followed a single path to achieve them.

While process is important—and there are specific processes that result in specific outcomes, it's the outcome that actually advances mission. Prioritize the outcome, and allow your people the flexibility to customize the process in a way that works for them. Especially if it delivers solid results.

MISTAKE #25

Overlooking Low-Cost, High-Value Employee Benefits

By Megan Klingensmith, PHR

As I write this, the US is seeing an 18-year low for unemployment[1], which is to say: *your employees have many options for where they work.* To win and keep top talent, we're going to have to work for it. And as we're aware, the nonprofit sector has a notorious reputation for requiring long, demanding hours for comparably little pay. So, what will compel a prospective employee to choose to work for *you*? Your organization's mission, while significant, may not be enough to attract and keep the talent you want and need. After all, not only are there increasingly other mission-driven avenues for employment like corporate social responsibility, social enterprises, and B-corporations, we can't discount that there are roughly a million other nonprofits in the US you're competing against, too. **To attract and retain great employees, we've got to give employees what they want.**

Here's what we first need to note about today's workforce: they care significantly about benefits. Oftentimes, more than they care about pay. This flies in the face of conventional wisdom, but consider the following:

According to Glassdoor, nearly 80% of workers would prefer new or additional benefits to a pay increase.[2] Let that sink in for a moment. We're trained to think employees care most about their paycheck, so it flies in the face of our conventional wisdom to consider that a dollar figure may not be most important factor in attracting and keeping talent.

Further, 90% of those 18 to 34 years old say they would prefer benefits over pay. This is, of course, the Millennial generation, who are likely already making up a significant portion of your organization's workforce. And if they don't now, they will soon, as Boomers continue to retire, and this comparably sized generation begins to fill their shoes alongside Gen X.

So, if benefits are perhaps more important to an employee than we assumed, are all benefits weighted equally? No, it turns out that three key benefits emerge as most highly correlated with employee satisfaction: health insurance, paid leave, and retirement plans. But let's first focus specifically on paid leave, because therein lies some of the greatest opportunity for nonprofits at the lowest cost. Unlike health insurance and retirement plans, there's no cash outlay for paid leave (Unless you count paying out employees their vacation time upon their leaving the company, but again, there's no cash spent until the employee terminates).

So let's consider paid leave—specifically, vacation time. What does it actually cost your nonprofit out of pocket to offer, say, an extra week of vacation?

It costs you nothing.

Suppose you upped vacation time from two weeks to four weeks. I know, gasp. But again, there's no cash outlay here, right? *The difference between two weeks' vacation and four weeks' vacation is zero dollars of actual realized cost.* To the organization, there's very little meaningful difference.

To the employee though, this is a world of difference. And for your organization's employer brand (how the general workforce perceives you), you're now differentiated among peers by your generous time-off policy. Your cache as an employer's just gone up, and you've spent virtually *nothing* to do it. And if you're spending little to no cash on a perk that's meaningful and motivating to the employee, I'd say you're doing something right.

I know some will want to argue that increasing vacation time will cost the organization employee productivity and results. Do we know this for certain, though? Is a well-performing employee going to suddenly not get their work done satisfactorily because they're utilizing your vacation policy? If they're a strong employee, the work will still get done. And if they're not a strong employee, I'd argue your root issue is with hiring and performance, not your benefits.

Let's take things a step further and consider another no/low-cost benefit that employees increasingly want: workplace flexibility. To begin, what do we mean when we talk about workplace flexibility? The most useful framework I've encountered on workplace flexibility was published in a study featured by Harvard Business Review, focusing on 6 types of flexibility:

1. **Unconventional hours:** ability to work outside a standard 9-5 schedule.

2. **Freedom to adapt/step away when needed:** ability to flex one's hours for a one-time event.

3. **Location variety:** ability to work at a location of the employee's choosing for some portion of their time.

4. **Location independence:** ability to work from anywhere, any time.

5. **Minimal travel:** employees have little to no travel expected as part of their job duties.

6. **Reduced workload:** employees are able to work on a part-time schedule.

Based on these six types of workplace flexibility, the study surveyed white-collar professionals to determine the demand and supply of flexibility: *how often is flexibility desired by employees, and how often is it provided by employers?* What they found is, 96% of employees said they need some form of flexibility (based on these six criteria), yet only 47% reported having access to the types of flexibility they need. **In other words, nearly all employees sought one of the six forms of flexibility enumerated here, and just less than *half* have the flexibility available to them in their present employment situation.**

And incredibly significant for the nonprofit sector, *95% of women need access to flexibility, but only 34% of them have access to the flexibility they need.* This is the largest flexibility gap among *any* employee demographic.

One could easily dismiss employees' desire for flexibility as a nice-to-have, not an actual business imperative. But employees without access to flexibility are twice as likely to report being dissatisfied at work, and half of employees say they would *leave their company if offered a more flexible alternative.*

Further, beyond employee engagement and retention challenges, "the lack of flexibility can also hurt the performance and productivity for as much as one-third of the workforce, with 34% of respondents reporting that the structure of their workday makes it challenging to perform in a sustainable way over time."[3] Given the impact that lack of flexibility has on the workforce, if we're focused on attracting and retaining great employees and being competitive against other potential employers, flexibility hardly seems a nice-to-have at all.

If we can assent to the notion that today's workforce cares about flexibility, we ought to look at our organizations to identify how we can offer more flexibility to our staff.

Which of the six types of flexibility is currently in place organizationally? Is this flexibility in any way built into the organizational culture, or offered only in special circumstances?

Assuming there's more flexibility to be had, the next step is to engage employees to understand which types of flexibility *they'd* most value, and would therefore generate the most engagement of current employees and attraction of future employees. These are not difficult discussions to have. But it takes a measure of proactivity and intention to move beyond the status quo and reshape our policies so they're working for, not against us.

In the competition for talent in the nonprofit space, don't make the mistake of overlooking free and low-cost ways to engage and retain talent by giving employees what they want. And don't just take my word for it, get this information straight from the source: your employees themselves. Chances are, they already know what it will take to keep them motivated and engaged, and it just might be something your nonprofit can actually provide—we might not win the competition for talent based on salaries alone, but to overlook free and low-cost, high-value benefits that are well within reach would certainly be a mistake indeed.

[1] Morath, Eric, and Sarah Chaney. "Unemployment Rate Falls to 18-Year Low; Solid Hiring in May." *Www.wsj.com*, 1 June 2018, www.wsj.com/articles/unemployment-rate-falls-to-18-year-low-solid-hiring-in-may-1527856298.

[2] Glassdoor, (2017). A Guide for Resourceful Recruiters: The Benefits Employees Want Most. Retrieved from http://b2b-assets.glassdoor.com/benefits-employees-want-most-2017.pdf

[3] Dean, A. & Auerbach, A. (2018, August 21). 96% of U.S. Professionals Say They Need Flexibility, but Only 47% Have It. Retrieved from https://hbr.org/2018/06/96-of-u-s-professionals-say-they-need-flexibility-but-only-47-have-it

MISTAKE #26

Not Establishing Formal Board Job Descriptions and Expectations

By Andrew Olsen, CFRE

Right now I serve on the board of the Minnesota Coalition for the Homeless. I love serving on this board—not just because the cause is vitally important to me, but because of the great experience I've had with the organization throughout my work with them. What I appreciate most is that from the beginning of my engagement with MCH, they've been crystal clear about things. During the interview process I had discussions with multiple board members and staff members. What struck me is that each person I spoke to in the process was speaking from the same script (not literally, but I think you get my point).

They were clear about the role I would play, the responsibilities I'd have, what was "in scope" and "out of scope" for my participation as a member of the MCH board, and what the expectations were for me as a board member.

What's interesting is the number of nonprofit boards that aren't anything like this. I frequently meet with board members who can't tell me what their role is within the board or the broader organization. They often talk about not knowing what the expectations are of their service, or what the organization needs or wants from them. Sometimes this .happens because no one in organizational leadership has experience serving on a board, so they don't know how to set expectations or craft a plan for the success of individual members of the board. And often, it happens because the board itself hasn't invested the time, energy, and focus to create a board member onboarding plan.

Clarity helps give people—especially volunteers—an understanding of what you expect from them. And the quickest way to get someone to do what you want them to do is to give them clear instruction. People don't want to guess at your expectations. Guessing is hard, and it leads to disappointment. People want to know, from you, what it is you want them to do. So give your board members what they want. Give them a clear set of responsibilities and expectations, and be upfront about what you need from them. It will dramatically improve their volunteer experience with your organization, and help you get what you need and want from them in a much more efficient and effective way.

MISTAKES #27-#28
Not Prioritizing Racial Diversity

By Zully Avila, MBA

Racial and cultural diversity inclusion, or the lack thereof, are gaining visibility due to the dramatic cultural change the US is currently undergoing. A palpable proof of this cultural change occurred on Thursday, January 3, 2019 when the most racially diverse class to date—the 116th—was sworn into the US Congress.[1] Although there is a noticeable rise of racially diverse leaders in politics and in corporations, unfortunately, studies have shown that the nonprofit sector is experiencing a racial diversity leadership gap and has remained stagnant for the past 15 years.[2]

Further reaffirming the racial diversity leadership gap, *The State of Diversity in Nonprofit and Foundation Leadership* study analyzed the leadership of 315 of the largest nonprofits and foundations in the US in 2017, and found that 87% of all Executive Directors and Presidents were white.[3] The nonprofit industry is clearly failing to reflect the racial diversity of the communities and individuals it serves. This chapter does not focus on the causes of the racial diversity leadership disparity, but more so on the importance of racial diversity in leadership within nonprofits by learning from two detrimental mistakes committed by nonprofits, which will help you avoid committing the same mistakes.

The lack of racial diversity in leadership has not only plagued nonprofits, but also for-profit companies. However, for-profit companies tend to take immediate action on improving their leadership diversity deficiency after a catastrophic error. For instance, in January 2018 Swedish multinational clothing retailer H&M made an epic mistake when it debuted a black child modeling a sweatshirt that read "Coolest Monkey in the Jungle." This mistake cost H&M millions of dollars, many celebrities publicly and vocally cut ties with the brand, and their target demographic took to social media to disparage the brand further, vowing to boycott it.[4] Within the first six months of 2018, H&M had dropped in profits by a third in comparison to the year prior.[5] To mitigate its failure, H&M immediately hired global diversity leader Annie Wu to promote diversity and inclusion, but at the same time the media noted that prior to Wu, the company's board of directors were all white.[6]

Another for-profit example that "missed the mark" by being culturally unaware was Pepsi's 2017 advertisement featuring Kendall Jenner. The commercial had pulled inspiration from the Black Lives Matter movement and intended to project a global message of "unity, peace, and understanding."[7] However, it received criticism due to the ad's climactic scene where Kendall Jenner defuses tension amongst the protestors and the police with a single can of Pepsi, thereby trivializing the Black Lives Matter protests. Bernice King, the daughter of Martin Luther King Jr., tweeted a picture of her father protesting with a Caucasian police officer pushing him off, with the caption "If only Daddy would have known about the power of #Pepsi."[8] As a result, Pepsi pulled the ad and halted all initiatives from further rollout. Clearly, Pepsi lost money in the production and the planned campaigns for this specific advertisement.

You may think that H&M and Pepsi are extreme and rare examples in the for-profit world of how the lack of racial diversity and cultural sensitivity in leadership can deeply affect the financials of a company. Sadly, there are several similar examples that have occurred in the for-profit world—but how does this relate to nonprofits? And why should racial diversity in leadership be important to nonprofit organizations?

Unfortunately, there are parallels to be drawn amongst both sectors. Therefore, nonprofits should take advantage of for-profit's colossal mistakes and apply them as lessons learned due to the lack of racial diversity in leadership into their own organizations. In the span of my 15-year career, I have worked in, worked as an agency partner, and consulted on projects for both commercial and nonprofit sectors. The following are real-life examples that I have experienced in the nonprofit sector, emphasizing two major types of mistakes that stem from the lack of racial diversity in leadership.

MISTAKE #27

Lack of Cultural Awareness & Sensitivity

A few years ago, I was working with a small but very well-known nonprofit in Washington, DC. All leadership was Caucasian, I counted fewer than five staff members who were of diverse backgrounds—one of whom worked under the Department Director I was consulting with for a specific project. For three months I worked on this project in an open area near a Development Coordinator named Lucia*, who was Mexican-American. Within the first month of me being there, I witnessed an awkward exchange between Lucia and one of her colleagues.

Lucia was a recent transplant to DC from Texas and had expressed how excited she was to have joined this nonprofit at the beginning of that year—she seemed ambitious and eager to make a difference in the world through this organization. One day, while working on a project, Lucia was listening to music through her headphones—something many of her colleagues were doing, as well. One of her colleagues, a middle-aged woman named Maureen, walked over to speak to Lucia. Lucia took off her headphones and proceeded to engage with Maureen. Maureen had asked Lucia a question, and when Lucia began to respond Maureen stopped her in mid-sentence and asked her if she heard "that noise."

Maureen quickly looked out the window and then rushed to look out the next window—a few feet away from Lucia's corner. With a disappointed look, Maureen walked back to Lucia and said, "I can hear the ice cream truck, but I don't see it." Lucia chuckled and looked down at her headphones and said, "I think you might be hearing my music." Lucia unplugged her headphones and played Mexican folk music over her computer speakers. Maureen looked confused and asked, "What is this?" Lucia excitedly shared that it was her favorite Mexican folk band. Maureen was shocked and asked, "Do you understand this music, do you speak Mexican?" Lucia smiled and proudly responded, "Yes, I understand because I am Mexican, and I do speak **Spanish**." Maureen then blurted out, "But you're educated." Lucia softly responded with restraint, "Yes, many of us are educated just as many of you aren't." Maureen apologized for her ignorance, and in the end Lucia seemed to have accepted the apology.

Shortly after the exchange with Maureen, I observed Lucia encounter uncomfortable open-air conversations with the Department Director, Brad. Brad was in his mid-thirties and a Georgetown alumnus, he was born and raised in affluent Bethesda, Maryland. As with most development teams in nonprofits, the staff was operating on a tight budget and was overloaded with projects. Lucia was managing multiple projects and her duty was to obtain final approval from Brad. Lucia was about to launch a direct mail campaign as she quickly passed by my designated work area and walked into Brad's office to show him the final artwork. He quickly gave his comments, marked the piece in red ink, and handed it back to Lucia. As Lucia was walking out of his office, Brad jokingly yelled out "You're as fast as a "drive-by. I know YOU know what that is! Get it?!" Brad drowned himself in his own laughter, meanwhile Lucia smiled uncomfortably, walked back to her desk, and continued working. Brad was referring to the stereotypical Mexican West Coast gang culture of drive-by shootings. Brad did not seem to be a malicious individual, he simply did not understand that his "joke" was not funny to Lucia. Instead it was hurtful and insensitive, just as the Pepsi commercial was to the Black Lives Matters protestors.

I was concluding the three-month project I was hired to consult on when I learned that Lucia had given her notice and was joining a top marketing agency. I walked over to Lucia's corner, congratulated her, and asked her what interested her about that specific marketing agency. Lucia shared that the increase in salary was certainly appealing, but what convinced her was the diverse talent she met in her round of interviews. She expressed that although she was passionate about the nonprofit's mission, she could see herself growing at the marketing agency in a manner that she could not envision at the nonprofit.

Unfortunately, I also have been on the receiving end of culturally insensitive and inappropriate comments. I had been hired to work with an international organization to lead and manage the Midwest's fundraising campaigns. I flew to meet with the leader of that region, Bob, to review quarter one's results and discuss the strategy for the remaining fiscal year. At the close of the meeting, Bob looked down at the corner of his desk and fixated on an article he must have printed prior to my arrival. He then spoke up and said, "He is out of his mind. Them illegals don't belong here, and we should not be helping them. It's easy for them to cross the border, but these Mexicans need to go back where they came from. Don't you think?" It took me a minute to register what had just been said to me, a Mexican-American daughter of illegal immigrants. The only response I could muster up without jeopardizing the agency I worked for was, "Can I have a copy of that article? I have been so focused on your region's performance and strategy that I haven't had the opportunity to read today's headlines." I walked away with a copy of the *New York Times* article, *Obama to Permit Young Migrants to Remain in US*—without a doubt, that day I was tested just as Lucia had been tested.

The difference was that the nonprofit organization that employed Lucia missed an opportunity to retain a rising star. It was evident that Lucia had joined the nonprofit because she was passionate about the cause—she had been quite vocal about what it meant for her to work there. It could be argued that if Lucia had stayed longer and documented each of the culturally insensitive comments she had received, she could have filed a lawsuit against the nonprofit. Whereas in my case, the culturally insensitive comments were from a client, not my employer. However, I later discovered that this organization had already experienced a PR nightmare when a leader in another region shared his negative views about the LGBT community, which resulted in a significant decline in fundraising dollars.

The solution to combat the lack of cultural awareness and sensitivity is the best piece of advice I can offer to all leadership in any nonprofit organization, which is to prioritize racial diversity throughout the organization and genuinely foster a culture of inclusion. Diversity initiatives must start at the top with cultural sensitivity training—it could save your organization from a PR disaster and avoid a significant loss of fundraising dollars.

There are no excuses for avoiding these initiatives. You may be thinking that it is unnecessary because your nonprofit is small, and you may also be questioning how exactly you can foster a culture of inclusion. There are plenty of manners in which you can create a comfortable, welcoming working environment for people of diverse backgrounds—such as setting up a committee, encouraging cultural potlucks, and creating mentorship programs.

Promoting racial diversity and nurturing a culture of inclusion will only benefit your organization. The new workforce wave is more diverse than ever[9] and has been described as a "largely optimistic group."[10] According to Gallup's 2016 report, *How Millennials Want to Work and Live*, 87% of millennials say professional development or career growth opportunities are very important to them in a job.[11] In Lucia's situation, she was unable to envision career growth in an organization that was not diverse. As the workforce grows in diversity it will be even more imperative for nonprofit organizations to prioritize racial diversity and foster a culture of inclusion.

MISTAKE #28

One Size Fits All Mentality— Strategy & Messaging

Just as our workforce is becoming more diverse, so are our donors. According to the Census Bureau, by 2030 over half of Americans are projected to identify as non-white.[12] This cultural shift presents a major opportunity for nonprofit organizations, which requires an adjustment in messaging and in the overarching strategy to appeal to diverse constituents.

Not revamping your overall strategy nor tailoring messaging to appeal to more diverse donors can be disastrous. For example, a couple of years ago I was hired to lead the fundraising efforts for another nonprofit organization that had a branch in Puerto Rico. For some odd reason, the Puerto Rico branch was siloed and had their donor database separate from the head organization.

As with any client I work with, in partnership with my analytics team, I dig deep in donor data analysis to understand past performances—this ultimately helps shape the strategy I recommend for the upcoming fiscal year. What we found was a drastic response rate spike with a shockingly low average gift of $5 in that fiscal year, which then plummeted even further the following year. We also saw that the number of pieces mailed was astronomical—they closely matched Puerto Rico's donor universe. I remember thinking, *this cannot be possible.* It was a conundrum. To better understand what transpired the past fiscal year, I flew to Puerto Rico and met with the leadership of that branch and asked for permission to do hands-on research.

Through my research, I discovered that the head organization had allocated a budget of $1 million for Puerto Rico, and had hired a consulting group to lead and execute their fundraising direct mail campaigns. Unfortunately, this consulting group evidently did not understand Puerto Rican donors and had applied broad strokes in strategy and messaging. There was no segmentation strategy nor an ask array strategy—the dollar amounts were open in the remits. Lastly, the messaging did not reflect the Puerto Rican community. For instance, the Christmas appeal had images of Caucasian folks in bulky sweaters asking for donations to help the community at large—

in Puerto Rico, a tropical island. To make matters worse, the appeal was in English.

I later uncovered that the consulting group had worked with the head organization's leadership and gotten their final approval to execute the campaigns. Ultimately, the organization's leadership is to blame for pretty much throwing away $1 million and insulting the Puerto Rican market with disconnected messaging. Nevertheless, I could not help but question how it was possible that nobody in leadership thought the images of Caucasian kids wearing sweaters were a good idea to appeal to Puerto Rican donors. Similarly, how is it possible that not one person at H&M questioned the image of the black child in the infamous hoodie? The H&M image must have passed through several dozen hands—from the photographer, the graphic design team, the digital team that uploaded the image to the website, and the marketing team . . . and yet not one sole individual raised their hand and asked, "Are we sure about this?"

I wholeheartedly believe that the lack of racial diversity in both situations is the culprit, as the lack of diversity produces groupthink and can result in a "one size fits all" mentality. Groupthink was first used in 1971 by psychologist Irving Janis. It is a term that describes "when a group of well-intentioned people make irrational or non-optimal decisions that are spurred by the urge to conform or the discouragement of dissent."[13]

The solution to overturn groupthink is diversity, because a counterbalance is positive for companies and organizations—it encourages diversity of thought and fights conformity, which is essential for the increasingly diverse donor base.[14] The ability to reach and relate to a diverse donor base is within each nonprofit organization's grasp, and successfully building relationships and connecting with diverse constituents will be easiest when the organization itself reflects diversity internally within its leadership and staff.

Conclusion

The mistakes differ in the details of each situation I described, but regardless of the details, the root of both mistakes is the lack of racial diversity. Nonprofit organizations need to adjust their sails by understanding and catering to the growth of America's multicultural population. Keeping in mind that multiculturalism is not a new concept, but how we interpret it must change.

Historically, the US was described as a melting pot of cultures, where cultures assimilate into a single homogeneous society. However, assimilation has deterred and as a result the salad bowl concept emerged. Also known as the cultural mosaic theory, the salad bowl concept proposes that peoples of diverse cultures not only assimilate into the new world culture, but also remain distinct by retaining specific cultural practices.[15] This further reaffirms that the manner in which nonprofit organizations communicate with the US' ever-growing diverse population requires a multicultural strategy, which includes tailored messaging that allows diverse donors to connect with a nonprofit organization's cause.

It is important to note that the survival of nonprofits will also begin to shift, to depend on the diverse donor base as it will soon be representative of US' majority/minority population. If your nonprofit organization has racial diversity organizational goals for 2019, congratulations—you are ahead of most nonprofits. For the nonprofit organizations that did not realize the importance of racial diversity, it is not too late. Start now, and your organization will reap the benefits from your diversity initiatives.

1 Panetta, Grace. "This Graphic Shows How Much More Diverse the House of Representatives Is Getting." Business Insider. January 12, 2019. Accessed February 05, 2019. https://www.businessinsider.com/changes-in-gender-racial-diversity-between-the-115th-and-116th-house-2018-12.

2 "Race to Lead: Confronting the Nonprofit Racial Leadership Gap." Building Movement Project- Social Service and Social Change. Accessed February 05, 2019. http://www.buildingmovement.org/reports/entry/race_to_lead.

3 Center, Foundation. "The Diversity Gap in the Nonprofit Sector." Philanthropy News Digest (PND). Accessed February 05, 2019. https://philanthropynewsdigest.org/columns/the-sustainable-nonprofit/the-diversity-gap-in-the-nonprofit-sector.

4 Nickalls, Sammy. "Brand Marketing H&M Is Under Fire for Modeling Its 'Coolest Monkey' Hoodie on a Black Child." *Www. adweek.com*, 8 Jan. 2018, www.adweek.com/brand-marketing/hm-is-under-fire-for-modeling-its-coolest-monkey-hoodie-on-a-black-child/.

5 Hodgson, Camilla. "H&M Profits Dive in 'tough' First Half of the Year." Financial Times. June 28, 2018. Accessed February 05, 2019. https://www.ft.com/content/4ea486fa-7883-11e8-bc55-50daf11b720d.

6 Fumo, Nicola. "H&M Hires Diversity Manager In Wake Of Racist Hoodie Fiasco." Forbes. January 19, 2018. Accessed February 05, 2019. https://www.forbes.com/sites/nicolafumo/2018/01/18/hm-diversity-manager-hire/#646b99d05337.

7 Victor, Daniel. "Pepsi Pulls Ad Accused of Trivializing Black Lives Matter." The New York Times. April 05, 2017. Accessed February 05, 2019. https://www.nytimes.com/2017/04/05/business/kendall-jenner-pepsi-ad.html.

8 IBID.

9 "Meet the US Workforce of the Future: Older, More Diverse, and More Educated." Deloitte United States. July 31, 2017. Accessed February 05, 2019. https://www2.deloitte.com/insights/us/en/deloitte-review/issue-21/meet-the-us-workforce-of-the-future.html.

[10] Gallup, Inc. "What Millennials Want From Work and Life." Gallup.com. May 10, 2016. Accessed February 05, 2019. https://www.gallup.com/workplace/236477/millennials-work-life.aspx.

[11] "How Millennials Want to Work and Live." *Gallup.com*, 2016, www.acceluspartners.com/wp-content/uploads/2016/09/2016-How_Millennials_Want_To_Work_And_Live-Abridged.pdf.

[12] Colby, Sandra L., and Ortman, Jennifer M. *US Census Bureau*, 2015, US Census Bureau, 2015.

[13] "Groupthink." Psychology Today. Accessed February 05, 2019. https://www.psychologytoday.com/us/basics/groupthink.

[14] Johansson, Anna. "Why Workplace Diversity Diminishes Groupthink And How Millennials Are Helping." Forbes. July 20, 2017. Accessed February 05, 2019. https://www.forbes.com/sites/annajohansson/2017/07/20/how-workplace-diversity-diminishes-groupthink-and-how-millennials-are-helping/#2c778b0f4b74.

[15] Mahfouz, Safi. "America's Melting Pot or the Salad Bowl: The Stage Immigrant's Dilemma." Journal of Foreign Languages, Cultures and Civilizations. ARIPD (American Research Institute for Policy Development). Vol. 1 No. 2, 2013, United States of America. ARIPD (American Research Institute for Policy Development). 1.

MISTAKES #29-#32

Not Leading Yourself Well

By Stacey Holmes Girdner, MBA

As a nonprofit leader, there are hundreds of responsibilities and priorities that demand your attention and distract you from doing the actual leading of your organization. While you are moving well over 100 mph dealing with a myriad of challenges, what might go unattended are your own leader behaviors, surrounding yourself with partners who think differently than you, using your leader influence for good, and caring for your leader vitality. Following are some common leader mistakes and suggestions to avoid these pitfalls.

MISTAKE #29

Lacking Self-Knowledge as a Leader

There were five of them, sitting around a conference table, talking about the difficulty of giving feedback to—or worse yet, terminating—employees who were failing in their role. There seemed to be widespread agreement that if they were to operate their nonprofit successfully and create the kind of culture they spoke of, they would need to demonstrate courage and address problem employees. The feeling of despair in the room was palpable because none were very skilled at acting on difficult people decisions.

After a heavy pause as the reality of what they were saying set in, two of them spoke up: "I totally agree and have already done a lot of this throughout my division." The other chimed in, "Me too. I think all my people are currently performing at the top of their game."

Again, there was a heavy silence. This time though, it was not despair, but disbelief. *Did they just say what we think we heard?* At that moment, these were two of the divisions that had the poorest record of addressing employee performance issues. But these leaders spoke with confidence in their own competence. How could they be so off? Were they really that blind to their own weaknesses?

No one said a word, but the question hung silently in the air, "Could I be equally deluded about my ability to lead?"

As leaders, we typically know our goals and what we are trying to accomplish, and we see ourselves through our good intentions. We are usually trying to do something important for our company and all its stakeholders. What we don't know, however, is whether our aims hit the mark. And the higher we go in an organization, the less accurate and timely feedback we'll receive about how our actions are experienced by others. Worse yet, the longer we are in a leader role, the more likely it is that we have growing blind spots that few—if any—in the workplace have the courage to point out to us. A colleague of mine who just got promoted to President of an organization said, "Overnight, I became funnier, smarter, and more in demand." Not because he had changed, but his positional authority had. As we continue to succeed as leaders, unless we are intentional about getting feedback, we may end up like the emperor with no clothes—walking around thinking we are beautifully adorned when in reality, we have nothing on and although everyone else sees and knows the truth, no one is willing to claim it. What to do?

Know thyself and all thy foibles.

A. Take assessments. Okay, I admit I can be an assessment-aholic. I love data. And leader assessments provide quantitative data of differing reliability and validity. Nevertheless, the good ones typically affirm a leader's known areas of strength and limitations, as well as make more conscious those behaviors they didn't overtly see in themselves. There are lots of online assessments with varying effectiveness, and each may measure a different aspect of your leadership style. A few I recommend are PeopleMap,[1] Everything DiSC Management Profile,[2] and Hogan Leadership Assessment.[3]

B. Ask for feedback. This can be tough for those working with you because sustaining a collegial relationship with you is not only important to their work, but may also be important to their sense of security in their employment. Ticking you off is usually not high on any employee's list, so going around asking people what they think of you might not be fruitful. Instead, you might enlist someone to gather the information for you through a 360° feedback assessment or through face-to-face interviews.

C. Work with a coach. The field of executive coaching is growing exponentially as corporate and nonprofit leaders experience the significant changes that can occur when they focus on their working behavior and knowledge. Ask around or find one through the International Coaching Federation (coachfederation. org).

D. Read. Some books I recommend are *Primal Leadership* by Daniel Goleman, *What Got You Here Won't Get You There* by Marshall Goldsmith, and *Crucial Conversations* by Kerry Patterson, Al Switzler, Joseph Grenny, and Ron McMillan.

MISTAKE #30

Hiring Your Twin

It was like a contest, although it shouldn't have been. Who can hire the most successful new employee? The hiring manager narrowed the field down to two candidates. Of the two, she liked candidate A. Candidate A was much like her—thorough, detailed, self-disciplined, responsible, and reliable. The boss's choice? Candidate B. Candidate B was as unlike the hiring manager as Candidate A was similar. He was creative, spontaneous, charming, persuasive, and easygoing. Ultimately, Candidate B was chosen because his style was seen as a better fit for a sales position. He brought a new set of skills and a different temperament to their work. Instead of hiring for chemistry and compatibility, they hired for capability and fit with the job. Within his first week, he took steps to sell their product that no prior employee had ever done. Within a month, he had brought on two winning clients. How he went about doing his job seemed like a mystery to the rest of the team. They just stood by and watched him with amazement while he did what he was hired and equipped to do, and in a way none of the others could have done. They hired him not just because he had the chemistry to work well with the team, but more importantly, because he had the skills and experience to succeed in the role.

Who was it that said about their spouse, "I looked in her eyes, saw myself, and fell in love"? WE are the center of our universe. Everything we say and do has been filtered through our unique mindset, thoughts, and beliefs. This natural self-anchored-ness, although grounding, can trip us up as leaders. Why? We tend to surround ourselves with leader teams that mirror our image of ourselves. We like to work with people who see things similarly; who share a common strategy for the company; who enjoy the same jokes we do; who have a similar pace and gravitate toward common preferences; who make us feel good about ourselves. We typically enjoy working with people who are like us. The upside? Work is more comfortable and enjoyable. The risk? This may lead to a lack of diversity of thinking, not having anyone to challenge us or get us out of a rut, not having a team who complements our skills with different capabilities. But if our natural inclination is to hire like-minded candidates, how do we break out of the norm?

Hire partners who complement your style.

A. *Don't rely solely on the beer test.* I've worked with numerous executives whose interview style is to chat with employment candidates, ask a couple of questions, then spend the majority of the time telling the candidate about their company and describing why the candidate would want to work there. If the two share a similar chemistry, the executive leaves the interview ready to extend an offer.

This approach is using the beer test criteria for employee selection. The beer test suggests you ask yourself, "Would I want to have a beer with this candidate?" and if your answer is "Yes!", the person gets hired. Unfortunately, it's not uncommon for six to eight months to go by when the hiring executive is surprised that the new hire is failing in her or his role. "But they were so likeable and seemed so competent when they interviewed!" the executive might say. In hindsight, the executive may realize the only competency that was screened through their interview approach was their ability to get along with others over a beer. Probably not the best way to assess someone's fit for a job and organization.

Don't get me wrong. Chemistry is important. But it's not the ONLY thing that is important when hiring for skills outside of your own. To ensure you develop a leader team that is complementary rather than duplicative, you must first understand the essential skills required to succeed in the company and in the role. What do they need to know and be able to do to perform this job well? How do they need to perform this job? What values do they need to share to fit with our culture? What leader style do they need to guide their direct reports? What are my own limitations that I need this person to complement? Rather than relying on chemistry to serve as your hiring criteria, take the time to define what the candidate needs before recruiting.

B. *Gather stories.* Armed with a clear definition of what it takes to succeed in the role for which you are recruiting, you can develop questions that will enlist stories from candidates. For example, if an essential skill is being able to close a deal with a major donor, the story you want to hear is how they've done it before. You might ask, "Tell me about your most recent major gift win. Talk me through, step by step, how you engaged the donor and what you did specifically that led to their making a donation." Ask them to tell you the story. Why? You will not only get a picture of WHAT the candidate can or cannot do, but also HOW the candidate goes about doing it. The best predictor of future success is past performance.

Stories give you a wealth of information about the candidate's real work experience. Also, it's hard to fake a story—so with this approach, you are less likely to get bamboozled in an interview. However, the stories should specifically demonstrate the essential qualities needed to succeed in the role. So, for each essential quality, create one question that will elicit a story from the candidate about how they've demonstrated that quality in the past.

C. *Focus on complementing your strengths.* In addition to hiring for competency in the role and fit with the organization's culture, also pay attention to hiring individuals who complement rather than duplicate your strengths. If you are a forward thinker who enjoys creative risk-taking and spontaneity, you may want someone on your leadership team who is a conservative and thoughtful planner. If you tend to color within the lines, your team and organization may be stronger if you have someone in your group who pushes the boundaries.

Whatever your circumstance might be, go beyond the beer test and actually define what it will take to succeed in the role, gather stories to give you confidence that what you need done is what the candidate has actually done before, and ensure they bring a different style and approach to the table so you aren't just hiring your twin.

MISTAKE #31

Abdicating Your Power to Influence your direct reports' success

She stormed into my HR office, exasperated, claiming she'd had it with her new employee.

"She isn't doing things the way she is supposed to. I'd like to let her go."

I replied, "No problem. Let's first be sure you've done everything you can to ensure her success. Did you make your expectations clear?"

"No. I wanted to see how she would naturally gravitate toward the work on her own."

"Did you provide training?"

"Well, no. She didn't ask for any."

"Have you given her feedback?"

"Um, no, that's not my style. I gave her the space and autonomy to perform."

"Did you do anything to help her succeed?"

"Well, I guess not."

I can't tell you how many times I've seen this happen. When leaders do not get what they want nor what the business needs from an employee, they tend to feel helpless and resort to letting the employee go. Have you been there? Well, here's the good news. YOU HAVE POWER. And I don't mean the power to fire someone (although that is one of your options). I am talking about the power to influence the performance of any of your direct reports. And you don't have to use coercion, threats, bribes, or monetary incentives! Here's what you need to do.

Take responsibility for the success of those around you.

A. *Make your* expectations clear. A common conversation I have with frustrated leaders goes like this:

"My employee isn't doing xyz."

"Well, have you told the employee they are supposed to do xyz?"

"No! They should know."

Maybe they should know, but they are less likely to do it if you haven't made it clear. Want to turn around someone's performance? Sit them down and describe what they would be doing if performing the job successfully. Describe your expectations. Specify their role and responsibility. Then, if they don't succeed, at least you'll know you've been clear about what is required.

B. *Provide training, mentoring, or coaching if needed.* One of the reasons employees don't perform as expected is because they simply don't know how. And if they are a new employee, it's not likely they will let you in on this. Instead, they blunder along on their own. Don't be that leader who hired someone and then set them up to fail. Instead, after you've made your expectations clear, find out where they need the most help.

Ask, "Which of these tasks have you performed before and which are new?" For the ones that are new, ask, "Would it help to have someone walk you through how we do that here?" Then offer training or arrange for training by a subject matter expert. It's

YOUR responsibility to ensure your employees have what they need to succeed and providing training, when needed, is one of the ways you can do this.

C. *Find out what's getting in the way and remove the barrier.* Employees fail to do what they are supposed to do either because they don't know it's their responsibility, they don't know how to do it, or something is getting in the way. Your job is to uncover the barrier and when possible, remove it. For example, maybe a member of your board is regularly provocative during your monthly board meetings. With curiosity, you describe the behavior you've observed and the impact you see it having on others in the meeting. You ask, "How do you see it?" Then you learn that the board member is tired of the lack of conversations and questioning during board meetings. She thinks the board should be more engaged during meetings and to stir things up, she makes confrontational statements. Her intent is good, but her method and timing are off. In this example, what's in the way? The board member's choice of time and approach to board development. When this kind of thing happens with one of your direct reports, dialogue with your employee. Find out what's getting in the way of performance. Remove the barrier for them.

D. *When all else has failed, invite them to leave the organization.* It may come to this. That's okay. But you'll only want to do this after you've exhausted your power to influence through being clear about performance expectations, providing training when needed, and removing barriers when they get in the way of performance.

MISTAKE #32

Believing it's Noble to Burn Your Candle from Both Ends

I remember he felt so righteous about his habits. He would frequently brag about his long hours at work, lack of sleep, and all the sacrifices he made for "the good of the nonprofit." He was overweight, irritable, drank more than he should, and rarely saw his wife or children. At the same time, he was proud of his work ethic and believed he was demonstrating to other executives what good leadership looked like. That was, until found himself in the emergency room with a heart attack. Only then did he start to evaluate the nobility of burning both ends of the candle.

There will probably NEVER be enough minutes in a day for all the things you'd like to squeeze out of each 24-hour period. Never. Also, have you ever heard anyone on their deathbed saying, "I wish I'd worked longer hours?" If you lead a company, you are responsible for taking care of yourself. All you've got is you. And if you don't take care of yourself, who will? Or, if you don't take care of yourself and land in the emergency room, who'll run the business then? A common leader mistake is believing it's noble to wear yourself ragged over work. This is a severe misnomer. If you are in an important leadership role, one of your most important responsibilities is to take care of yourself.

You have one life to live—so live it!

A. *Start by getting a good night of sleep.* I knew a leader who was being rapidly promoted up the ranks because his energy seemed inexhaustible. He was everywhere doing everything. Nothing seemed to stop him. Soon, however, he started getting irritable, short, and grumpy. His decisions started to produce less-than-desirable results. His health started to suffer, as did all his relationships—especially his marriage. It turns out he was compromising his sleep so he could get more work done each day. He was averaging four hours of sleep per night. It was really beneficial to his career, until everything started to fall apart.

According to the American Academy of Sleep Medicine and the Sleep Research Society,[4] our health is dependent on getting at least 7 hours of solid sleep each night. And if you are not currently getting that much sleep, you are not alone. Overall, Americans are sleep deprived. Nevertheless, strong and clear-minded leadership starts with getting at least 7 hours of sleep each night.

B. *Eat well and hydrate.* If you are working endless hours and neglecting yourself, thinking you are being a responsible leader, think again. Did you know your brain consumes more of your glucose than any other organ in your body? After your 7 hours of sleep, the first thing you can do to further your career and to be a responsible leader is to eat breakfast! Your brain cannot operate well without sustenance. The same goes for lunch. Research shows that those who eat lunch away from their desk are much more productive in the afternoon than those who do not. Why? Lunch feeds your brain. Want to ensure the success of your organization as a leader? Eat breakfast as well as lunch. You will notice the difference in your attitude, ability to solve problems, temper, and clarity of thinking.

When it comes to hydration, although there is no scientific evidence that you must drink 64 ounces of water each day, your body stops working properly when it is low on water. And if you wait until you get thirsty, you've waited too long. Get a cool-looking water bottle. Fill it up. Drink throughout the day. In addition, drink water during your meals. Your body will thank you for it.

C. *Move.* Sitting is the new smoking. Prolonged sitting time is a health risk. It's tough if you have an office job not to find yourself sitting for eight, nine, ten, or more hours per day. But even just 10-minute snatches of movement can help. Have walking meetings. Get up and go down the hall to talk face-to-face with someone rather than sending an email. Take the stairs. You know the routine. The USDA's Dietary Guidelines for Americans[5] encourages at least 150 minutes of exercise per week and the US Department of Health and Human Services claims that regular physical activity can lower your risk of early death, coronary heart disease, falls, weight gain, breast cancer, colon cancer, high blood pressure, type 2 diabetes, stroke, and depression. In addition, regular physical activity (remember . . . even 10 minutes at a time) will improve cardiorespiratory and muscular fitness as well as cognitive function. When given the chance, move rather than sit.

D. *Focus on the top five.* According to the Center for Disease Control, there are five physical behaviors that, when consistently demonstrated, could mitigate

75% of deaths worldwide caused by diabetes, heart disease, lung disease, mental illness, and cancer. What are the five? Eating healthy, drinking alcohol in moderation, refraining from smoking, walking at least 30 minutes per day, and keeping your waist size at less than ½ of your height.[6]

E. *Make time for things that give you joy.* Schedule at least one joyful activity per week—whatever it is. Feed your spirit. Feed your soul. Feed yourself as a leader!

[1] *PeopleMap.com*, www.peoplemapsystems.com/.

[2] https://www.thediscpersonalitytest.com/

[3] https://www.hoganassessments.com/

[4] Watson NF, Badr MS, Belenky G, Bliwise DL, Buxton OM, Buysse D, Dinges DF, Gangwisch J, Grandner MA, Kushida C, Malhotra RK, Martin JL, Patel SR, Quan SF, Tasali E. "Recommended amount of sleep for a healthy adult: a joint consensus statement of the American Academy of Sleep Medicine and Sleep Research Society." J Clin Sleep Med 2015;11(6):591–592.

[5] U.S. Department of Health and Human Services. *2008 Physical Activity Guidelines for Americans.* Washington (DC): U.S. Department of Health and Human Services; 2008. ODPHP Publication No. U0036. Available at: http://www.health.gov/paguidelines. Accessed November 8, 2018.

[6] Johnson, Nicole Blair, et al. "CDC National Health Report: Leading Causes of Morbidity and Mortality and Associated Behavioral Risk and Protective Factors—United States, 2005-2013." *Www.cdc.gov*, 31 Oct. 2014, www.cdc.gov/mmwr/preview/mmwrhtml/su6304a2.htm.

MISTAKE #33

Failing to Implement Board Term Limits

By Andrew Olsen, CFRE

I was in Toledo, OH meeting with a faith-based social service organization that had asked for my help to improve their direct-response fundraising results.

It was, I thought, the perfect scenario. The Executive Director understood that they didn't have the necessary expertise in-house, and he was motivated to solve the problem. He had involved the board chair in our earliest conversations, so there was alignment at the board level as well.

But wow, was I wrong!

As we settled into the final board meeting where we'd decide on the organization's fundraising strategy for the following year, I noticed there were three empty seats. About 10 minutes into the meeting, three other board members showed up. They were clearly unhappy and looking for an argument.

Each of these three board members began to verbally attack me and the organization's Executive Director. They weren't just arguing over costs or questioning specific elements of strategy. They were making inappropriate personal attacks, and fighting against the idea of the organization changing or evolving in any way.

One particular board member went so far as to look at the Executive Director and say, "You're not even half the Executive Director that Peter was."

Get this. Pete was the Executive Director 12 years prior. Yes, TWELVE YEARS.

This organization's bylaws didn't include board term limits, so when someone joined the board, they were essentially a board member for life, unless they chose to leave. This stifled creativity, limited the organization's ability to gain fresh perspectives, and resulted in a board environment that celebrated historical approaches simply because the people around the table were the ones who created them.

Here are five reasons board term limits are important:

1. Regular, planned volunteer leadership transition helps create an environment that values and embraces change as a cultural principle.

2. Recruiting new members means you can bring a more diverse set of talents and lived experiences to the forefront of your organizational leadership.

3. It provides you an opportunity to remove board members who are disengaged or toxic.

4. Term limits give you the opportunity to strategically recruit volunteer leaders who can positively impact philanthropy, either through personal capacity, community relationships, or both.

5. You can be more nimble and responsive to the organization's need for strategic volunteer talent by recruiting people with specific and evolving skill sets if you have established term limits.

As I hope you can see, board term limits are critical to the long-term health of any organization. They aren't always easy to implement, but getting them in place is well worth the time and effort necessary to put them in place. I'm a fan of three year terms for board members. If you want to retain talent over the long-term, you might also consider allowing two consecutive three year terms. You should also create a policy structure that allows for your board to release a board member who is behaving inappropriately or is disengaged from their role as a board member.

STRATEGY & PLANNING

"Strategy is about making choices, trade-offs; it's about deliberately choosing to be different."
—*Michael Porter,*
Bishop William Lawrence University Professor
at Harvard Business School

"However beautiful the strategy, you should occasionally look at the results."
—*Unknown*

I F, AS MICHAEL Porter says, "strategy is about making choices, trade-offs," then what does it mean for strategy development in the nonprofit sector?

Often our sector is characterized as the *will do because we must do* sector. That is, we take things on because we believe they are essential, and likely because no one else is addressing them.

But the question is, when we do things like this—and it happens often in our sector—do we consider the consequences?

I would propose that in many cases, we don't. This is likely the result of simply not understanding that there are real trade-offs that must be made anytime we add or subtract a goal or initiative. This is why strategic planning is so critical, even if it is often overlooked in our sector.

MISTAKE #34

Not Having a Strategic Plan

By Andrew Olsen, CFRE

You might be thinking, "WHAT!?!?!? How can any organization operate without a strategic plan?!" And you wouldn't be alone in thinking that. I don't know how any organization—commercial or nonprofit—runs successfully without a strategic plan. How can you know the direction you're headed is the right one if you don't have a plan? How do you benchmark progress? You'd be amazed, though, at the number of nonprofit organizations that don't engage in a strategic planning process and don't operate from an established strategic plan.

Often when I challenge an organizational leader running an organization without a plan, I get responses like, "We don't have the time. We don't have the money. We don't have a strategic planning expert on staff." Honestly, I think these are all deflections. This is about priorities and accountabilities. It's much easier to disregard when you miss the mark if you don't have a strategic plan guiding your efforts. If you haven't established key performance indicators, it's easy to slide by whether you're successful or not. The reality is, most nonprofits that operate without a strategic plan never really go anywhere. They don't grow. They don't solve big problems or accomplish big things. They simply exist. And in my opinion, that's a waste. Build a plan. Work the plan. Measure against the plan. You'll see the results pay off in big ways!

Here are 6 steps for developing a solid strategic plan:

1. **Understand your reality:** Where is your organization? Not where do you see your organization, or where do you want your organization to be, but truly, objectively, where are you in your lifecycle? What is working? What isn't working? Where are you succeeding, and where do you have room to improve? The best way to get at this information is to conduct an objective audit process, both internally and externally.

2. **Define your priorities:** What are the critical things that must happen, and why? What are the non-essential activities that might be *important* but aren't essential to your success? This is where you take out your red pen and start striking out the non-essentials so that you free up time to focus on the true priorities (hint: you can do this same thing with your budget!).

3. **Define your goals:** What must be accomplished for you to be successful? What will happen for those you serve, for your organization, your team, and you personally when you are successful? What will be the result if you don't achieve these goals?

4. **Identify accountabilities and responsibilities:** Create a list of the people who are ultimately accountable for each goal on your list. Under their names, identify the other members of your staff, external partners, and volunteers who will be responsible for some aspects of each goal.

5. **Execute:** Documenting your strategy is meaningless if you never execute against it.

6. **Measure and pivot:** You need to regularly revisit your strategy to make sure that the activities you're executing actually map back to the strategy and goals you set, and that what you are doing is bringing you closer to achieving those goals. If you're out of alignment, adjust either your execution plan or your strategy to adapt to your new reality, then begin executing again

MISTAKE #35

Making Decisions Based on Cost Instead of Value

By Andrew Olsen, CFRE

Several years ago while I was leading the Rescue Mission business unit at a large fundraising agency, a new low-price competitor entered the market. They aggressively pursued our clients and convinced four of our largest to leave us and begin working with their firm for direct-response fundraising services. The claim they made was that they would provide the same level of value for significantly lower cost to each organization.

Half of their promise ended up coming true. Their costs did come in lower. However, because they lacked the same level of expertise in media strategy, creative, offer development, digital, and channel integration, each of the four nonprofits ended up experiencing significant increases in donor attrition, and revenue losses of anywhere from $100,000-$400,000 year-over-year. These organizations are homeless service providers in four major cities across the US. When they lose revenue at the scale that these organizations lost, that means there are people left without access to emergency services like overnight shelter and meals. **There are real and significant impacts to decisions like this.**

Negotiating to get the best value you can is a great idea. It's the smart thing for any organization to do. However, focusing only on cost—and not on value—is dangerous (as it was for my clients). If you only ever look at the expense side of the ledger, and are always chasing cost reductions instead of striving to raise the most money possible for your organization, you're destined to fall into this trap.

MISTAKE #36

Not Understanding the Value (and Cost) of Your Time

By Andrew Olsen, CFRE

It's easy to think of your time and that of your staff as "sunk costs," and not consider that time when you develop strategies and plans. What I mean by this is, as you're looking at a strategy you might fret over the external costs to execute that strategy, but because you're using existing staff resources to deliver that strategy, you may not even consider those staff costs in the process.

The place where this is most frequently an issue is in event fundraising. A charity might show on paper that they raised $100,000 at an event, and only spent $30,000 to put on the event. That's a net of $70,000 for this event, which is a decent return on investment.

However, that $30,000 doesn't account for all the hours that staff and leaders invested to put the event on. Once those costs are accounted for, you see that the true cost of the event is $65,000 ($30,000 in hard costs, and $35,000 in time, or soft costs). This means the net revenue on this event is actually only $35,000.

Seeing the fully loaded cost in this situation should (I hope) cause your organization to think seriously about whether an event like this is worth the cost. Alternately, you might choose to spend those resources on individual donor relationship building, where your return on investment is likely to exceed 5:1.

Next time you evaluate an opportunity for your organization, you need to make sure you're accounting for all of the costs, including:

1. Hard costs of development

What are the external costs (i.e., money you have to spend) necessary to develop your idea to the point where you can test it?

2. Soft costs of development

How many hours do you need to spend to develop this concept, and at what cost are those hours? Will it require 100 hours from your Development Associate to create this, or does it require 100 hours from your Chief Financial Officer? The cost of those two sets of hours is *very* different. This should also include the cost of overhead.

3. Hard costs of rollout

What are the external costs necessary to continue executing your idea, program, or campaign at scale and over time?

4. Soft costs of rollout

What are the internal costs (i.e., staff time, overhead) related to executing at scale and over time?

5. Ongoing management

In addition to the individual staff member(s) responsible for executing these programs or campaigns, what are the ongoing management costs of overseeing the execution and expansion of these programs?

6. Opportunity cost

What might you lose (i.e., the cost) by executing this program or activity instead of another option?

MISTAKE #37

Failing to Understand How Your Organization Generates Revenue

By Andrew Olsen, CFRE

One thing that surprises me when I meet with departmental leaders (and even many CEOs) in nonprofit organizations is how many don't fully understand how their organizations generate revenue. They might understand how they personally generate revenue for the organization, and some might know how their department contributes to this, but the majority don't completely grasp their organization's financial model.

This is a huge mistake! If your people don't understand how your organization makes money (I know, I know—making money isn't your mission—but that doesn't matter for this exercise), and how you spend that money, they won't be able to fully participate in leading the organization. Don't keep this information under lock and key. Healthy organizations share this information on a regular basis so that everyone has vision to the health of the organization, how they contribute both to revenue and expenses, and what they can do to improve each side of the ledger.

As a nonprofit leader—whether you lead the entire organization, a major department, or even just a small team—here are the key financial elements you need to understand in order to successfully contribute to managing your organization:

1. What are each of the revenue streams generated by your organization?

2. What are each of the expense lines in your operating budget?

3. How can you, in your role, impact both the revenue and expenses in meaningful ways that help you maximize net revenue?

When you fully understand these elements of your operating budget, at a line-item level, you can have meaningful conversations with your staff, your supervisor, key leaders, and even your board to identify ways to increase revenues and reduce costs.

MISTAKE #38

Failing to Embrace Change and Manage it Well

By Kathryn Landa, CFRE

Change is hard. Organizational change is harder. And, 50%-70% of organizational change initiatives fail. Why? And, how can you be one of the success stories?

After experiences with two start-ups and managing a multi-year corporate change initiative, I've seen the best and worst sides of change.

Here is what people who get it wrong fail to realize: **change is not about the organizational goals or the outcomes; it's about the people who will be making the change.**

If it was just about putting machinery in a new order or programming new features into your software, we wouldn't even call it change. We would call it an update. But we can't "update" people. *People* have to change. And if you've ever tried to change someone, you've realized that you can't. People must *choose* to change and be committed to it.

Now, this is where a lot of leaders start to shift in their seats because we start to talk about feelings. As much as we pretend that employees check all of their emotion and feelings at the door and simply stop being human the moment they enter the workplace, it just isn't true.

Try as we might, we remain human and we carry our life experience, vulnerabilities, fears, and hopes with us every day. They are what makes us who we are and what brings our unique talents to bear on the organization.

Some of us are more naturally comfortable with change, while others feel genuinely threatened or unsafe as the environment shifts. Our job as leaders is to consider the field as we plan for change. Now, there is certainly a place for the "this is the way it's going to be; get on board or get on out" approach, but you have to carefully weigh the consequences of that tactic. If you have really good people doing really great work, you are risking an exodus of talent.

So, who is on your field? Who will take to the changes naturally? Who will take convincing? And who will need extra investment? Sometimes it is those people with the most initial resistance who end up being the biggest advocates for the change.

Failure to pivot

Why is change even necessary? Well, it isn't—until there is pain. Sure, we can change something or someone anytime. But, when there is no pain, most people don't even think about changing or innovating. Usually we don't make a move until it's too late or the situation has gotten much more difficult to change than it would have needed to be.

When the pain gets bad enough—the financials are slipping, relationships are struggling—we realize we have to change things. But we often don't know how to articulate exactly what is wrong or what we need to do differently in a way that moves people forward.

And, though the impetus and push for change can easily come from within any level of the organization, in the end I believe it absolutely falls on leadership to anticipate the potholes down the road and adjust the path. Unfortunately, some leaders are reluctant to look for the next turn in the road—especially when things are going well. Some leaders are afraid to admit they've made a mistake. This is a people problem. My colleague calls this navel-gazing (and not the positive, meditative kind.)

In 2007, Nokia, the telecommunications company, was earning 50% of all profits in the mobile phone industry. I'm sure we could all still recall the famous ringtone if we wanted to. Unfortunately, Nokia failed to understand the gravity of the transition to smart phones. Nokia had hardware engineers who could build cool phones vs. other companies with software engineers who could build great operating systems. They also thought their brand was big enough to overcome being slow to market with developments. Nokia was subsequently annihilated by Android and Apple. *They failed to pivot, and most likely they failed to do so because things were going pretty well.*

In the nonprofit space, we see droves of organizations that have failed to keep up with donor trends like aging donor populations and recognizing shifts into digital communications and commerce.

In an analysis conducted by the National Center for Charitable Statistics, data showed that 36% of all nonprofits that obtained tax-exempt status in 2005 were no longer considered active just 10 years later.[1]

We still see organizations whose entire files are built on low-dollar, premium-addicted donors who aren't growing in numbers or giving. These organizations have failed to diversify audiences or offers to build a more solid base for the continued success of their mission.

A model for managing change (and people)

Marcella Bremer's book, *Organizational Culture Change* lists 7C's for success:[2]

1. Commitment from the top
2. Clarity on current and desired situation and goals
3. Consensus and commitment from workers

4. Continuous communication

5. Copy-Coach-Correct: Consistency

6. Create critical mass

7. Carry on

A similar framework is shared in various forms by many experts in this arena. Each step—or one like it—is critical to a successful implementation.

The steps that I've personally seen go most awry are those that require the highest degree of personal change from employees, and those usually involve clarity, consensus, and continuous communication.

Clarity: Vision Casting That Actually Works

Let's take *clarity*, for instance. A lack of clarity from the start of (or throughout) a process of change will leave your initiative dead in the water. If people don't understand the need for change or how the new direction will address the existing problem, they will not easily get on board.

And still, there is a delicate balance here. If you are going to run out to tell your staff that you are all standing on the proverbial "burning platform," yet you aren't able to provide some level of hope or a compelling new plan, you risk being left stranded on the platform by yourself, surrounded by flames.

Staying on the Nokia case study, former Nokia CEO Stephen Elop is a most classic case of oversharing about change. Elop came on in 2011 when Nokia was already in rapid decline, and he communicated to the company (and even issued a memo that was later leaked) that they were all quite literally standing on a burning platform and would need to take a leap of faith with him into a partnership with Microsoft to save the company. I don't envy his position. Frankly, at that point Nokia's success would have been an incredible turn-around for anyone—and in the end, Nokia did partner with Microsoft, only to be promptly dissolved.

Elop took deep criticism from employees, the board, and the general business community for his tactics, but most especially for that memo. In my opinion, he essentially reduced the entire company's investment in upcoming operating systems and software to a memo asking everyone to throw all of their R&D out the window; or more appropriately, to exchange it all for a Windows operating system.

Regardless of whether that could have been the right move, Elop lost the faith of almost every employee in that company as soon as he issued that statement. He forgot that his company was made up of people, and that not all of them could make the transition to drastic change that quickly.

A new vision should be positive and authentic. Yes, it must address the *need* for change AND it must have a clear, hopeful strategy for the future. Not everyone will see the writing on the wall; not everyone will understand the need to change the way they've been doing everything for so long. But, with a clear roadmap about where you are headed and an understanding of *why*, they can begin to adjust.

Consensus: A Delicate Balance of Who's In Charge

Your job as the leader of your organization is to build consensus around the new vision. It's not your employees' job to "get there." It's not up to the lieutenants in your charge to drive things forward (though, certainly, if you've done your job well they will); it is up to you.

You have chosen the new direction, you have carefully evaluated the necessary changes, and you have to do the difficult work of anticipating the needs of all the stakeholders in your organization and where you are willing to meet each of them.

If you barrel through change on your own path without so much as a nod to your employees, you will fail. If you democratize the process, backing off of your position and attempting to accommodate every dissenting opinion in the group, you will fail.

Managing change is a time for conviction and for care. Consensus literally means " a general agreement," and that is where you are trying to get to. It is essential to have enough agreement to bring your best people along with you on this journey.

Like the basis of most long-term, successful relationships or partnerships, you'll need to do far more listening than talking to get to consensus. Many people involved in the process will need to talk through their feelings, doubts, and concerns about the direction you have given. Don't speak, just listen.

One of the best pieces of advice for me when working with people has come from the parenting book, *How to Talk So Kids Will Listen & How To Listen So Kids Will Talk*, by Adele Faber and Elaine Mazlish. One of the tactics that is shared is to bite your tongue as your child is working through a challenge that has arisen, using simple utterances like "hmmm, oooh?, mmmm."[3] It worked brilliantly on my kids, who then felt emboldened to open up and share, and came to their own understanding and resolution without me saying a single word.

I've employed this strategy across all of my relationships and business partnerships, and you would be shocked at how valuable it can be for you as well, in any highly emotive situation. Once you've done a good bit of listening, there may be no need for you to speak at all. A knowing smile or nod might be the cap on the consensus you needed to build. If you do need to address a misconception, do it clearly and calmly. Restate the need for change and why you've chosen the current path.

Continuous Communication:

If you think you have communicated enough, you haven't. Say it, say it again, and then remind everyone what you said. I remember when I was on a team responsible for communicating change, many times we felt as if we were talking the change to death—only to find that employees were hungry for even more information. They were still crystalizing and clarifying the concept, and every employee moved at different paces through that process.

Then, when we were rolling out phases of the change, we had to communicate even more. And communication in this equation is not a one-way street, not by a long shot. We collected feedback in every step, evaluated any tweaks to the roll-out plan, and communicated back to the field. We reminded, coached, and clarified all along the way. Once we moved through a phase, we looked at outcomes. We talked through our goals again and we talked even more about the next step.

There were times when teams were quiet—they weren't asking questions or raising concerns. It turns out that these were some of the most crucial moments and required even more communication than normal. These were points where people had grown weary, were frustrated, shut down, or simply just didn't understand the junction we were at. We had to dive even deeper and pull information out of our teams to find out what was really going on, and then re-double our efforts to inform and inspire our people through consistent and open communication.

There is a caution here as well. Similar to sending the "burning platform" memo, consistent communication and organizational transparency does not mean that everyone in your company should know every detail of the crisis you may be facing. This is a tricky position because I advocate 100% for transparency and authenticity, while at the same time not everyone can handle the naked truth. For some, it's like yelling *Fire!* in a crowded movie theater.

Too much focus on the hard realities with not enough hope for the future will leave employees stuck in despair. Too much focus on our bright and rosy future while people are miserable will result in a feeling that leadership is completely out of touch with the existing realities, which leads to mistrust and disillusion.

Our job as the leaders is to balance the good news and the bad.

Pilot and Pivot

Finally, go confidently in the way of your path. This doesn't mean you won't have to make small pivots along the way as needed. In fact, you shouldn't hesitate to tweak the strategy as you begin to execute the change. I like to call this the "pilot and pivot" approach. Pilot a portion of the changes, watch for success in implementation, and pivot as necessary until the strategy is working.

Every plan must be fluid in order to adapt to the change in the landscape, time, and other factors involved.

If you remember that in as much as donors should be the center of your fundraising universe, your employees are the center of your organization, you will succeed at change and continue your mission for decades to come.

---

[1] Gore, D'Angelo. "Ben Carson on Nonprofit Failures." *Factcheck. org*, 21 Oct. 2015, www.factcheck.org/2015/10/ben-carson-on-nonprofit-failures/.

[2] Bremer, Marcella. *Organizational Culture Change: Unleash Your Organization's Potential in Circles of 10*. Kikker Groep, 2012. pp.13

[3] Faber, Adele, et al. *How to Talk so Kids Will Listen & Listen so Kids Will Talk*. PTS Publishing House, 2017. pp.13

MISTAKE #39

Hiring the Wrong Players and Coaches (Employees and Consultants)

By Kathryn Landa, CFRE

We all know and love the *right people on the bus* analogy, which reminds us to focus on the *who* of our organization before the *what* we are doing next or the *where* we are going.

Players

We need the right people on the bus, the wrong people off of it, and we need those chosen few to be sitting in the right seats.

I've personally spent time in both the commercial and nonprofit spaces, and in each case, the "people" part of business is where we all trip up the most. Very few of us are truly excellent at assessing talent and growing people. The reality is that your talent, both in-house and outsourced, will make or break your organization.

One bad apple can cause a toxic chain reaction within your culture. One dynamic individual can energize your entire team. We need to do better. And, the formula is simple.

Need, fit, balance, pivot
Assess your **need**
Assess their **fit**
Balance the team
Pivot when needed

Assess your need

Whether you are new to your organization or you've been around for a while, you must constantly evaluate the human resource needs of the team.

Especially now, as employees are turning over at ever-increasing rates and you've likely found yourself with constant holes that require rebalancing. What do you need? How do you know what will work for your department or organization?

First, think critically about the existing goals and challenges of the organization. What direction is the strategic plan pointing to, and what will it take to get you there?

You may need to upgrade, add, or even downgrade a position based on where you are headed. You may need to consider part-time or contract workers.

We have to stay creative, stay flexible, and realize that staff shifts—such as an unexpected resignation or transfer—don't have to be devastating. It could be a shift or opportunity like this that opens up new possibilities for a creative new structure. But that won't happen if we just replace a position out of sheer panic over "getting the work done."

Assess their fit

Budgets are tight, and when you do get a position approved, qualified candidates are often hard to come by. Some of us are located in areas where there just aren't any job seekers.

First, we MUST resist the temptation to just get a butt in the seat. In the past I personally fell for the philosophy of "a warm body." Sometimes we are afraid we'll lose a position if we can't fill it, or we are beleaguered by the pileup of work from the vacated post. So we give up, settling for a candidate we know isn't right.

In the long run this will always be counterproductive. You'll spend more time, stress, and investment over that hasty decision than you ever would have experienced by holding out just a little longer for the right person. In other words, you may not pay for it now but you will pay for it later.

Second, recognize that some people are just poor judges of talent. I know some very strong, effective leaders who aren't great at interviewing or selecting talent. They can still be effective by bringing other trusted colleagues in on staffing decisions. Don't be afraid to admit the same and ask for help.

Third, maximize the interview process. The typical process is a lot like speed dating. You may or may not even be included in the 20 seconds involved in scanning résumés, and then you are thrust into a room with a stale copy of a résumé and a stiff professional whose future is literally on the line.

You have 30-60 minutes to decide both of your fates. HOW are we supposed to successfully select someone who can make or break the organization? Even NBC's *The Bachelor* gets a few dates, and a whirlwind weekend before he has to make that final choice.

To get as much information as possible in that interview, I like to ask behavioral questions. Behavioral questions sound like, "Tell me about a time when you . . ." Because I don't just want to know what someone *says* they will do, especially when they are on their best behavior in an interview. I want to know what they *have* done. You want to know how they have put the skills and characteristics you are asking about into practice and what the outcome was.

"Tell me about a time when you managed competing deadlines . . ."

"Tell me about a time when you were under-resourced . . ."

"Tell me about a time when you asked for a six-figure gift . . ."

Also, don't stop at the first answer to your question. Go deeper. "Why did it go so well when you were in charge?" "What about your organizational system makes you more effective than the next gal/guy?"

Your job is to pick up as many individual data points as possible in the short time that you have. You don't want to make the decision on 4 pieces of information, you want to make it on 40. Overall, you need to talk less and listen more.

For higher-level positions you need to have more than one face-to-face interview. Anyone can have a good day or a bad one. I personally like to see someone in a natural setting like dining out. You might be one lunch away from finding out that your prospective employee doesn't have table manners, talks down to those in service positions, or genuinely can't carry on a conversation.

And one final tip on the interview itself: if you have someone else joining you to interview an applicant, have a pre-determined signal for "This interview is over." It respects your time—as well as the applicant's—to wrap things up if you already know there is no fit. I would simply turn over the résumé as a signal to my panel that we aren't moving on with questions and politely wrap up the conversation with the applicant.

Balance the team

Most team sports have different positions that contribute a variety of skills to the overall performance of the team. Your department should be no different.

Too many strategists and too few executors will get you

in a bind. An entire team that is strong in details but not in relationships can spell disaster.

You need dreamers *and* doers, leaders *and* followers—or you'll just be out of balance. In very small team environments, this may mean balancing a combination of skills in just two or three people; it takes skill, but it can be done.

There is also something to be said for the right combination of A and B players. Early in my career I made the mistake of believing that I could and would hire only the top talent for every position on the team. I later learned that this doesn't always make for the best team chemistry or success outcomes. Some employees will be top performers but require a high level of maintenance, while others will be solid average producers but need much less oversight. Again, it's a delicate balance, and your job is to make sure that you've diversified your portfolio well.

Pivot

Here's the last area where we get into trouble building success-ful internal teams: we fail to pivot when things aren't working. For some of us, it's a fear of conflict or of failure that stops us. For others, it's difficult to separate personal feelings from the professional task at hand—and yet when we do not address failings in the team dynamic, we only hurt the organization and all the employees on the team.

When team dynamics aren't working, we may simply need to re-shuffle. It's likely that the team already feels this and will welcome a change that makes everyone feel like the proper course correction was made and they are headed in the right direction again.

When things are more serious, and that new hire just isn't working out, we usually make one or more of several mistakes:

- We wait too long to manage them out of the organization.

- We tell them multiple stories (often with conflicting messages) about what isn't working, because we are afraid to tell the truth—and leave them more confused than when we started.

- We move them around the organizational chessboard.

- We ignore the problem.

- We pander to the problem.

You may have heard of the concept, *Hire smarter, fire faster* or *Hire slow, fire fast*. Both statements illustrate my point that we have to be intentional about who we bring onto the team, and we have to bravely manage them out if it's the wrong fit for us.

Coaches (a.k.a., consultants, agencies, partners of any kind)

Have you ever experienced a conversation like this?

"Mary, these costs are getting ridiculous . . ."

"Well the program has grown 20% in the last three years, John. I feel like costs have been appropriately commensurate."

"Even so, I've got to get the board off my back. Let's do a (wait for it . . .) R . . . F . . . P . . ."

You aren't in fundraising for long before this exact situation surfaces. It may have even been your own instinct.

The truth is, there is nothing wrong with being fiscally and strategically responsible for your organization. We will always need to closely evaluate our use of the dollars donors entrusted to us. At the same time—and like anything else—finding the right partners is a skill that has to be learned and honed if you want to reap the biggest rewards.

The *need, fit, balance, pivot* formula applies here as well, but the dating process is different. Whether you've had the same partners for the last 10 years or you've been trying something new, it's wise to evaluate all of your development partners annually. You have to ask: what is it that you really need at this time, and are your partners delivering the value you need to meet your objectives?

Running an effective RFP to find the right Coaches

For the love of all that is good in this world, please stop issuing dry, templated, cobbled-together RFPs/RFIs. I know RFPs are an undertaking and they pile up on top of your regular slate of work. But, if you are going to take the time to run one, make it worth your while.

Dos and Don'ts

Don't issue an RFP when you already know what decision you are going to make. If you know you plan to change partners, just cut the cord. Don't make your existing partner jump through hoops when it won't amount to anything—it's unnecessary. Inform them sooner rather than later, and continue the process. The odds of them pulling the plug on your existing work are VERY low. They want to keep your business as long as possible and then win it back as soon as possible.

Don't invite people to the RFP that you know you wouldn't select. Similarly, if you know exactly which new partner you are going to pick, don't make other contestants jump through the hoops either. These filler participants are outlaying a lot of resources for the chance to work with you. If they don't have a fighting chance, don't invite them. If you must show that you've vetted multiple options, have partners submit pricing and modified/simplified answers to your largest questions.

Don't ask your current partner to respond to the written RFP. Now, this one is a bit more radical, but it's more logical than you might think. First of all, you know your partner already. You know how they are treating you, what their offerings are, and what the outcomes and even chemistry are like. Don't put them through the task of documenting that in 70 pages of dry reading. Instead, have them submit budgetary projections in line with the RFP request and bring them in to do the final presentation.

Don't hold a cattle call. I've participated in RFPs that have a dozen initial respondents and 7 finalists. That is pure overkill. There is no reason to vet that many partners, and it's not likely that more than 3-4 options have the general services and culture you are looking for.

Don't use a template. A framework and a template are two very different things. Inherited templates can be very poor. I've seen requests that have sections I-III and then sections A-F with half of the questions nearly overlapping and a disclaimer that says to follow the exact format or be disqualified from the response group.

Since we still need a place to start from, it is best to use more of a framework. A framework is different because it is designed to identify the core and common areas of evaluation that are necessary for you to make an informed procurement decision. Then you can color that framework with what you really hope to learn about the new potential partners.

What does success look like? What are the budget parameters? What are the non-negotiables? Do you just want to see how the partner thinks? What is it you need to learn from them, and what kinds of questions can you ask to be able to grab the essence of that from a few written pages or visuals?

Do get to the point. Keep it simple. If you follow the "no template" rule, this is easy to follow. Your questions should be focused and pared down to the basic information you really need. Personally, I think it's helpful to use word count or page number ceilings. This forces partners to get to the point about what they can uniquely offer. It also prevents them from using canned responses that tell everyone what they want to hear.

More pages does not mean a more informed decision. I learned one of my favorite quotes about communication in my 9th grade English class (though its attribution is a bit of a debate, with some crediting Fyodor Dostoyevsky and others claiming George Bernard Shaw said it) "I'm sorry this letter is so long, I didn't have time to make it shorter."

Do give ample time and resources. This one is simple. The time you allot should be commensurate with the level of work you are requiring. Two weeks for a 12-part response is pretty thin, but if you follow the "keep it simple" rule, you should be able to offer a 3-week response time and partners should have ample time to prepare something illustrative.

Do be mindful of timing. I once had an RFP due during a national conference that fundraisers and partners would all be attending. And I once had an RFP due on January 1st, which meant that all prospective partners worked through two holidays—on top of fall fundraising activity—and the organization staff had to be available during that time as well for questions and follow-up. It was unnecessarily bad timing.

Do provide all the necessary details if you are going to ask for extensive insights. I once saw an RFP that asked for a deep data analysis but didn't provide a data file until days before the end of the response timeframe, and allowed for no follow-up questions (threatening disqualification).

Do meet finalists in person. For any decision involving more than 10% of your annual expense to run your programs, meet the partner in person before selection or contract approval.

Understand the cost of an RFP. You don't pay (directly) to conduct an RFP process. Right? Well here's something to consider. Responding to the average RFP in the nonprofit sector costs consultants and agencies anywhere from $10,000-$25,000 (costs can exceed $100,000 if you ask for deep analytics and/or creative concepts in the process). If you include five companies in your RFP, that's an investment of $50,000-$125,000 that those companies are collectively making. Don't think for a minute that those costs won't find their way into a budget line somewhere—in your budgets and those of any other nonprofits those consultants work with. One simple way to reduce costs in our sector is to be mindful of the cost of responding to an RFP, and limit the frequency with which you issue RFPs, and the number of respondents you invite into your process. If consultants and agencies are able to save those costs, you're more likely to find flexibility in pricing in the future.

In summary

The cost of change is high. Though these methods of hiring and procuring may take a bit longer and require more investment on your part, they should improve organizational fit, reduce turnover, and produce longer-lasting and more beneficial partnerships.

---

[1] Faber, Adele, et al. *How to Talk so Kids Will Listen & Listen so Kids Will Talk*. PTS Publishing House, 2017. pp.13

MISTAKE #40

Not Involving Your Development Team in Strategic Planning

By Andrew Olsen, CFRE

As I met recently with a seasoned Director of Development, I could tell she was frustrated. We were meeting to review the organization's strategic plan, but it was clear she wasn't aligned with the plan. The development goals she outlined for me didn't map back to the strategic plan at all. As we discussed further, she said something that shocked me: "I wasn't involved in creating this strategic plan, and I don't agree with it. And I wasn't involved in creating my goals, either. My boss gave them to me, and I don't see how I could accomplish them. If he actually understood our donor base and our community, he'd know these goals are not possibly achievable. I just wish I could have been in the room when these were decided. I'm afraid of what will happen if I don't achieve this insane income number."

There are three reasons it's important to involve your development team in your strategic planning process:

1. **Buy-in:** Inclusion in the process increases alignment around priorities and ownership of the defined outcomes. Involving people on the front end of the process increases the likelihood that everyone on the team will mobilize around a shared set of goals and priorities.

2. **On-the-ground intelligence:** Development staff will
   provide you with a realistic understanding of what
   is possible on the revenue side of the equation. They
   know what is going on with your key donors, and they
   understand the trends across each of your revenue-
   generating programs. This is especially important
   information when your strategy includes any kind of
   program expansion or growth initiative.

3. **Diversity of perspectives:** People who work in
   development tend to think differently from those
   in administrative or program management roles.
   This diversity of perspective can help you hone and
   improve upon your plans by exposing the planning
   process to viewpoints that might not have otherwise
   been considered.

You don't need a complicated mechanism for getting your
development team's feedback—you can start with a conversation. Prepare some open-ended questions for your team to
consider about the direction of the organization—where they
think you should be focused, where donors have indicated they
think the organization should be focused, and what level of
funding might be available to achieve those goals.

Or conversely, share your strategic planning thoughts with
the staff and ask for their feedback. "What do you like about this
plan? What aspects of the plan seem incomplete, or unrealistic?
What would you change to better reflect the realities of your
day-to-day experience at our organization? How do you think
our donors might react to a plan like this? Which of our donors
do you think might be most willing to invest to help us achieve
the objectives in this plan?" Listen closely to their feedback,
especially when it challenges your own perspective on the
organization and its direction.

Make sure your team knows their input is a vital part of the plan's development, lest they think you simply want an echo chamber for your own views.

MISTAKE #41

Not Diversifying Your Revenue Streams

By Andrew Olsen, CFRE

Many nonprofits suffered heavy losses from 2007-2009 when the US economy fell apart. The organizations that were impacted the most were those with the fewest revenue streams. Of those, some of the worst stories came from organizations that generated 50%+ of their revenue from local and state contracts and grants.

In one such case, a Catholic social service agency in California was reliant on state and local contracts for 98% of their operating budget. For decades this meant a highly predictable budget with minimal fluctuation from year to year. However, during the economic downturn many of these contracts were cut, forcing the organization to discontinue several service lines, and reduce staff by more than 25%. Unfortunately, because this organization hadn't invested in developing multiple revenue streams earlier, they had no choice but to cut programs and staff.

Another nationally recognized organization had a similar crisis during the 2007-2009 economic downturn. The majority of their revenue prior to 2007 was generated through dues payments from their membership. This represented more than 80% of their revenue, and over decades they had amassed an endowment worth billions of dollars. By all accounts, this organization was incredibly financially healthy. That is, until the markets crashed . . . in a matter of days, the endowment fund for this organization was cut in half. That's right. They lost a full 50% of their endowment funds.

What this organization did immediately after that is commendable. Instead of accepting the loss and beginning to cut staff and services, their board met to discuss a strategy to grow their way out of this crisis. They set aside money from the remaining reserves and allocated it to building a base of individual supporters. Then they went about executing a plan to grow the organization's funding base—and that they did. I doubt they've fully recovered from that major financial loss yet, but they now have over 100,000 supporters, and I'm certain they are generating millions of dollars in charitable gifts each year.

They were lucky. Most organizations that aren't financially diversified don't get a second chance when something like that happens. They end up shutting their doors, or cutting staff and programs so deeply that they aren't effective.

The same thing happened in 2010-2012 for organizations that were largely reliant on direct mail fundraising for their revenue. What we experienced in the sector during this period is that fewer donors were giving. Those who continued giving expected more and better engagement from the nonprofits they supported. However, organizations that relied exclusively (or significantly) upon direct mail found that this was a tipping point—and that long-term success required more focus on building individual relationships with donors. Organizations that made the pivot (or better yet, had begun to pivot before this happened) weathered this situation more effectively. Many that didn't are still suffering today.

In a best-case scenario, your revenue mix should look something like this:

Optimal Revenue Mix

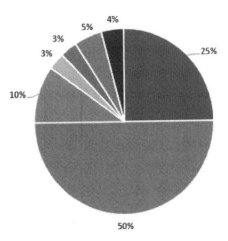

If your organization is currently reliant on only one or two funding streams for the majority of your budget, you should act now to fix that.

The more revenue streams your organization has, the more flexible you can be. And the more likely you'll be to weather unexpected financial storms.

MISTAKE #42

Ignoring the "Micro-Conversions" of the Donor Experience

By Lindsey Talerico-Hedren

You might already be familiar with Google's "Micro-Moments" philosophy on consumer behavior and brand interaction. It's the self-evident truth that consumers today are making decisions in micro-sized steps in their journey as they tramp through the universe of brand engagement.

Translated into nonprofit-speak, donors and prospects today are forming opinions of your organization in micro-moments that live in the crevices of the path to conversion. Meaning, *a donor will make an undetermined number of decisions about you long before they donate to you, and long after.* It means we have the opportunity—rather, the responsibility—to convert donors not just at the point of acquisition, but at all the points along the way: **the opportunity of micro-conversion.**

The problem is, nonprofits are still largely ignoring the way donors and prospects (as regular, normal, 21st-century consumers) behave today. Many are still marketing *at* donors, using a traditional marketing funnel as the guide to their approach. Most still see their fundraising with a one-dimensional view for attribution.

The mistake with the first part, by believing donors can funnel down the path to conversion, is that it completely disregards the value that micro-conversions have in their journey with your organization. The mistake with the second part, a 1-D view of attribution, is that it limits a donor's journey to a single source of influence. The reality is much different: donors are influenced by a variety of experiences—a variety of words, channels, and tactics on multiple screens, in multiple platforms, across any length of time, and in combination with one another.

So, how can you start changing the way you think so you can change the way you market?

1. **Start with the donor journey.** If you don't have one, start one. Every donor journey I have ever created or tracked has begun in a 99-cent, college-ruled spiral notebook. Map your donor's micro-moments: when and where the places are that a donor might interact with you. First, look at channels you own (website, social media). Next, look at channels where you earn value (reviews, PR, volunteer WOM). Then, look at channels you pay to be in (search, display, radio, TV, print).

2. **Begin determining the value of a channel or tactic (or team or staff member) based on the full donor journey and their full path to conversion.** It's like *Chutes and Ladders* in donor decision-making—when does a donor get to step B because of step A, and when does a negative step C bring them back down to step A? What value does a positive step A mean in getting a donor to step Z?

3. **Don't let single-channel attribution control how you fundraise and where you invest.** Even while source code management (still) requires that a donor be tagged with a single, last touch source, that doesn't mean you should see this as the full conversion

picture. Don't forget a donor's journey just because they've arrived.

4. **Intentionally round out your organization's approach to ROI measurement.** Rather than measuring ROI at the tactical level (single team, single effort), measure it at the program level (whole program, whole effort). Yes, this means social media and your volunteer coordinator and your CEO's newsletters are all playing a part in a donor's decision to give, as they should (otherwise, why are you doing them?). This will undoubtedly change the way you make budget investments and, hopefully, better serve your fundraising *and* the donor.

MISTAKE #43

"This" or "That" Choosing of Digital Tactics

By Lindsey Talerico-Hedren

I've been fortunate to have put together many proposals and digital scopes of work. In doing so, it's foundational to consider the client's needs, desires, and budgets. But if I'm doing what I believe I am hired to do, I'm also thinking about what is *right* for the organization—where they should invest because it's working well, where they should stop investing, and where they should start investing. Then I confidently hold thumbs and send the proposal into the abyss that is new business.

More times than not, the response is generally the same. Whether a big nonprofit, small nonprofit, international medical care service, or local food bank, the organization prefers to shape their programs against chosen tactics, rather than choosing tactics based on program strategy. Nonprofits are making choices based on a perceived à la carte-style menu of digital tactics. Yes to paid search but no to social advertising. Yes to lookalike prospecting but no to upgrade remarketing. Yes to email, but without investment in a strong donation page platform.

The result is that nonprofits are only able to derive value from a single tactic, and not the whole. If we are acknowledging and planning for the way consumers and donors interact with brands and nonprofits today, we understand that the success of a program is the sum total effect of many tactics. How do you expect to grow your brand awareness if you only choose to invest in direct-response tactics?

The next time you're issuing an RFP, annual planning, or strategic brainstorming, refer to one or more of these effective ways to ensure your digital program reflects the right combination of tactics:

1. **Ask your agency why.** Agencies are hired consultants. Challenge them to always provide you with strong rationale for their recommendations. And if you have ideas, take them to your agency. Pose questions. Get to the bottom of the "why" behind every digital decision.

2. **Consult with a trusted third party (or person).** I'm convinced the only way we ever really grow is by listening to the sage advice of others. Consult with a friend or an industry peer. Ask them what they know, how they go about planning for it, and what

their major challenges are. Then work to ensure those challenges never become yours.

3. **Consider your "must-haves" and your "nice-to-haves."** In digital, as in every program, there are critical areas of investment and there are areas you can manage to trim. But how can you tell the difference? Consider the value of each investment based on the role it plays with conversion, the amount of time it saves your organization, and/or the amount of value it provides to other programs. Then start to separate your "must-have" investments from your "nice-to-haves." Tactics I generally believe are critical (although there are always exceptions to the rule): email, paid search, display advertising, social, and native advertising. Tactics that are awesome but are only critical with the right challenge: video advertising, investment in every social media channel, blogging, and online affiliate marketing. Tactics I encourage every nonprofit to see as "must-haves": conversion optimization testing, SEO, and organic and strategic social media.

4. **Have fluidity in your investments.** One of the things nonprofits are terribly guilty of is locking down their budgets by channel or tactic with no fluidity in moving funds to tactics as plans evolve and performance is proven. Consider a budget for your offline program, and a separate budget for your online program. I have experienced many times where an agency partner is rather forced to overspend in a channel that has reached its performance ceiling, all because they have the dollars earmarked to be spent in that channel. How much more effective our dollars

would be if we could move them across programs and between tactics that are best performing, that are showing potential, and can achieve more with greater investment. It's a no brainer.

MISTAKE #44

Not Strategically Prioritizing Your Efforts

By Andrew Olsen, CFRE

When I walk into a development office and ask what the most important activities the organization is focused on and I hear, "It's all important!"—or when I sit with a Director of Development and ask her who her most important donors are and she says, "All of my donors are valuable and important!" I know there's a problem.

We only have so much time in a given day, week, month, year—and you have a finite amount of money to invest in order to achieve your strategic objectives. If your job is to raise the most money possible for your organization so that you can accomplish your mission at the greatest level of impact, you have to get really good at prioritization.

Often, one of the biggest challenges for nonprofit employees is not knowing which task is his top priority, or whether what he believes to be the top priority is his boss' or the organization's top priority. This breeds confusion, frustration, and inaction.

Several years ago I was fortunate to have the opportunity to study organizational leadership through Omnicom University, a program presented at Babson College and staffed by leading Harvard Business School professors. One of those professors was Frances Frei. She's a brilliant thinker and business strategist. One of the things she shared that I will always remember—and that is relevant here—is that *we can't be great at everything.* In fact, in all of her research and consultation with dozens of Fortune 500 companies, she's discovered that the essence of achieving excellence in a particular area requires that we accept mediocrity in other areas. That is, *if you want to be great at one thing, you need to be willing to fail at others.* You de-prioritize other areas to such a significant level that you essentially are bad at them. And only then will you have the mental and physical capacity to achieve greatness in your desired area.

I find this to be so simple and so insightful. But it's also really difficult, because who of us wants to fail at anything, right? The important takeaway is that if you don't get to the point where you can strategically prioritize like this, two things will happen: first, you won't achieve excellence at anything—instead, you'll be forced to settle for being mediocre at everything. And second, you'll likely burn out very quickly because you're trying to do everything at the highest level possible.

The process I've used to help multiple development teams and individual contributors in organizations focus their efforts is a simple rubric called Keep/Stop/Start. Yes, it's pretty close to what you're probably imagining right now.

First, we sit together in a conference room or office and make a list of duties and tasks based on job descriptions, roles & responsibilities documents, and team assignments. Once that's complete, we turn our attention to the second list, which is the list of things that must be done in order for the person, department, and organization to deliver on the organization's strategic plan goals. You'd be surprised—I think—at the number of times those two lists are completely different.

Typically we find that at least 50% of the "must be done" items are not adequately reflected in roles and responsibilities documents or in team assignments. This results in an overloading of responsibilities if we simply add the two lists together. And that's where the fun of the Keep/Stop/Start process begins.

On a whiteboard we create three columns (one each for Keep, Stop, Start). The first thing we do at this point is create a list of things we need to start doing in order to deliver on the organization's strategic plan goals. These, remember, are "must do" activities, so it's imperative they make it onto the Start list.

Next, using "must be done in order to succeed" as our filter, we go line-by-line through the combined list to decide where a task is to be kept or stopped. Most people, for one reason or another, are reluctant to admit that they have too many responsibilities or that they're overwhelmed. So getting items into the Stop column can be difficult. However, as someone is staring down a potentially long list of new tasks that must be started, it becomes easier to convince them that there might be things that can be given up in a daily or weekly schedule.

The final outcome of this process is a set of agreed-upon tasks that must be started in order for the individual contributor or team to achieve their portion of the organization's strategic plan goals, as well as a list of tasks that must be kept in order to meet those same goals. And importantly, a list of tasks that must be stopped (because they are not truly essential to success) in order to free up the individual or team to focus on those other two key sets of priority tasks.

CONSTITUENT ENGAGEMENT

"Martin Luther King did not say 'I have a mission statement.'"

—*Simon Sinek*

"Fundraising is the gentle art of teaching the joy of giving."

—*Hank Rosso*

I TITLED THIS SECTION Constituent Engagement because it's such a bigger topic than fundraising or marketing. For starters, what we talk about in this section is reflective of more audiences than just financial donors. It's inclusive of volunteers, advocates, partners, financial donors and other key institutional stakeholders.

Importantly, we also discuss more in this section than simply the art of telling and asking. Success in this arena is about crafting a thoughtful and intentional journey for each constituent, including building awareness and preference, engaging, building relationships, asking for support, and delivering on the promises you made in the process (i.e., stewardship). That's also why we start this section with Craig DePole's section on creating positive donor experiences. That's key to the success of everything else we'll talk about in this section.

MISTAKE #45

Not Considering the Donor Experience

By Craig DePole

If you search "thank you note" on the internet, you'll get pages and pages of links explaining the etiquette of the thank you note, how to write a proper thank you note, and so on. The one thing that is clear among all the posts is the act of expressing gratitude by sending a thank you note is important and expected in our culture. By the same standard, not expressing gratitude sends a powerful message of ungratefulness, rudeness, and many other qualities deemed unattractive in our society.

My mom would hound me to send thank you notes to grandparents, relatives, and friends after receiving birthday or graduation gifts. I hound my own children the same way, and it is met with the same resistance I expressed as a kid. I have often wondered why writing thank you notes is such a dreaded process. It's not from a lack of appreciation for the gift. Could it be the obligation of the action or the repetition of writing a typically bland and uninspired message? At some point we realized that the majority of the obligation was in the action of sending the note, and that the written message mattered less.

Unfortunately, nonprofit organizations often have a similar outlook on their donors' experiences: The donors make gifts, the charity sends a thank you letter. The thank you note obligation has been fulfilled and the experience is expected and unemotional. In a crippling blow, acknowledgments are deemed "fundraising opportunities" and direct asks for additional support are added to the letters with reply slips and gift arrays. And the expression of gratitude dies.

Unlike our grandparents and relatives who continue to send gifts unconditionally, donors today expect more from their charities—more gratitude, more relationship, more accounting of impact—before they decide to make their next gift. Charities that go beyond obligation and exceed expectations to create a positive donor experience will be rewarded with committed donors and increased revenue.

Donor Expectations

The donors of today are not the donors of our grandparents' and great-grandparents' generations. Donors (and consumers) today expect and have come to demand more from the brands they purchase and the causes they support. These "buyers" expect to have a seamless and integrated experience, whether connecting via an organization's website or phone system or through direct mail. They expect companies to understand and remember their preferences, whether stated or unstated. And these expectations are warranted. From their music and video services to their retailer and social media accounts, consumers are expecting personalized service, and companies are spending millions to deliver.

These consumers are applying these same expectations to the organizations they care about and the causes they love. Unfortunately, as consumer expectations grow, the nonprofit sector has been slow to respond. For a nonprofit organization, the highest level of customized service would mean that donors at every donation level could expect to be stewarded at a level typically reserved for major donors. While this may seem unreasonable, the organizations that can meet and exceed these expectations will be rewarded with donor loyalty and increased long-term value.

The charities that can fulfill a donor's expectations, articulate the donor's impact, and celebrate the donor's generosity with regularity and consistency will thrive. A simple thank you letter, which still plays a critical role in an organization's relationship with a donor, is only the first step in the process.

The Value of Customer Experience

The corporate world is spending billions to garner insight into their customers' preferences so they can deliver a positive experience—which will ultimately drive retention, loyalty, and future sales. A few brands are known for doing this well. Southwest Airlines, Starbucks, Zappos, and many others are brands that, while they have their faults, also have a visible focus on being customer-centric. Why does this matter? Because these brands have rightly figured out that the three most important reasons to improve customer experience are to 1. Improve customer retention, 2. Create customer evangelists, and 3. Increase revenue. These brands have calculated that if customers have a good experience, they are more likely to tell their family and friends, and that positive "advertising" is worth far more than the most expensive direct mail campaign, television ad, or email marketing effort can deliver.

Seeing stewardship as a revenue driver and not as a cost center is at the heart of this cultural shift for the nonprofit sector. Donors who have the best experience will donate again, and they are more likely to share that experience with friends and family. Word-of-mouth recommendations are by far the most credible source of advertising. One study reports that consumers are three times more likely to view content created by an individual as "authentic and trustworthy," as opposed to content created by a brand.[1]

Creating a positive customer experience is not a fad. It's not going away, and smart companies and nonprofit organizations are investing in ways to keep improving the experience they deliver. In a survey on digital marketing trends, brand marketers were asked to rank the most exciting opportunity in 2018. The result? Customer experience came in first! Making the experience easy, fun, and valuable for customers is cited as their top priority.[2, 3]

How can fundraisers move the needle on donor experience?

Start by reevaluating the acknowledgement process. Put yourself in your donors' shoes. What are they thinking and feeling after they make a donation? What are they expecting? Does the quality of the communication match the level of the relationship? What does the organization look and feel like from the donors' perspectives? This evaluation can cause a culture shift within many charities. Despite paying lip service to donor-centricity and message integration, many charities still see themselves as the reason the donor exists—"donors give because they love our mission"—rather than seeing that the charity exists because of the donor: "We can further our mission only because donors care." There is no magic wand or silver bullet. Donor experience improvements are complex endeavors that require dedication from all levels of an organization.

Donor experience spans across all touchpoints within the organization—from outbound direct mail, email, and social media posts, to donor services calls, the website, and programs. Does the website draw donors closer or keep them at arm's length? Are donors presented with a menu of endless and potentially frustrating options when they call, or are they welcomed with a friendly and helpful human voice? Is there a seamless continuity between the local office and a national office? Is the mission-delivery articulated as meaningful and impactful? The cumulative impact of each positive experience will increase revenue and retention when executed well.

A Donor Experience Case Study

So where does one begin?

A national nonprofit turned the table on acknowledgments and started focusing on the donor experience:

> *Two years ago, one organization launched a plan to* **reinvent the donor experience.** *They embarked on a multi-pronged, multi-year approach to help engage and cultivate donors in a way that was more intentional and donor-centric with the goal of increasing various performance metrics including second gift conversion, retention, and long-term donor value. Borrowing from corporations that are doing this successfully, they developed a series of touches that would aim to surprise and delight their donors.*

> *Central to this strategy was the welcome phone call made by one of the founders. This action has proved profoundly impactful. Analysis showed that those donors who received the calls had a 53% increase in lifetime value by their second year. Donors regularly credit this welcome call with being one of the main reasons they still give many years later. The welcome phone calls were scaled beyond the one founder to include additional volunteers and staff so that more donors could be reached.*

A special anniversary card to recognize the donor's loyalty was implemented to supplement the thank you letters and welcome packages new donors receive. The first five years are when the relationship is the most tenuous and vulnerable, so the strategy focused on donors during these first few key years. The goal was to show that the organization recognized and celebrated the donors' relatively newer commitment, and to make sure they felt appreciated. A card might appear unnecessary or wasteful by some donors, so the card was designed to also serve as a branded frame that could be used to display a favorite photo.

Improving the donor experience is as much about eliminating negative experiences as it is about creating positive ones. Donor frustrations can build up over delayed acknowledgments or feelings of powerlessness over the number of communications and solicitations they receive. Speeding up the acknowledgment process to increase donor gratitude was an area of keen focus. Donors were also given more power to choose the number of contacts they received. A brief message was added to the mailings to encouraging donors to customize their communication preferences. Donor relations teams were instrumental in this process as well.

The donor-experience efforts at this organization continue. Stewardship communications and programs are being evaluated regularly and adjusted to remain focused on the donor. The website and social media accounts are continually being refocused to delight and engage. The donor-experience commitment has gone to the highest level, with a new Chief Experience Officer position created

*to ensure the focus on donor experience is consistent
throughout the organization. Taken cumulatively along
with all the other efforts, revenue increased 14% and
donors are being retained at a rate that is nine percentage
points higher than the industry average.*

Creating a Positive Donor Experience

Being truly successful in driving a better donor experience
starts with an organization's leadership. Its board and C-level
executives must decide to make donor experience a priority.
Nonprofit leaders must decide that donors are not a metric to
be counted, an endless source of revenue, or easily replaceable.
Donors need to be viewed as a precious resource to be valued
and cultivated. The donor needs to be seen as the backbone of
the mission and treated as such. Align staff and volunteers under
the presumption that each of them is personally responsible
for executing on donor experience. **Articulating this simple
premise is critical to start.**

Next, **articulate the organization's vision** to the donor.
Whether it is that every child is fed, every animal has a safe
and loving home, every family has a roof over its heads, every
ocean is clean and sustainable, every disease finds a cure, every
historic and artistic institution is preserved and promoted, or
something else, donors want to buy into the ideal world vision
and the plans to achieve it.

Get the details right. All the best efforts fail if the data isn't
accurate and the details aren't mastered. Things like misspellings,
gifts not attributed correctly, and wrong information lead to a
lack of trust and a feeling that the organization is not on top of
its game or that details don't matter.

Show your humility and your humanity. Yes, despite our

best efforts, sometimes we get it wrong. But it's how an error is resolved that sets apart the best from the rest. In the age of social media—when one person's complaint or slight can go viral—the brands that put the donor first will succeed.

And finally, deliver content and service that aims to **surprise and delight the donors.** This may sound easy enough, but this is where organizations can get caught navel-gazing. Dig deeper and go beyond the boilerplate language and the same-old, same-old. Use creative and engaging ways to report back to the donors about the positive impact they are making, such as personalized videos, on-site reporting, or handwritten notes. Chances are good that the beautiful annual report you spent months on didn't even register with them, and that Thanksgiving card was perceived as nice, but not much more.

Throwing out the tried-and-true is risky, but failing to innovate and bring forward fresh ideas is far riskier. Find your organization's voice and personality, and capitalize on it every way you can. Your donors and your organization will be richer for the experience.

[1] Molly St. Louis, "Why The Best Marketing Dollars Are Spent Improving the Customer Experience," *Inc.com,* Inc. Magazine, https://www.inc.com/molly-reynolds/why-best-marketing-dollars-are-spent-improving-customer-experience.html

[2] Econsultancy in partnership with Adobe, "2018 Digital Trends in Retail," Digital Intelligence Briefing.

[3] Jeff Rajeck, "How brand marketers are optimizing customer experience in 2018," Digital Intelligence Briefing, Econsultancy, https://econsultancy.com/how-brand-marketers-are-optimizing-customer-experience-in-2018/

MISTAKE #46

Not Having a Written Development Plan

By Andrew Olsen, CFRE

I've worked with and met with thousands of nonprofits in the last 20 years. What's amazed me in these discussions is that so few of these organizations actually have written plans for how their organizations will achieve their goals in a given year.

What's crystal clear for me is that the nonprofits that have a written development plan and consistently manage to it are far more successful than those that don't.

If you don't have a written development plan, creating one may be easier than you think.

Here are the 9 essential elements of a great development plan:

Historical Analysis: What worked well last year? What were your biggest challenges? Where did you end up on total income, cost, and return on investment? How do those numbers break down by program, channel, and audience? It's even better if you can include a rolling 3-year average on these performance metrics.

Goals: Include a high-level narrative outlining your goals for the coming year. These should be specific, measurable, realistic, and time-bound. They should also be reflective of your historical performance. If your goals are significantly different from your historical results, you'll want to include a rationale outlining why you expect things to be different. For example, if you raised $150,000 from events last year, and your goal this year is $500,000 from events, you'd better have a significantly different plan in place to hit that goal. Equally important, if your goal is to raise $2 Million from individual donors, but last year's results show you raised $3 Million from individual donors, you'll want to provide a detailed explanation of why you think your numbers will come in below last year's actual results.

Responsibilities: Who is responsible and accountable for delivering against each of your goals outlined in your plan? What resources are needed to ensure your and their success in the coming year?

Themes/Messages: This is where you'll outline the key themes and messages that you'll map all campaign activities to throughout the year. It's also a great place to outline any message testing that you are planning for the coming year. Bonus points if the themes/messages you detail here actually align with your organization's strategic plan goals!

Audiences: Who are the unique constituent audiences you plan to engage in the coming year? What makes each of these audiences unique, and what behavioral (i.e., giving, volunteering), demographic, or other details can you share to help inform your leadership team about the relative differences and similarities of these audiences?

Channels/Programs: Include a comprehensive list of all funding channels and programs. For each channel/program, restate the topline goals and prior year's results. You should also list any significant changes that you're planning to make in any channel, any new testing, new vendor selection, or variations on what was done in the prior year.

Cost & Income Estimates: This is where you roll-up all of your estimated revenue and cost numbers from each channel/program, any consulting or agency fees, etc. It's critical that this not be simply a cost estimate. To be most valuable, you need this to outline gross income, cost, net income, and return on investment.

Calendar: If you don't have one, I encourage you to build, borrow, or steal a fully integrated calendar. On this calendar you can list all of your audiences, then outline every communication that audience will receive throughout the year. You should have sections for each different channel or program so that you will have vision to how each of your channels or programs layer on top of one another, and exactly what the typical donor's experience will be of your organization.

Progress Checks: As with any good plan, you need to build in progress checkpoints. Here you'll outline the timetable for reviewing your progress and results, both internally on your team, as well as with any executive stakeholders.

MISTAKE #47

Not Evolving with the Times

By Adam Morgan

As Bob Dylan sang, "The Times, They Are A-Changin'"[1] . . . and for the nonprofit sector and for philanthropy in general, that saying has never been truer.

Philanthropy is evolving. Are you evolving with it?

With the sweeping tax reform legislation that was passed at the end of 2017 and the changes to charitable giving that it is expected to bring—coupled with the rise of Donor-Advised Funds and the abundance of registered charities, churches, and other organizations to give to—the competition for donor dollars has never been greater.

2017 saw the most money ever donated to charity in a single year by the American public in the United States. For the first time ever, charitable giving broke the $400 billion mark ($410.02 billion, to be exact) according to the 2018 Giving USA Report on Charitable Giving (pg 17). However, even with charitable giving at an all-time high the US still doesn't contribute more than 2% of GDP (Gross Domestic Product) to charitable causes. This is a plateau that the nonprofit sector has struggled to overcome for decades, so while it may seem like donors are giving more money to charity, one thing is certain—donors are changing the way that they give to charity.

In recent years, organizations that house Donor-Advised Funds have become some of the largest charities in the US (when calculated by dollars received), and the list of the top 11 charities now includes 5 Donor-Advised Fund holders. The landscape of how donors invest their philanthropic dollars is changing, but are we keeping up with it? With the rise of the Donor-Advised Fund, many donors have found them to be a simple and convenient way to support charities they are passionate about. These days, a donor can set up a Donor-Advised Fund through a website in only a matter of minutes, and can direct their philanthropic giving from the comfort of their home.

However, while donors are adapting, many nonprofits are struggling to keep up or are blindly ignoring the trends. Many organizations don't fully understand how to properly acknowledge, track, and account for gifts from Donor-Advised Funds. Often a tax receipt will be issued to the donor—or worse, to the fund holder (think Vanguard, Fidelity, or Schwab)—showing that the organization doesn't understand the nature of the gift, the intent of the donor, or the basic laws and structures that regulate and govern Donor-Advised Funds. This lack of a basic understanding not only creates more work within the organization, but can also be harmful in furthering the relationship with a donor who gives via DAF.

Donor-Advised Funds aren't just for the ultra-wealthy, either. They are becoming viable options for families who don't want the hassle and headache of setting up a private family foundation, and for those who want to invest and manage their philanthropic dollars in an easy and manageable way. A young board member of an organization I work with told me that upon being elected to the board, he immediately opened a DAF and put in enough money to cover his annual contribution to that organization for the next six years! He was in a profession that was known for having an unpredictable income stream, and didn't want the organization to suffer if he had a "bad" year.

If you're having trouble soliciting gifts from Donor-Advised Funds because you don't know who your fund holders are, check out the DAF Widget (dafwidget.com) that's been developed by the folks over at MarketSmart. It's a free tool that makes giving via Donor-Advised Fund to your organization visible and easy on the part of the donor.

Donor-Advised Funds aside, most nonprofits struggle with developing new revenue sources and coming up with innovative fundraising ideas. Some become overly reliant on one, or too few, methods of fundraising—leaving them open to disastrous effects caused by a bad year, a bad mailing, or a bad event. For decades, the direct mail channel has been a major source of income for nonprofits, both large and small. And while it can still be a great way to acquire new donors and provide revenue to an organization, changes in how donors give and respond to mail solicitations have forced nonprofits to think outside the box and diversify their funding sources. Nonprofits that can't adapt to this shift have been struggling for years as their donor file decreases and once-stable and even abundant revenue streams start to dry up.

Equally challenging to nonprofits are the shifts that foundations, corporations, and governments are undertaking in how they award grants and funding to organizations. Increasingly, foundations and corporations are looking for nonprofit partners whose missions align with their philanthropic or funding priorities, not just organizations who are doing "good" work. Governments, when faced with tightening purse strings, have been cutting aid to the nonprofit sector. Those are dollars that can be difficult to see put back into budgets, since there are so many other demands on taxpayer dollars and an abundance of important public works projects that need funding.

In all of these cases, one of the underlying factors for organizations that struggle with adapting to the current trends is being afraid of change until it is too late. This goes for non-fundraising-related issues as well, such as updating HR policies (for example, including paternity leave options for new fathers), and upgrading technology and CRM platforms and resources so that you remain competitive and relevant to new audiences. Most important of all, organizations need to evaluate their programming to stay relevant and up-to-date for the communities and clients they serve.

What can you do?

There are so many ways to stay current with the trends and changes in the nonprofit sector. Watch any number of free webinars, attend local seminars, or even set up a conversation with your local community foundation to better understand how Donor-Advised Funds work. If you're not up to speed, make sure to ask how to accept them, how to acknowledge them, and how to solicit for them. If you're interested in general trends and information in 2018, Giving USA did a special report on Donor-Advised Funds. You can purchase the report or view a free recording of the webcast that discusses it by visiting https://givingusa.org/tag/donor-advised-funds/. For a basic tutorial-type webinar regarding DAFs, *The Chronicle of Philanthropy* has a good one entitled "Donor-Advised Funds: The Basics". In addition to those, the Association of Fundraising Professionals (AFP), Veritus Group consultancy and blog, and MarketSmart blog and podcasts are all can't-miss ways to find free or affordable information on how to adapt and thrive in an era of rising DAF popularity.

If you outsource your direct mail, work with your agency partner to develop multi-channel campaigns that integrate into your mid-level, major gift, planned giving, or event programs. This will ensure that you are communicating with your donors where they are, and not forcing an ever-decreasing segment of donors to take on more and more of your funding challenges. If you are working with an agency that doesn't allow the flexibility for you to operate like this, you need to find a new partner.

If you have a foundation, corporate and/or government relations staff, have them invest time in building personal relationships with their counterparts at each foundation, corporation, or agency that funds you. Look for natural partnerships where your mission aligns with their stated philanthropic priorities, so that you are developing a relationship that goes beyond the transactional nature of writing a grant and accepting a check.

Change isn't easy, but it is necessary for continued success—especially in the nonprofit sector. Focus on the changes that you can manage, and spend time developing a plan and strategy for staying up to date with trends and new technology. Don't be afraid to try new things, as long as you learn from the things that both do and don't work.

[1] Dylan, Bob. *The Times They Are A-changin'*. Columbia, 1964.

Donor Advised Funds -
1) Make a tax deductible donation
   Irrevocable contribution to charity
2) Grow donation - tax free
3) Support charities

MISTAKE #48

Not Investing in Major Gifts

By Andrew Olsen, CFRE

If you are willing to hire a social media manager, add another signature event to your calendar, double your investment in direct mail acquisition, increase the frequency of your direct mail and email solicitations, but refuse to hire more major gift staff, you're likely making a mistake.

Many nonprofit leaders are more comfortable investing in very tactical, easy to measure fundraising activities that they can typically see a return on investment from within a very short period of time. Even if, in the case of new donor acquisition, that return is a negative. In that case, I often hear something like, "*At least I have new donors to show for it.*"

The addiction to short-term gains and returns in our industry is significant. It is most often what drives this unwillingness to invest in major gifts. Successful major gift fundraising requires infrastructure investment that you likely won't see a return on for at least 18 months, and in some instances it might look like 2-3 years before you start to reap the full reward of these investments.

What leaders miss in this short term thinking is that the return on investment of a successful investment in major gifts can be anywhere from 5X—100X better than investing in these other programs. I'm not suggesting an organization should not invest in any of the tactics I've listed above. But the investments should be measured, and should reflect a long-term investment mentality rather than just focusing on your current budget year.

If you can raise five times more money by hiring a major gift officer than by investing in more new donor acquisition, you'd be insane not to take that tradeoff. But if you're only thinking about this year's budget, you'll force yourself into making the wrong decision and ultimately hurt your organization's long-term potential for success.

MISTAKE #49

The Devil is in the Data

By Jenny Floria

My husband and I have "collaborated" through several home remodels or redecorations. One time, we were picking out what was to be a gray carpet for our bedroom. We went to the store with the tiniest of paint chips to find a complementary carpet color.

With 20 shades of gray in front of us, my husband preferred a color called "Gray Slate." I insisted that it looked blue. He insisted that because it was called "Gray Slate" it was gray. We argued at length until I finally gave up. Color wheels meant nothing to him so I finally relented; fine, we'll go with "Gray Slate."

A few weeks later, the technician installed our selection. Sure enough, once the carpet was laid down it was a beautiful light blue. My husband came home, took one look at it and said, "But . . . it looks blue." He argued with the installer that it was not the carpeting he had wanted. Both the installer and I showed the remnant piece with the name "Gray Slate" imprinted on the back.

"It may not be what you wanted, but it's what you asked for," the installer said.

My husband finally agreed that no mistake had been made, and we lived with blue carpet in that bedroom until the day we sold the home.

What does this story have to do with fundraising, and—even more unlikely a scenario—with data?

When it comes to fundraising, the most important part of the equation is not the creative. It's not the channel, or even your mission. It's your audience. **Who** you are asking is most critical to your success, more so than any other aspect. Yet the most important piece of that effort is often buried in a data request that no one but a database manager or specialist will review. *When working with data, sometimes you get what you ask for and not what you need.*

This often happens for one of three reasons:

1. Data decisions are made by non-strategic data staff. This does not mean that these people are incapable of being strategic, but often they are not given enough information about strategic goals to provide valuable input.

Once, while relatively new at an organization, I requested the file of "active donors" and the database manager gave me the same exact number of names from mailing to mailing. This seemed suspicious to me, especially because we had been successfully reactivating lapsed donors who should now have been classified as "active," so our active donor counts should have been higher.

After much discussion, I learned that she was defining "actives" as people whose donor ID had been created within the timeframe specified AND they had made a gift. Someone who had been in the database for 5 years and recently donated was excluded from the criteria, because their ID was not within the "active" time frame. We were working hard to reactivate lapsed donors, only to never ask them for a second gift! Once I explained the purpose of the data selection and why I needed a different definition of "active," the query was revised and our active donor counts increased, as did our renewal rates.

2. People making strategic decisions do not understand the data. Do you know what kinds of data are available in your database? Are you regularly updating your records so you have current addresses? Does everyone on your staff understand which data go into which fields? It is worth getting your "hands dirty" by digging into the database.

When I was a new staff member at an established health organization, I began building my strategy by investigating what information was available. Only a fraction of the database was considered "active," yet there were tens of thousands of records in there! Why was that? I discovered that many people who gave to us through events had never provided a postal address, so they had never been solicited via the mail—which was this organization's primary fundraising channel. Prior to my arrival, no one had ever looked at the records that had a blank address field; all the mailing reports only pulled those records that had a "good" address. No one had thought to look at records with no addresses, so we were missing a big opportunity with people who already had an interest in our mission but had never been asked to donate!

We spent the money to do address appending and updating, and suddenly had a new pool of potential prospects who had not heard from us in a while. They were our top-performing prospects for quite some time.

3. Organizations do not spend the time to think strategically about audience. Nonprofits are accountable to ensuring that they spend money wisely, so when the expense line gets bigger, the stakes get higher. Nonprofits will have a strategic discussion with their top creative minds, consultants, directors, and others who have a stake in the campaign. They may spend hours debating the best wording for a fundraising appeal, or the most effective channel combination. Email followed by postal mail, or vice versa? What are the best subject line tests? Should we test a 6 x 9 envelope versus the control?

What's often missing from these conversations? Audience selection and segmentation. *The smartest people in the world can build the best fundraising strategy, but if it's sent to the wrong audience, it will fail miserably.*

I was once at one of these strategy sessions. A client of mine was experiencing declining response rates over the past two years, and deep thinking was in order. Top strategists from two consulting partners were flown in, as well as the organization's Vice President, Director of Development, and others. As an afterthought, the person closest to the data was brought in as well, since he lived near the client and it was easy for him to get to the meeting.

As we were discussing creative, offers, ask arrays, channels, and many other tactics, the data person asked a question about the client's suppression file. (He even apologized for asking a question that seemed "off topic.") He had noticed that more than 30% of the prospect names we were renting were being suppressed through a significantly large file called the "house suppression" file. This particular suppression file had grown by 300% about 18 months prior. Did anyone know who was on that list?

It turns out that for a single internal mailing, an assistant had marked all of the people whom they did not want to receive that particular mailing as "do not mail." She did not know that they could create temporary suppressions, nor did she understand that she was eliminating these constituents from all future communication. Instead, all of their former board members, volunteers, former and retired staff members, and a laundry list of other key constituents had been permanently suppressed from all direct mail efforts.

Thankfully, they were able to determine the timeframe when these suppressions were added, and reverse them. For the next mailing, more names were mailed and response rates flourished once more.

If you are cringing right now, then you probably understand the impact these missteps had on these programs' performances. Or, perhaps you are wondering which of these oversights could be happening right now at your own organization.

Here are some things you can do to ensure you are talking to the right audience through your data selections:

1. Deploy leadership or other strategic resources toward your data needs. Don't leave your audience selection in the hands of someone who is not versed in your fundraising strategy. Whether you have a data operations team, information technology team, or whatever name they are given, make sure that department's leader understands your fundraising goals and how data helps make those goals happen. Bring that person into strategic discussions so s/he is versed in the role that the department will play in the organization's fundraising success. Ask that person to ensure that the right resources are working on your data to make your fundraising dreams come true. Connect with the person whose hands are on the data, and make sure s/he understands the importance of the work.

If you don't have that expertise within your own organization, then bring in a consultant who can help you ask the right questions and optimize your data to work for you.

2. Do an annual audit of data processes and procedures.

Yawn, right? Here's why this is important: Walk down your hallway and ask three people what defines an active donor at your organization. Is it the time period in which they gave? What IS that time period, by the way? In the past year? Two years? Calendar year or rolling 12-month window? Are they active from the time when they FIRST gave to your organization? Do they have to give a certain amount—say, more than $5—to be considered an active donor?

Now are you convinced that a data audit is a good idea?

The purpose of the annual audit is to ask these kinds of questions and make sure everyone is on the same page as to what the data means and how it should be used to define audiences. Build the *specific* definition of active donors, lapsed donors, prospects, and the plethora of fields that are probably languishing away in your database. You may uncover data that are currently being captured and not used. Oftentimes I'll have a list of new audience segments to test come out of this exercise because I uncover information I didn't know was available.

This is also an ideal time to make sure that everyone is aware of the definition of suppression fields. I've been in long, challenging discussions about when a "do not solicit" field should be used as a suppression, depending on the nature of the mailing being planned. The most disconcerting part of those discussions is that people *within the same organization* weren't even clear as to when "do not solicit" names should be suppressed; sometimes they abided by donors' wishes and sometimes they didn't, depending on who performed the query.

At the same time, people who process communication requests from donors may be unclear as to when to mark people "do not solicit" versus "no contact" or other variances. When donors write "please don't mail me," does that mean no email either? Make sure clear procedures are written and followed precisely by everyone who touches the database.

3. Make the data team aware of the goal each time you ask them to select data for fundraising efforts. This is done easily and simply through a comprehensive data request form. The two key pieces that must be at the top of the request form are, in plain English, 1. Who you wish to communicate to, and 2. Why.

The rest of the data request form is often checkboxes of field values that should either be intentionally included, excluded, or ignored. It sounds rote, but I've had the best cases of getting exactly what I needed by using a specific request form.

One time, I was asked to help with a data query for my organization's event team. They had a new event they'd never held before, and were unsure how to navigate the database to get to prospective attendees—could I help? I asked them a few questions about the event and its goals, and filled out the data request form on their behalf. I got a call back from the database manager who had questions, since he had seen that this was a data query for an event. Did I want to limit my data pull to within a 10-mile radius of where the event was to be held? (I had accidentally left the geographic select to my standard select for direct mail, but it was a selection the event team hadn't even considered). He happened to have data on people who had attended a similar event that the organization had held a few years ago, did I want to include those names as well? (I hadn't known about those people—yes, I did want those names!)

We spent maybe 10 minutes on the phone clarifying certain field selections. He performed a single query and got precisely the audience the event team was looking for. They were pleased that they had gotten what they needed and not what they would have asked for, and he was pleased that he did not have to build a query over three or four times with new clarifications.

When it comes to data, the devil truly is in the details. Remind yourself that data equals audience, and audience is the most critical piece of your fundraising strategy. Pay as much attention to the data element of your fundraising program as you do to creative, funding priorities, and offers.

Otherwise you, like me, may end up living with blue carpet for a time.

MISTAKE #50

Treating Donors Poorly and Damaging Donor Perception

By Jayson Matthews

Like many nonprofit professionals, I get a lot of questions from family and friends asking me what exactly I do for employment. Besides the *hilarious* and old joke "Oh, I guess that means you don't make any money!", I get a majority of questions based on bad fundraising experiences versus questions about the actual work of the organization. While I'm not offended that it appears that very few of my family and friends actually care about what I do for 50-60 hours per week (I actually feel like Chandler from *Friends*—does anyone actually know what I do for work?), I am more saddened to hear story after story of a bad fundraising experience. I hear about "being sold," "pushy," "relentless phone calls and emails," "no thank you," "I have no idea what I actually helped with," and many other stories. After years of these stories, I quickly concluded that the ONLY personal interaction that most donors and volunteers have is with development staff. And for the most part, they are screwing up donors' and volunteers' entire worldview of nonprofits and the work they do.

In short, this piece could be titled *Stop treating donors like ATMs* and we would be done. Yet, there is more to explore. In this section, I'll cover three key points: *1. Fundraisers need to be better friends with our donors; 2. Fundraisers need to draw donors out of their comfort zones to get closer to the work; and 3. Fundraisers need to be more aware how small the nonprofit community is, and be more aware of the impact of job changes.*

1. Fundraisers need to be better friends with our donors

Yes, I know. ALL OF YOU believe in the power of relationships and would do nothing to damage the relationship between the donor and the organization. And there is no such thing as "pressuring donors" to make quarterly revenue goals. Yet, the things that you tell a Chief Development Officer during a job interview and what you actually practice during the day-to-day may be slightly different. This is not a lecture on why it is important for fundraisers to build relationships with their donors. This is more a lecture on what that relationship is.

I have a saying that "A true friend helps you move in July when it is 110 degrees outside." Obviously, this is a very Phoenix-centric statement, but the point is still true. A true friend will be there for you even when it is inconvenient and not fun. It is EASY to be a friend to someone when everything is going well and times are great. It is less easy to be a friend to someone when you are incredibly stressed and everything is falling down around you. Some of you may be thinking to yourself, "Jayson, I don't want to marry this donor. Give me a break." I am not asking you to marry all of your donors (which would be weird) or enter into personal relationships with your donors that you are not comfortable starting. *I am asking you to increase the level of honesty with your donors.*

True friendship is telling your buddy that he/she has a booger hanging from their nose. It is a level of honesty that cuts through possible embarrassment and gets to serious conversations. I tell everyone that if they see that I have a visible booger in my nose or food in my teeth—and they DON'T tell me it's there—then I guess we aren't friends. I always point this out for my friends because I am looking out for them through demonstrations of honesty.

As this pertains with our donors, we need to demonstrate honesty by *telling them into the work.* They need to see that the work can be hard. They need to see that there may be factors out of our control that prevent success. They need to know that times are stressful and there is more pressure to raise money. They need to know that a program is failing and that efforts are being made to evaluate and maybe stop it. We need to have honest conversations with our donors. This "everything is fine" while the house is on fire mentality is lying. I also believe that just telling donors what they want to hear is ingenuine. It means that I only care enough to tell you *what I think you deserve you know.* That isn't honest and that isn't friendship.

Now, it is also important to point out that—like all friend-ships—trust has to be built over time. There is a difference between telling someone you just met that they have food in their teeth, and telling them about your last three failed rela-tionships. That is a little too much, too fast. Would you be big and bold with your story on the first solicitation for $25? Probably not. I like to use the dating analogy: the first few dates are used to get to know each other and earn trust. Then as you earn trust, you share more information. You become partners.

2. Fundraisers need to draw donors out of their comfort zones to get closer to the work

I am obsessed with getting donors closer to the work. I know this annoys some of my fundraising colleagues, as they are very protective of "spooking" the donors through difficult subjects. And to be fair, I have seen donors disappear into thin air because of a couple of hard conversations. Yet, I believe in retrospect that my colleagues in those cases kept the donor in a bubble and weren't being honest about the work.

Now, before I continue with this point, I know that donors give for a number of reasons. Ideally, I wish all donors gave without any incentive of tax breaks, wanted to change systems, and wanted to truly end the reasons why people need emergency food assistance. Unfortunately, that is not the case. Or, to borrow language from the section above, some donors don't want to be friends, don't want honesty, don't want to get closer to the work. That is a reality.

Yet, I am optimistic that more donors are curious and compassionate. You don't get much of a tax break for a $100 donation per year. Donating to a cause may be the first action that demonstrates interest over years. I have heard amazing stories from donors who educate me on childhood cancers, art, and animal issues because they started with one donation—and then they got closer to the work.

I define "partnership" as active engagement that includes co-creation and honesty. When fundraisers have a chance to generate excitement and curiosity, then channel that energy into learnings that uncover more knowledge that can be applied—that is creating a philanthropic partnership. And through these partnerships, a fundraiser can work with their programmatic colleagues to thoughtfully bring the donor close to the work.

This typically starts with volunteering and may develop into advocacy. The beauty of bringing donors closer to the work is that you can increase honesty around the challenges, co-create opportunities for action, and develop partners that are out there raising awareness and funds to support the same cause. One needs to look no further than to witness Jimmy Kimmel talk about his son's medical experience. I have learned so much about his son's experience (and the amazing work of Children's Hospital of Los Angeles) through what Jimmy expresses. This is what it means to bring donors closer to the work.

3. Fundraisers need to be more aware how small the nonprofit community is, and be more aware of the impact of job changes

This last topic will be the hardest because it will sound the most naggy. First and foremost, I am not judging anyone for changing jobs. Everyone has the right to leave an organization that isn't treating them well, to move to an organization that pays more, to pursue all of their hopes/dreams/aspirations, etc. Keep on, keeping on, cowboy . . .

Yet, people do notice that. I have been working in the nonprofit community in the Phoenix metro area since June 2004. With exception of the 20%-30% who float in and out, it seems like I have worked with the same 150-200 people in nonprofit fundraising, programs, and management. Granted, there are ONLY 4.7 million people in this metro area. But I have seen the same trend in national ending-hunger organizations.

I have heard my father-in-law, who has been involved in art museums for over 40 years, joke that he sees the same staff rotate around the country. And as a patron to the arts, he notices this movement of staff.

I make this point because I have heard from many donors who feel like they are being used to help someone achieve their professional goals. Some of my friends who run corporate giving programs watch as a new fundraiser bounces from small start-up, to large established, to healthcare foundation. They watch and wait as ambition moves talent to more lucrative jobs.

I have had a colleague challenge me by telling me that this is simply "the game" which exists in almost every industry. While I agree that this does exist in many places, there IS a difference between the industries. If you are someone who is a TV journalist and you are bouncing around to a new job every two years, then cool. That doesn't hurt anyone. If you are a fundraiser who bounces from an ending-hunger agency, to a hospital, to an art museum—and you expect to retain your donor relationships—then you may be causing harm.

There is another perspective. I have a few dear friends who have bounced around to a number of jobs. They have bounced around for a number of valid reasons, and cosmetic reasons. They have invited me to a gala or event using the same appeal (which is funny), then it comes down to "C'mon, just come to this event. I need the bodies" (which is less funny, but real). I make the case that our donors are feeling this turnover as well. This impacts larger gifts and gifts over time, as most donors also want to give to stable organizations.

Being mindful of these three points will help you not screw up the relationship between the donor and the organization. Practicing these points with humility and humor will only pay off in big returns over time.

MISTAKE #51

Setting Arbitrary Fundraising Goals

By Andrew Olsen, CFRE

This weekend I received an email from a nonprofit asking if I could help them decide on an acceptable year-over-year growth goal. Was 15% right? Maybe 20%? The development team had been asked to decide on a rate of growth that they would commit to on an annual basis.

My guidance to this organization was that setting an arbitrary goal like this is a really bad idea. Instead, I recommend setting goals based on the data available to you.

Review the status and health of each revenue stream. What do you know about the donors in each area, and whether they will maintain, increase, or reduce their giving in the coming year? What will you need to change to hit your goals in each different area? Consider what has changed in the economy over the past 12 months, and how donor giving behavior has changed—both in your organization and nationally. Assess what your expense budget is for all fundraising, stewardship, travel, and associated activities. Has it increased year over year? Decreased? All of those elements should be factored into your organization's development planning process and contribute to the assumptions you use to get to a goal for the year.

MISTAKE #52

Measuring the Wrong Things

By Andrew Olsen, CFRE

It's always surprising to me when I see a nonprofit's RFP, or talk to a development officer and the focus of their inquiry is on increasing average gift, doubling direct mail response rates, or getting 15% more new donors. These are fine goals for any organization to have, but by themselves, they do little good for an organization.

Here's why . . .

If an organization has 1,000 donors, they could simply focus only on the top 50 donors and thereby increase their average gift. However, disregarding the remaining 950 donors would significantly reduce the total revenue the organization raises annually.

Similarly, if an organization's goal is to double response rate, they could change their ask strategy and only request that each donor give $5 in support of their cause. This could dramatically increase response rate, but also decrease their overall revenue by downgrading donors who had been giving gifts of $100, $500, or even $1,000+. And if the goal is to get 15% more new donors in a year, a similar effort to bring donors into the organization at, say, an initial gift of $3, $5, or $7 would be very effective at fueling growth in the number of donors on their file. Unfortunately, new donors who join at those levels will likely never pay for themselves. They will have very low retention rates, and won't upgrade.

Let me give you another real-world example of how measuring the wrong things can really hurt an organization:

After analyzing the donor file from one nonprofit several years ago, we discovered that 20% of their total donor base (more than 10,000 donors) would NEVER generate net revenue if they continued direct mailing them in the way they had for the last few years (i.e., high volume of uninspiring, generic, and expensive mail). Quite to my surprise, after informing them of this and suggesting that they remove those people from their regular mail program so they didn't waste money on them, I was met with a stern and resounding "NO!"

The reason?

Apparently, one of the key performance indicators set by this organization's board was cost per piece of mail sent. Now, when you reduce your mail quantities, your total cost of mailing decreases. However, because you're dealing with a lower quantity, your per-piece cost of mailing goes up (but again, total cost goes down). This unfortunate and arbitrary indicator—set by a board that had no level of marketing or fundraising expertise—was causing this organization to waste money and to continue to bombard donors with mail that clearly wasn't motivating them to support the organization.

Here are the key performance metrics you should measure to ensure you have a healthy and growing donor file:

- Total number of active donors (i.e., donors with a cash gift in the last 12 or 24 months)

- Percent of donors retained year-over-year, both in aggregate, and by life-stage (i.e., first year, multi-year, reactivated lapsed)

- Cost per new and reactivated donor (ideally, look at these two numbers separately as well as blended together)

- Net yield per new and reactivated donor (again, look at these separately as well as a single blended number)
- Total income
- Percent of donors upgrading, downgrading, and giving the same year-over-year
- Number of mid-level and major donors who upgraded, downgraded, or remained at the same level year-over-year
- Number of gifts per donor
- Average gift per donor
- Annual revenue per donor
- Second gift conversion %
- Long-term value per donor

MISTAKE #53

Not Focusing on Loyalty and Retention Over the Long Haul

By Aubrey Bergauer

Audience Development: The Long Haul Model

A New Paradigm that Solves the Problems of Audience Attrition, Churn, and Aging

(Adapted from original article on Medium.com)

The problems in the orchestra world (*where I spend my time and energy*) of declining audiences, aging audiences, and audience turnover have been well articulated, belabored even. In response to these problems, we as a field often talk a lot about incremental gains and successes—such as an orchestra that sold 5% more tickets than last year or trimmed expenses enough to balance the budget. Make no mistake, these are big successes under the current model, but when we know as an industry that our fixed costs will continue to rise and outpace the operational tweaks and incremental revenue gains we can achieve, the model needs to be reexamined.

To give away the end of this story, over the last four years—after a calculated change in approach to audience development strategy—the California Symphony has seen profoundly different results from the national trends for orchestras:

NATIONAL TREND		CALIFORNIA SYMPHONY
-10%	Overall Audience Size	97%
28%	Season Ticket Holders Who Also Donate	43%
-5%	Season Ticket Revenue	29%
-1%	Total Ticket Revenue	32%
20%	Contributed Revenue	41%

Source: National data from the League of American Orchestras "Orchestra Facts" report (published 2016); most figures reported over a four-year period (2010-2014) versus the last four years at the California Symphony (2014-2018). Figures adjusted for inflation where possible.

Even though most nonprofits outside the arts sector aren't as reliant on ticket sales and earned revenue as performing arts organizations, all of us are reliant on donations. And through reconstructing a new audience development strategy, in addition to the results above, over the last four years the California Symphony nearly *quadrupled* its donor base, grew its overall operating budget by 40% (meaning we are serving a lot more people), and ended three of the last four fiscal years with a sizable surplus.

So what's the mistake a lot of nonprofits (not just orchestras) are making? *Not focusing on loyalty and retention over the long haul.*

This chapter examines first what the current/typical audience development model looks like, followed by reasons why organizations do it this way (spoiler alert: there is a long list of explanations to support the traditional approach, which are barriers to change). We'll end with counterpoints on why changing the model is worth it—namely, because there is big money on the table, which in turn allows us to better serve our mission.

What Audience Development Typically Looks Like

Arts organizations have a lot to offer to our patrons, which is why when a first-time attendee comes to a concert, what ensues is essentially a marketing and development free-for-all. That person goes right into all our campaign mailings for subscriptions ("New blood! They came once so they must be willing to at least consider season tickets!"), right to the phone room for telefunding ("They clearly like us enough to attend, so they might be willing to make a modest donation!"), into all the single ticket marketing efforts like email and online ads ("They completed a purchase on our website, so we are smart and savvy and have that tracking cookie showing them ads everywhere now!"), and into pretty much every direct mail solicitation for single tickets or for donation appeals ("Recent attendance is a great indicator of future engagement!"). That's a lot of offers and messages . . . and by a lot I mean a deluge. Then, this same free-for-all takes place again if that person becomes a repeat attendee ("Now they really must be interested in us!"). Then all again if someone takes a chance on a season ticket package, large or small ("They drank the Kool-Aid! They obviously must want to consider donating now!!"). At some point around the time someone becomes a renewing donor or major donor, we sort of get our act together and often have a pretty clear path of next steps for cultivation and stewardship.

To a degree, the current model works. Organizations do make money, and a lot of it, this way. But when 90% of first-time buyers don't come back—a well-documented national stat for orchestras made famous by former head of marketing at the Kennedy Center and later Vice President of the League of American Orchestras Jack McAuliffe—this is a problem. And when first-year season-ticket-holders —a critical group because being a season subscriber is the number-one indicator of future donation proclivity—are the hardest segment to renew, averaging a 50% or less renewal rate for many orchestras, that's a problem. It's a giant pipeline problem we have created for ourselves.

What We've Done About It

In short, the California Symphony decided we would do everything we can to create a flowing pipeline. For us, this meant calculated changes to the approach described above, shifting to a strategy focused on patron retention. Now, no matter who you are—whether a first-time attendee, or repeat buyer, or new season subscriber, or longtime donor, or anywhere in between—we have a specific plan for you and a specific next step in mind, and everything we do points you toward that one next step and nothing else.

For example, a first-time attendee now receives four different invitations to come back again, from a letter on their seat when they arrive to a follow-up postcard, to email reminders; all we want is for them to return. Not get season tickets; not donate—just come back. Equally important to what we do now is what we don't do now. That is to say, we do not solicit a donation before a patron is a second-year subscriber. (This is usually when jaws drop.) The new approach is a long-term, disciplined strategy, and one that has proven lucrative for us. We've grown our audience by a sizable 97% over the last four years—having to add concerts to keep up with the demand—and have nearly quadrupled the number of donor households. We completely reconstructed how we do audience development, and we're in it for the long haul.

Why the Industry Does it the Current Way

Change can feel risky, and it turns out there are several genuine reasons why organizations feel the risk and are reluctant to divert from the traditional model:

Revenue attached to old ways

Again, organizations do make money the current way. Some people do subscribe after attending one or two performances, and some people do make a donation when they're called after their first visit. And when we are dealing with a pipeline problem, it can be painful to purposefully limit that pipeline at first, such as when you're pulling a list for a direct mail appeal.

Let's say it's for a fiscal year-end campaign when all the low-hanging fruit for donations has already made their annual gift, and you know how many more people you could add to that mailing list if you pull recent new ticket buyers. It's tempting to add those people to the prospect list because some will respond, and those moments make it hard to think about how we're contributing to that 90% no-return rate because we're making the wrong ask too soon.

Wrong metrics

Another reason change feels risky is because we often measure the wrong things. A bigger database is not the right metric, as an example. Bigger databases do not implicitly mean we are serving more people; a bigger database often means we serve a lot of people once, and that's bad when our jobs are to cultivate loyal lovers of our art form. In the example above, a larger mailing list is the wrong measure. Looking at the response rate would be a healthier gauge of success (more on that later). Bigger is not always better, and bigger is almost always more expensive (more on that later, as well).

Short-term emphasis

This is especially true since the 2008 financial crisis, and again in the new normal of declining corporate support and changing tax laws: there is incredible pressure to run our organizations with short-term outcomes. When I was first brought into the California Symphony to lead a financial turnaround in 2014, one major institutional funder said to me that if we did not immediately have balanced budgets for the next two years, consecutively, then they would pull their funding. And they said this knowing the organization was in crisis and knowing I was implementing a three-year turnaround plan (largely built on the audience journey strategy outlined herein).

Nonetheless, the directive was firmly to balance the budget in one year. (Side note: we did it, but talk about pressure to NOT take a long-term approach to sustainability!) I pick on that one funder, but the truth is nonprofit leaders see that kind of pressure a lot. Not just from funders, but from watchdog organizations like CharityWatch and GiveWell. And from our boards as well. When the budget does not balance, how often does the board want plans and ideas that promise a quick fix? By the way, if there truly was a quick fix (besides cuts, which are the epitome of a short-sighted solution), wouldn't we all have implemented that fix a long time ago? The short-term pressure is real.

No culture for failure

This stems straight from the previous point. We all have lean budgets with little to no room for any experimentation to try new things. This isn't because no one wants to experiment, or find a new model that we all know we need, it's because we usually must have every penny go toward everything else we've committed to do as an organization. We all have top-notch artists, quality programming, and education initiatives that make a difference (or for other nonprofits, we all have programs and services that are meeting deep needs and in many cases saving lives). Failure to fund on any one of those fronts because an experiment did not result in a profitable outcome in its first iteration is generally not an option. As charitable organizations, we are often required to produce results in an organizational culture with no real appetite for failure—or innovation, or even delayed gratification—because a lot of us simply cannot afford to have a miss.

Don't know how to do it differently

Having siloed departments—particularly siloed marketing
and development departments—and a focus on acquisition
(both patron and donor acquisition) make it so that our staffs
don't always intuitively know how to do work a different way.
We are taught that acquisition is key, and in a broken system
it is, because we have to fill the declining audience and short-
term revenue voids somehow. We are taught, in different
words, to treat new patrons like a land grab. "Who 'owns' those
names?" we ask, when trying to figure out a way for marketing
and development to play in the sandbox together, when the
reality is that's the least customer-centric question we could
be asking.

Patty McCord, who served for many years as Chief Talent
Officer at Netflix, said (on the FRICTION podcast with Stanford
Professor Bob Sutton) about maintaining a customer-focused
culture, "Siloes are just gonna slow you down . . . Companies
that are really, truly successful are collaborative and solving for
the customer, and you can't solve for the customer in siloes.
You can't do it." As an industry whole, we sort of know only
one way to generate the revenue we need and don't really know
how to do it any differently.

Don't have the discipline

Maybe this is in the category of "Don't know how to do it
differently," or maybe it points back to an emphasis on short-
term revenue, or even not having a culture for failure. Back
to the example of wanting to run that fiscal year-end appeal
mailing list, when we first instituted this new strategy, we
could have mailed to twice as many people if we had included
recent ticket buyers, and we all know that some of those people

would have made a donation. In a time when we were digging
ourselves out of the ditch financially, it was incredibly difficult
to have the discipline to say, "No, now is not the right time to
be making a donation ask of this group. Instead, we will wait
until people from this group are renewing subscribers when we
know they are times over more likely to respond, give more, and
ultimately renew that gift. We are vying for a higher lifetime
value of these patrons." Also, having discipline takes time, and
that's a currency we don't usually have, which brings us to last
reason we keep doing things the current way.

Don't have time

We often don't have time in two different ways: 1) no time
to wait for results of a longer-term strategy, and 2) no time
in the work day to even think about changing the status quo.
To the former, it takes a while for the full process of having
a first-time attendee come back as a repeat buyer, then get
converted to a season ticket holder, and then to renew that
subscription, and then finally to have the chance to solicit
them for a donation. For the marketing folks, those first
few steps from new attendee to subscriber can happen in a
year or so if all goes according to plan (which when you are
disciplined, it does nicely play out that way more often, but
I'm getting ahead of myself). For development folks, however,
that's at least two years of patiently waiting to get their hands
on those prospects, which is very different than the current
approach. To the later point, changing the approach means
time in the day is spent differently—not adding more to
the plate (which feels impossible at times), but mixing up that
plate a bit.

Why a New Way is Worth It

More revenue

There may be revenue attached to old ways, but there is way, way, wayyyy more revenue attached to a disciplined, strategic approach. Through shifting our focus from patron acquisition to patron retention, the California Symphony has grown earned revenue by 32% over the last four years compared to the national average of a 1% decline, and that's while increasing both single ticket and season ticket sales compared to national season ticket revenue on the decline (source: League of American Orchestras "Orchestra Facts" report, 2016).

Yes, that's insane. More important though, that's indicative of the flowing, growing pipeline we're going for. Lest anyone think this growth is through price increases alone, total subscriber households have grown by twice the national average over this same time period. Oh, and our prices have held flat the last three of four years, except for dynamic pricing on single tickets (like the airlines do, where high-demand flights cost more), which—when performances are consistently selling out as they are now—you better believe those last-minute buyers are paying a pretty penny because supply is scarce and they didn't plan ahead. We're not talking about *Hamilton* tickets here; we're talking about an orchestra defying the national trends for the industry by smartly responding to the ample research available to us, and building loyalty.

Contributed revenue follows suit, despite us soliciting fewer people than before. In fact, the California Symphony's percentage of subscribers who also donate actually surpasses the industry average: 28% nationally versus 43% here. If we remove first-year subscribers from that count since we don't solicit that group, this means 62% of all season-ticket-holders who are asked make a donation—who else wants that kind of a response rate?! Furthermore, total contributed revenue has grown 41% for us (double the industry average of 20%) in conjunction with nearly quadrupling the number of donor households.

It's worth mentioning that we've realized expense savings, too. Now that virtually every mailing list for marketing and fundraising appeals is smaller and more targeted, it simply costs less. We now put that money toward other things, like talent development and innovative programming.

Better metrics

If the wrong metrics are things like the size of our database and how many new names we've added to our list trades, then metrics that reflect how the audience is engaging with us and responding to our work are the right ones. In other words, metrics that measure retention and loyalty matter. If attending our organization is a bucket list item for people—meaning they come once and check us off the list—we've done something very wrong. And for 90% of new visitors nationwide, this is exactly what's happening. Who cares if the database is gigantic if none of those people have any future value to us, especially when all the research shows that converting a customer to a second/repeat visit within 12 months of their first experience makes their lifetime value skyrocket? While lifetime value of a patron is incredibly difficult to measure with most CRMs, we can measure three-year value or five-year value of patrons who've gone through the old model versus the new model . . . which is very telling. Or in its very simplest form, we can measure annual patron revenue and associated expenses when the focus is acquisition, versus patron revenue and associated expenses when the focus is retention.

CRM = Customer Relationship management

A New Way: How to Do It

If the mistake nonprofits are making is not focusing on loyalty and retention, and we know there are some compelling reasons why we make this mistake, how do we do it differently?

Take a long-term view

People often ask how we have achieved the financial results that so dramatically outpace our peers, and the answer we give is that we're playing a long-term game. We may have said no to some short-term revenue in year one of this transition, but by year two we were seeing across-the-board growth, and now long-term results as we're into year five of this strategy are undeniable. When our organizations have such an over-reliance and emphasis on short-term revenue, admittedly the most difficult, risky-feeling part is at the beginning. The opposite is also true though: doing it this way—this long-term, disciplined, strategic way—feels really right and really smart, and the revenue follows. The services our nonprofits provide matter too much to not be in it for the long haul.

Less lean budgets

This is easier said than done, but it can and must be done, and it does get easier. Going back to that foundation's mandate to go from years of big shortfalls to a balanced budget in one season, we did it by recalibrating how we spend our money per this reconstructed plan, and that first year the budget was indeed pretty lean. But by year two of the new model, the organization had built into the budget several new programmatic experiments. Yes, we actually had risk capital by year two. In years three and four, we ended each fiscal year with a 10% surplus and paid off/eliminated a portion of the organization's accumulated deficit. In year five (the current season), we were able to offer our professional musicians a significant raise, as well as secure a new seven-figure endowment gift because the donor was so impressed with this growth—what a virtuous cycle!

Structure the org so people know how

If siloes make it difficult to do this work, discipline makes it easier. "Process slows you down 100% of the time," continues Patty McCord, former Chief Talent Officer at Netflix (in the same FRICTION podcast quoted above), "But discipline can often speed you up." At the end of the day, people want to be on a winning team, and sending the right message to the right people at the right time results in higher response rates, lower campaign expenses (marketing and development, digital and direct mail), and a lot more money to fund our mission. We're no longer scratching our heads trying to figure out how we're going to make the revenue goals when subscriptions are down, or stressing over who else we can add to that fiscal year-end solicitation because we just need more names (side note: we didn't even run a FYE campaign the last two years because we knew we were ending in the black, and instead sent a thank you mailing to all our donors . . . what a change of pace that was). We also created a new position, Director of Patron Loyalty, to oversee both marketing and low-level annual fund functions because we were so serious about removing the siloes.

FYE - Fiscal year End campaign

Spend time differently

If all this sounds like a lot of work, it is. It does take a lot of work to pull a report of first-time attendees after every single concert, and then to send each of those people a postcard inviting them back again, and then to follow up with an email reiterating how much we're glad to have them and reinforcing a discount offer to come back, and then sending yet another email reminder approaching the expiration date of the offer. It takes work to run three different versions of the season brochure and five different versions of the renewal invoices so the right people get a tailored solicitation for a donation upgrade and the not-right-yet people don't. But it's different work than what we were doing the other way.

We're not running all those lists and scripts for telemarketing and telefunding, we're not paying for all those hours of phone calls because we're not calling most of the people we used to. We're not running around doing tons of list trades and flash sales because our acquisition mailings need to be bigger and prices lower if we have any hope of selling those empty seats. We're not pursuing empty corporate sponsor leads with the board, and instead building the list and file notes for board members to call and personally thank donors who gave less-than-major-gift donations, because calls to this group have made a dramatic impact on renewals and particularly upgrades (which is part of the "one next step only" plan to get that segment closer to major gift territory). We cut out all that old, somewhat desperate-feeling work and replaced it with work that matters over the long haul instead.

Final Thoughts

Once again, in its simplest form, this is all about solving a pipeline problem. And through a new model focusing on customer loyalty, an orchestra has realized a growing audience, secured more donors at every giving level, added more programs on stage and off to better fulfill the mission, and consistently balanced the budget through it all. I am in this business for the long haul, and I hope you'll join me.

MISTAKE #54

Not Creating a Major Donor Plan

By Andrew Olsen, CFRE

Have you ever been exposed to a major gift program where the staff doesn't actually follow a defined plan? What that typically looks like is a lot of activity—often in conflicting directions—that's not necessarily delivering any value. I've been involved with a few organizations like this where there is a commitment to raising a lot of money, but no commitment to strategically building long-term relationships with donors or developing the systems and infrastructure necessary for long-term success.

Sadly, organizations that skip the planning and go straight to the asking often find that they never achieve what they hope for.

Just like you need a strategic plan for your organization and a development plan to guide your full development efforts, if you're going to be successful in major gift fundraising you're going to need a written major gift plan. It doesn't have to be an encyclopedic document, but it should cover the key elements of a successful major gift operation, including:

1. **Goals:** What do you realistically expect to accomplish—both in donor participation and revenue generation?

2. **Objective:** Do you have a well-defined, compelling, and urgent case for support?

3. **Budget:** What can you afford to spend to achieve your objective, and how do you plan to allocate those investment dollars?

4. **Pipeline:** How many prospects do you have in each relationship phase (qualification, cultivation, solicitation, stewardship), and taken in total, are those enough donors at your various target gift levels to help you reach your ultimate funding goals?

5. **Timing:** Based on what you know about the donors in your pipeline, when do you expect to make each ask, and when do you anticipate closing each gift?

6. **Staffing:** What staff do you have in place to lead and manage this program? What training, coaching, and support structures will they need in order to be successful?

7. **Board & Volunteers:** Does your board fully support this initiative? Is each board member willing to support this effort in one way or another (they don't all have to ask for money)? What other key community influencers and leaders have you engaged in the process?

8. **Performance Tracking:** What tools will you use to know you've been successful, and on what schedule will you track your progress?

We consistently find that organizations and individuals that plan for major gifts at this level have a much higher rate of success in both building long-term donor relationships and in securing significant major gift revenue compared to those organizations and individuals who forego this level of planning.

MISTAKE #55

Not Creating a Plan for Each Major Donor in your Caseload

By Andrew Olsen, CFRE

I'm not sure who first coined this phrase, but that old adage of "What gets measured gets done" is true even in fund development. In my experience, one of the areas where this tends to be most difficult for some nonprofits is in their major gift efforts.

In the last week I was with two nonprofit organizations. Both organizations are actively involved in large-scale fundraising campaigns, seeking to raise several million dollars each. In the first organization, they have defined plans for each of their top 30 donors. As I sat with their team, they updated me and one another on the status of each donor relationship, what the last interaction was with the donor, what the goal was for that donor for the current year, what the next step in moving the donor toward an ask would be (and when), and finally, what amount they planned to ask the donor to give, and the particular program or project in which they'd ask the donor to invest. The process is working well for this organization. In fact, by following this process, the organization has doubled their revenue in each of the last four months compared to their plan.

A few days after meeting with that organization, I sat with another during a similar meeting. The big difference in the two is that the second organization hasn't applied the discipline of creating individual development plans for their major donors. So instead of walking through the specifics of each donor relationship, they talked broadly about who might be interested in supporting their project, what kind of numbers they might possibly be able to ask for, and spoke in general terms about their next steps—things like, *we should host an event*, or *maybe Jim could invite some of his network to a dinner with us.*

From a results perspective, this second organization is struggling. They aren't raising the money they need, they're in jeopardy of coming in well short of their campaign goal, and some of their most committed donors are at risk of withdrawing support because they aren't seeing the kind of progress they expected.

If you haven't done so yet, start creating your individual major donor plans. Create them, work them, track them, and watch your results begin to improve as you bring more structure and consistency to your development efforts.

MISTAKE #56

Assuming Fundraising Isn't Your Responsibility

By Andrew Olsen, CFRE

On one assignment several years ago, I was working with a demanding nonprofit CEO. Prior to taking the leadership role at this organization, he spent 20-some years in sales and operational leadership at a major manufacturing company in the Midwest. He was recruited for this nonprofit role through a nationwide search. The board of the organization was looking for someone who could turn around what they felt was an organization teetering on the edge of failure.

He and I were discussing the organization's challenges one afternoon as we started to explore the idea that his organization lacked a culture of philanthropy. They had a VP of Development and three other development staff. Beyond that, no one in the organization (from bottom to top) had anything to do with the organization's philanthropic efforts. As we started to explore this together—and I began to explain to this CEO how critical it is to develop a culture of philanthropy where every person on staff at an organization plays a role in development—he cut me off. Mid-sentence he interrupted me and said, "Let me be clear with you, Andrew. I'll never be heavily involved in fundraising. That's why I hired a Vice President of Development. That's her job and her team's job. The rest of us have real work to do."

I was stunned by this CEO's utter lack of understanding of his role in the organization's financial and operational success. After all, if they aren't raising the money, they won't need anyone on staff to do the "real work." Unfortunately, too many nonprofit leaders and boards have this opinion—and it's directly impacting organizational revenue, culture, and staff turnover. All negatively.

CEOs and Executive Directors must be their organization's chief fundraisers. That's not to say they need to be the person making the ask in every case. However, they do need to lead the team, lead all major fundraising initiatives, and make it a priority to engage with individual, corporate, and institutional funders. They should be heavily involved in major gift activities—at a minimum by being in the room during key meetings to share the organization's vision for the future and to convey their deep (and hopefully sincere) appreciation for every key partner.

Here are three other ways that all nonprofit staff need to be involved in your philanthropic efforts, and why they're essential to the success of your fundraising efforts:

1. **Share:** Every employee in your organization has the ability to share the stories of impact from your nonprofit and promote the great work you're doing with their friends, family, and others they come into contact with on a daily basis.

2. **Attend:** Staff and leadership should regularly attend the events hosted by and for your organization. One surprising thing we often see is that many nonprofits *charge* their employees a fee to attend and work the events they host. This is just plain stupid, and you should avoid it.

3. **Connect:** Not every person working for your organization will be comfortable asking for money. And that's not everyone's job. But connecting you with others in the community who might want to support your critical work is essential.

MISTAKES #57-#59

Go, set, ready! Common Mistakes in Capital Campaigns

By John Kozyra

One of my most memorable campaign experiences was with a museum that needed to relocate to a larger building. Their programs had become very successful and every day they had long waits due to their limited capacity. After months of discussion, the board of directors voted to move forward on a campaign that would fund the relocation and expansion of their museum facility. Everyone was aligned on the goal: expand so we can serve more youth in our community. Yet, they had one major problem . . . it took more than a year to find a bigger, better building to call home. This was a classic example of "putting the cart before the horse." The details of the project were not sorted out before the fundraising had begun and it took many months to regain alignment among board members, donors, and the broader community. This is one example of many that we will explore in this section of what can go wrong in capital campaigns and how to best prevent missteps along the way.

Over the past ten years, I have had the opportunity to design and lead close to 20 capital campaigns, raising a total of nearly $200 million. These campaigns have ranged from small Catholic parishes in the Midwest to large hospital systems on the West Coast. Through these efforts, I have observed many barriers that can stand in the way of success, most of which are mistakes that can be avoided with proper planning and execution. The most common mistakes include:

- Feeling rushed to raise money fast and thereby bypassing the early planning phases of the campaign, which oftentimes results in many missteps and a much longer, tougher campaign effort.

- Allowing financial need to drive goal setting, which often results in an unrealistic campaign goal.

- Lacking clarity on project specifics and how they will impact the organization and community in the future, which will fail to instill confidence in donors considering a gift.

- Not securing alignment of leadership on the direction and vision of the campaign, which nearly always spells disaster once those same leaders are asked to make a gift and will inevitably hurt the credibility of the effort among external donor prospects.

- Recruiting a "band of the willing" as campaign leaders instead of being patient and strategic when cultivating and recruiting the most effective volunteer campaign leaders who can offer the much-needed affluence and influence to spearhead the effort.

- Rushing the campaign process by having unrealistic expectations of when the funds need to be received, which often results in lower gift amounts and damaged donor relationships.

- Not asking for specific, major gift pledge amounts, which will inevitably yield lower gift amounts and fail to achieve the campaign goal.

- Bypassing the "quiet phase" and "going public" too soon, which typically negatively affects the credibility of the campaign and its chances of success.

- Being overly focused on making asks and forgetting to effectively steward campaign donors throughout the campaign pledge period, which can jeopardize the amount of pledges that are fulfilled.

- Making the campaign exclusively focused on the organization's needs rather than emphasizing its benefits to donors and the community, which almost always yields lower gift amounts and less donor and community engagement.

- Forgetting to build a marketing plan to create awareness of the campaign project and its benefits to the community in advance of and during the campaign. This fails to honor the need for prospective donors to understand the goals of the campaign, ask questions and truly "buy in" before being asked to consider a major gift.

- Creating a generic recognition plan that is not personalized for each donor, which is a critical mistake—especially for top-level prospects who are making this campaign part of their personal legacy.

These mistakes can usually be explained by a few common causes. First, most nonprofits have never conducted a campaign and do not fully grasp the level of work that needs to be done to prepare for the effort. Therefore, they often skip or skim over the required due diligence and necessary momentum-building work that increases their odds of success. Second, launching a campaign is often decided by the organization's board of directors and subsequently handed to fundraising staff for execution. This can be an unfair process, as boards rarely have the expertise to think through fundamental areas of campaign planning, including establishing a realistic campaign goal, developing a compelling case for support, and setting effective timelines that honor best practice campaign strategy.

Lastly, many nonprofit campaigns are thwarted by the egos of their leaders, as these leaders sometimes believe they can conduct a campaign on their own, with limited help. Perhaps some leaders take this approach as they strive to impress their board or executive team, but this is a failing strategy. It takes a strong team and influential leaders to make a campaign successful, and—from the beginning—it must be a highly collaborative effort.

While the list above is not exhaustive, it should give you an idea of common missteps in the capital campaign process. In my opinion, the three most detrimental campaign mistakes from this list are: *insufficient preparation, a lack of strong volunteer leaders, and neglecting to maintain a high level of campaign activity.* I'll share a few personal experiences to demonstrate how these mistakes can be problematic for a capital campaign, and then we will dive into how to avoid these mistakes in your own campaign effort.

MISTAKE #57

Lack of Preparation for the Capital Campaign

Again, nonprofits that have never conducted a campaign are often unaware of all of the necessary preparation work that is required to make a campaign successful. I experienced this lack of knowledge firsthand, as I was recently working with a social service organization that had an urgent construction need that was going to cost more than $5 million. During the campaign planning phase, I discovered that several of the basic preparation tasks had not been done or had been glossed over. For one, the board of directors was not aligned in regard to the specific construction needs of the project, which resulted in the first four months of the project being wasted on securing their approval to proceed with the campaign. Second, the construction project had not been prepared for city approval as part of campaign planning, and the timeline for construction was questionable.

Due to this lack of planning and awareness building, it was difficult to secure early major gifts. It was also difficult to recruit highly influential and effective campaign leaders, because they lacked confidence in the overall construction plan and whether or not it would actually be approved. While the campaign will still likely be successful, it will end up taking many more months (possibly even years) to complete than it could have taken if the planning and due diligence were conducted more effectively.

Another critical aspect of preparation is the work done externally to prepare donors for the upcoming campaign. While this organization's leaders were not prepared for a campaign, their donors were even less prepared. In our initial cultivation meetings, donors were often surprised to hear of the plans and unsure whether or not they would be the correct solution for the organization and community's needs. Some prospective donors questioned whether the construction plans truly reflected the real priorities for their community. This early lack of buy-in from major donor prospects creates a major barrier to success. I share this example because it highlights the need to gain alignment during the early stages of campaign planning. If alignment is lacking, it can create a snowball effect throughout the effort because highly desirable volunteer leaders are often very selective about which projects they will associate themselves with.

MISTAKE #58

Lacking Strong Leadership in a Capital Campaign

There is a certain magic formula to cultivating and recruiting effective campaign leaders. Without strong volunteer leadership, a campaign will struggle to gain access to top major donor prospects, as well as gain the necessary credibility and momentum for success. I will explore this in more detail later on in this section.

I recently worked with a large healthcare organization that struggled to recruit effective campaign leaders. Prior to the campaign, they spent much of their time fundraising from employees, physicians, hospital vendors, and through special events. While these were effective channels for achieving their annual goals, they did not cultivate strong relationships with leaders and philanthropists in the community. Therefore, when the time came to recruit effective leaders with seven-figure or higher gift potential for a major campaign, the number of prospects was very limited. The problem created by their historically internal focus on gift giving was further compounded by a lack of leadership availability to cultivate substantial major prospects. Again, this can create a snowball effect when it comes to securing early major gifts and generating momentum for a successful campaign.

MISTAKE #59

Limited Capital Campaign Activity

Success in a campaign largely depends on sustaining a high level of the right kind of fundraising activities. These activities may include donor research, individual cultivation meetings, small gatherings or salons, and other events to engage and educate donor prospects.

I recently worked with a Catholic parish whose priest refused to make personal visits to parishioners and other potential donors to solicit support. I am still unsure if this was due to him being shy, lazy, or some mixture of both. This priest believed that all that was required was to host a nice dinner party and that everyone would come and give generously at the event. As any campaign expert could have predicted, the single event raised a small portion of the campaign funds but did little to accomplish the overall goal. *A campaign approach that does not incorporate sustained donor interaction almost always predicts failure.*

Now that I have walked you through examples of my top three campaign mistakes, let's take a look at how to best avoid these mistakes.

Getting Prepared

Take time to fully and effectively prepare for the campaign. Depending on your organization's situation, getting prepared for a campaign may take several months to several years. First and foremost, it is critical to gain alignment on the goals and anticipated outcomes of the campaign between your board of directors, organization leaders, major donors, and community leaders. Gaining alignment may also require cultivating and recruiting new board members who share the vision and have the affluence, affinity, and influence in the community to turn the vision into a reality.

It is critical to build a robust donor pipeline of major gift prospects. If a major donor is hearing about the goals and vision for the campaign after the campaign has begun, then you are too late. Major donors need to be actively involved in helping shape the goals of the campaign. This is often accomplished through conducting an extensive campaign planning and feasibility study. This type of study, typically conducted by a third-party consulting firm, usually involves having strategic conversations with your top donor prospects to better understand their perceptions of your proposed plans and assess whether or not they would be ready and willing to consider a major gift. This process also helps fundraising leaders identify other prospective major donors who need to be included in the campaign cultivation plan. Overall, this process will provide insight into the desires, goals, and motivations of your best donor prospects, which will inform the design of the campaign plan.

Ultimately, thorough planning and preparation gives major donor prospects confidence and trust in the vision of the campaign. It is important to be prepared with answers to questions, alternative scenarios that were considered in the planning process, and a clear rationale for why you are doing what is planned. If donors do not have confidence in your planning process, they likely will not trust you to use their dollars well. Clearly, this will jeopardize your chances of success in securing a major gift.

I recently completed a timeline for a hospital that reflects all of the items, and anticipated timeline, for the preparation period (pictured below).

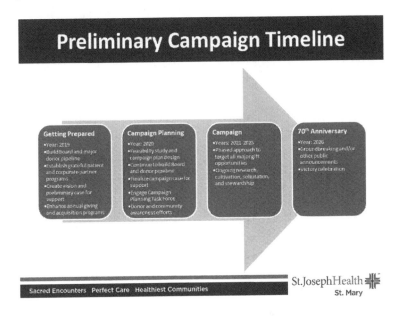

Identifying and Recruiting Leaders

Recruiting, training, and deploying effective volunteer leaders is possibly the most challenging aspect of a successful campaign. The ideal campaign leader will have all of the following characteristics:

- Ability and willingness to make a major gift to the campaign, ideally the largest gift of the campaign.

- Relationships with major donor prospects who your organization would not otherwise be able to access.

- Influence to effectively serve as an ambassador for the effort—internally among your board of directors and staff, and externally in the community.

- Credibility within the community that will further instill trust and confidence in your prospective donors.

Finding a leader with these characteristics is never easy. Why? It is likely that this person (or persons) is professionally successful and busy. They are also likely involved in other nonprofits and are being asked to support and lead other efforts. It will take time to cultivate them as a prospective leader and donor, and gain their buy-in to your vision for the campaign.

The most effective way to cultivate a prospective leader is to involve them in the planning process. When preparing for a campaign effort, I will often look at the organization's top cumulative donors and assess whether or not they might be effective campaign leaders. Once the list has been culled down to five or more prospective leaders, I will look for ways to give them a meaningful role in the project and campaign planning process. If the project plans are already finalized, then it may be more effective to invite these prospective leaders to serve on an advisory committee, often called a Campaign Planning Task Force. The Task Force's primary responsibility is to advise fundraising leaders on the campaign plan and case for support, and identify leaders and prospective major donors. I usually ask this Task Force to meet monthly for three to six months during the campaign planning phase before we officially begin reaching out to prospective donors.

Sustaining Campaign Activity

Once your campaign has launched, it is important to sustain a high level of fundraising activity. This activity includes prospect identification and research, cultivation, solicitation, and ongoing stewardship. I realize this does not sound like groundbreaking advice, but a successful campaign requires a level of activity that professional fundraisers and executives are not accustomed to. If you work with campaign counsel, you will likely be provided a Table of Gifts that can serve as a roadmap to success. It will show you how many donors you need at specific giving levels to be successful. The challenge is that these tables only share part of the story for success.

The best advice—and it is actually quite simple—I can offer are the following ratios:

- For every dollar you need to raise, you need to solicit $3. Therefore, in a $20 million campaign, you will need to solicit a minimum of $60 million.

- For every donor you need to support the campaign, you need to solicit three donors. Therefore, if your Table of Gifts requires 150 donors to complete a $20 million campaign, you will need to solicit gifts from a minimum of 450 prospects.

In my experience, nonprofit leaders often cringe a little with this type of calculation because they have worked so hard to build strong donor relationships. Some feel that this aggressive approach will jeopardize those relationships and hurt their ability to secure future gifts from those same donors. While this is valid concern, it is hardly ever substantiated. Donors want to be part of something meaningful and, if cultivated well, will enjoy the invitation to participate in an effort that will advance your organization's impact in the community and add to their personal legacy.

Campaigns are hard work and you will be served well to

begin preparing months—or maybe even years—in advance. Taking time to prepare and gain alignment among your board of directors, major donor prospects, and the broader community will pay dividends when you are seeking to raise unprecedented levels of funds. Additionally, you may need to use this time to build your board and major donor pipeline so that you have the necessary leaders and prospects for a successful campaign.

This extended preparation process will enable you to identify and cultivate your best prospective campaign leaders. As I mentioned earlier, effective leaders truly make or break a campaign. These leaders, along with your organization's leaders, will be essential to driving a high level of campaign fundraising activity. The passion of your leaders will ensure that the campaign maintains the necessary momentum for success.

While a major campaign is perhaps one of the most difficult fundraising efforts, it is also the most rewarding. Campaigns are typically only conducted to facilitate a transformative opportunity for an organization. Therefore, the chance to lead a campaign is a special opportunity to build the future of a community and truly make an impact for many years to come, and avoiding the mistakes above will make your campaign that much more successful.

MISTAKE #60

Failing to be Real: What Nonprofits can Learn from Reality TV

By Greg Warner

Can't we be "real" with one another?

As of the writing of this chapter, 14 of the top 50 television shows in the United States are reality shows, including the NFL games (sporting competitions *are* real—not scripted), *Dancing With the Stars*, *The Voice*, *60 Minutes*, *American Idol*, *The Bachelor*, and *Undercover Boss*.

Reality TV is popular, there is no doubt about it. But not for the reasons you and most self-appointed experts might think. They wrongly figure that reality TV viewers watch because they are not very smart, and they want to talk to their friends about the shows.

According to an article in *Psychology Today* by Steven Reiss (professor of psychology and psychiatry at Ohio State University) and James Wiltz (Ph.D. candidate at OSU at the time of their research), the truth about why people watch reality TV is something to which nonprofits might want to pay more attention. Their research found that people like reality TV simply because the shows deliver really good stories—drama, suspense, morality, and more. But, on top of all that, the shows provide watchers with prestige.[1]

Now, you might be saying to yourself, "Huh, I don't understand. What does prestige have to do with it?" Stay with me on this.

Reiss and Wiltz found that reality TV makes an ordinary person who is watching along feel that the ordinary people on the TV show are important (because millions of people are watching them). And, in a somewhat voyeuristic way, the ordinary viewer gets a "secret thrill" imagining that the reality stars could actually be them.

"But what's this got to do with fundraising?" you might ask.

Nonprofits fail to deliver to their supporters what reality TV delivers to millions of viewers every night. And advertisers pay dearly for those eyes and ears. Nonprofits fail to provide good stories, or they don't tell their stories well. They don't give their supporters enough drama and suspense. They don't offer enough chances for supporters to demonstrate their morality. *Therefore, what nonprofits need is more reality!*

Every top fundraiser and every fundraising expert knows that campaigns succeed when they are *real*. Reality makes stories better. Reality gives supporters a chance to save the day. And, unlike reality TV, nonprofit supporters can get involved. They don't have to be just voyeuristic bystanders. They can donate, volunteer, sign a petition, or lobby congress.

All of these kinds of decisions to get involved are influenced by emotion. That's why telling real, true stories moves people. They are powerful, motivational, and inspirational. And the "secret thrill" donors get makes them feel really wonderful.

After all, that's truly what everyone wants, deep down inside—to feel good. Therefore, nonprofits need to stop being so stodgy. They need to open up and become more transparent. They need to invite their supporters to view live-feed streaming videos of the good work they do while it's being done. They need to turn on a camera at their board meetings so supporters can watch them work (like on C-SPAN). And they need to provide windows into how the money is being spent—for instance, with interviews of researchers seeking a cure for cancer, viewable via online webinars.

Yes, indeed, nonprofits need to be more real. Failing to match reality TV for their supporters' eyes and ears is holding us back.

---

[1] Reiss, Steven, and James Wiltz. "Why America Loves Reality TV." Psychologytoday.com. 1 Sept. 2001. www.psychologytoday.com/us/articles/200109/why-america-loves-reality-tv.

MISTAKE #61

Not Getting Face to Face with Your Best Supporters

By Roy C. Jones, CFRE

> "For clinking money, you can shake the can. For folding money, you should go ask for it."
> —Harold Seymour, legendary fundraiser

Without a doubt, failing to visit your top supporters and prospects in person is one of the worst mistakes in fundraising.

I have met hundreds of nonprofit CEOs over the last decade who truly are bad stewards. They do not understand their responsibility to meet with their top financial supporters, and they have grown lazy by depending on the direct response program to provide all the operational income for the organization.

The entire objective of your direct response program (direct mail, website, digital marketing, telemarketing, special events, etc.) is ultimately to put you in front of financial partners who are ready to make a huge investment in your organization or cause. Philanthropists who partner with charities NEVER begin their relationships with a HUGE gift. They usually begin by making regular gifts through your direct response program. High-capacity investors in charity view their giving just like they do their stock investments: they make initial "small gifts" to measure the impact of the organization, and if they believe the charity is providing a great return on their investment . . . they will donate more.

The goal of all of your direct-response fundraising is not to just provide net revenue for your charity. It is designed to help you identify and glean from the program individuals who are willing to make five-figure and six-figure investments into your organization.

The courageous CEOs and development professionals are nearly always the most successful. They make it a priority to identify top prospects from the direct response list and meet face-to-face with them every year, every month, every week, and yes, every day.

The best nonprofit managers also know how to say thank you. They go to great effort to build relationships. They identify supporters' interests and ask them to invest in great causes to change the world!

Start doing it . . . knock out that email, pick up that phone, send that text message and ask a supporter with capacity to meet you for a cup of coffee.

MISTAKE #62

Overcomplicating Your Fundraising

By Jim Shapiro

Most organizations make their fundraising <u>too complex</u>, and <u>too much about their organization</u> itself. That's because they know so much and they know the value of their organization.

But remember that your fundraising is not meant to convince *you* to give a gift!

The vast majority of your donors don't know as much as you do about the cause your organization supports. So your fundraising needs to meet the donor where she is at—and talk about what she understands—using words she understands. This isn't selling her short, by the way. She doesn't think about your cause 40+ hours a week like you do.

It can seem like a difficult and counterintuitive thing, but if your fundraising materials are doing their job you most likely won't like them. Great fundraising for your organization will seem overly simple to you. It might even feel "misleading" because you know your organization does so much more.

But it will meet the donor right where she is. And it will compel her to action.

Think about it this way: if you write to engage your Executive Director, your program staff, and your board members, then your fundraising potential is pretty small. But if you write to engage anyone who cares about your cause or the people you serve, your fundraising potential is much larger.

Something else you should realize is that your donors

don't care how special your organization is, and telling your donors your organization is unique doesn't help you raise money. In fact, it usually causes you to raise less money. That's because *most donors care more about who needs help, and the improvement in the beneficiary's life if the donor gives a gift.*

How you make that improvement happen just doesn't matter to most donors. We've done test after test, and they all come to basically the same conclusions:

If you talk about the need and the improvement that will be caused by the donor's gift, lots of money pours in.

If you highlight your uniqueness by talking about how your organization serves its beneficiaries . . . a little money drips in.

Most donors are simply much more interested in the *who* their gift helps, and the improvement that happens when they give. Yes, a few major donors (and your staff and board) are very interested in how your organization does its thing. Save your talk about uniqueness for them instead of in your messaging to donors. Focus on what the donor can do with their gift, not how you make it happen.

MISTAKES #63-#65

Grant-Seeking Missteps

By Coral Dill

Last winter, I was sitting in a coffee shop waiting for Dan to arrive. He is a marketing executive who I met in a past life, during my brief layover in communications and PR, before landing solidly in grant writing. One of his long-term corporate clients had recently parlayed their corporate vision into a nonprofit mission and they needed funding "yesterday."

Dan had been working with them to gain traction on the public relations front, but had taken them as far as he could. Without a background in nonprofit work or a solid understanding of fundraising, he wasn't quite sure what else he could do for them. He invited me for coffee under the guise of picking my brain, but I had a suspicion that he really wanted me to take this client on and help with fundraising in general—grant writing in particular.

He walked in the door already frazzled from the busyness of the city and the frigid cold. Before he had a chance remove his hat and gloves, he began telling me about his client and their mission. He explained that the organization had, until now, been funded solely by the corporation that they grew out of. But less than a year later and hundreds of thousands of dollars invested, *the corporation had decided* it was time for the nonprofit to begin the task of grant-seeking, in order to offset their expenditure.

Ten minutes into our conversation Dan had unknowingly outlined one of the most frequent mistakes that I see nonprofits and their well-meaning advisors make. Based on an assumption that grants are a quick and easy source of revenue, they decide that fundraising efforts should *start* with grants.

MISTAKE #63

Starting with Grants

Frequently I receive inquiries after a well-meaning board member or staff person recommends that a prospective client hire a grant writer to bring in some "quick" money. The truth is that grants can be an extremely expeditious way to bring dollars in the door—the actual act of writing the proposal, submitting the request, and receiving approval *can* be quick. Last year I submitted a grant the evening before Thanksgiving. By the time I was back in the office Monday, it had been approved! The total turnaround time was five days, including Thanksgiving and a weekend!

That is quick. What *wasn't* quick however, and what is often overlooked, is the time and effort it takes for an organization to become grant-ready and the time spent cultivating relationships with grant-makers. Those are the most important elements of any grant application and *those* elements can take years—literally!

Similarly, I frequently encounter new organizations that interpret their 501(c)3 designation as a green light for grant-seeking. While in theory this is true, the reality is that there are very few grant-makers who will fund new or start-up nonprofits. Most grant-makers require at least three years of funding history and proven success. While there are exceptions to every rule, grant-makers who fund new or start-up organizations are, by and large, the exception rather than the rule. An IRS designation is just one small piece of the grant-seeking puzzle.

Becoming grant-ready can be a lengthy and onerous process, and grant-seeking should rarely, if ever, be the first step in fundraising.

How to Avoid Mistake #63:

#1 Remind that well-meaning board member or staff person that *a grant-maker is like an investor*. Like an investor, a grant-maker is looking for a safe investment with a great ROI. Rather than a financial return on their investment though, they are looking to you to provide the programs and services that result in measurable outcomes—outcomes that help achieve their shared goals. Your commitment as a grant recipient is to follow through on those deliverables.

Grant-makers, like investors, need to ensure they are making a wise investment. To do this they will gauge the overall effectiveness of an organization, which includes its long-term sustainability as well as its capacity to carry out the proposed program or project.

#2 Design _programs and projects that are worthy_ of being funded. Focus on creating solid programs and projects with specific goals and objectives. Conducting a needs assessment may help you formally identify the need that exists, while also helping you determine the gaps in services that currently exist in your community.

As you build your projects and programs, begin to establish methods of evaluation asking what real success looks like for each program. Remember that you don't have to reinvent the wheel. If you are struggling to determine outcome measurements, look to organizations that are doing similar work and see how they measure outcomes. There may be an opportunity to adopt some of their tools for measuring success.

Then, begin to establish a history of successes! Once you are ready to apply for grants, you will already have the data to prove that your programs or projects are providing _real solutions—_ you'll have the outcomes to prove it!

#3 Develop a fundraising strategy that _does not_ depend on or even include (gasp!) grants, initially. Begin to build partnerships with individual donors, sponsors, and other key stakeholders. In addition to helping build a financial history, this support can be leveraged for additional funding. To a grant-maker these partnerships illustrate that you are actively seeking to sustain your mission, while also highlighting the fact that community partners find value in your work *and* are willing to invest their time and resources to further your mission.

* * *

As our conversation continued, I asked Dan to tell me more about his client's potential funding sources, apart from the support they had been receiving. He stated, rather matter-of-factly, that there were no other sources of funding and other than "half a million in grants" that he didn't anticipate would change. I shifted awkwardly in my seat.

"Don't worry, the board chairperson has done her research and has identified over a million dollars in grants for us to pursue," he said.

"Done her research?" I asked tentatively.

"She has made a list of the 10 largest foundations in the state, and 10 largest nationally. Combined they are worth billions!" Dan said. "We are confident that if we research the social media footprint of each and reach out to each trustee personally, we will secure at least a million dollars towards our initial project."

I've always wished I had a better poker face, but perhaps no time more than this moment. While hesitant to be the naysayer, I knew that they could rip that entire list up and be no further from their goal.

Unfortunately, a list of 20 foundations—even if they have millions to give—is futile if you've failed to identify their funding priorities. Out of the thousands of foundations that exist throughout the entire world, there may only be 10 that share your goals or want to support your mission—and that is ok! The purpose of *good* grant research is to unearth those grant-makers and reveal your best odds of finding funding.

This is the second-most-common mistake I see grant-seekers make, regardless of the age or success of the nonprofit:

MISTAKE #64

Overlooking the Importance of Quality Grant Research

Good prospect research is key in creating a successful grants pipeline. Not only will effective research help you identify grant-makers with giving potential for *your* organization, it will also help you avoid wasting limited time and resources on long-shot grants with a slim likelihood of being funded.

When conducting research, it is important to focus on what the foundation gives *to*, rather than how much they give *total*. If, for example, your organization is Beef Eaters of America, and the largest grant-maker in your state is the Vegan Friends Family Foundation, it is incredibly unlikely you'll receive funding, no matter how much they have to give or how little you ask for.

But sometimes it's not that straightforward. A few years ago, as an in-house grant writer, I was working with a team to develop a fundraising strategy for the organization's youth program. This particular meeting included the CEO, two VPs, and myself. The greatest need at the time was for a new 16-passenger van. While not a large request, a van is a very specific kind of request and not something that *just any* grant-maker is interested in. While not impossible to fund, I knew it would take a bit of research to find the *right* grant-maker.

As the team discussed potential sources of funding, one of the Vice Presidents slid me a shallow stack of website screenshots and announced to the team that the *Ford Foundation* would fund our van. As everyone began to rejoice over the perceived slam-dunk solution, I knew I had my work cut out for me. Not only was the Ford Foundation *not* a likely source of funding, but it was now up to me to be the realist and explain that to the team.

Yes, the Ford Foundation traces its roots back to Henry Ford and the Ford Motor Company, but what this well-meaning VP had missed entirely was that the foundation itself has nothing to do with transportation or motor vehicles and their funding priorities had zero alignment with our current need. The likelihood of receiving funding for a van was exactly 0%. Had he conducted *quality* research, he would have saved himself the paper, but also saved the room's disappointment as I explained why we would not be seeking funding from the Ford Foundation.

During my tenure as a grant writer I have discovered that, whether in-house or as a consultant, one of my primary responsibilities is to help educate the board and staff about the grant-seeking process. While often straightforward, grant-seeking is not always simple. It can be a delicate balance of art and science, attention to detail, and a little bit of finesse; but mostly it comes down to understanding the priorities of the grant-maker and ensuring that your programs or projects help the grant-maker achieve *their* goals.

How to Avoid Mistake #64:

#1 Find a *good database* or hire a professional to assist with grant research. Good grant research is worth the investment. When I started out as a grant writer, I simply wrote whatever my boss gave me—which was mostly renewals. When it came time for me to begin researching new opportunities, I fumbled my way through the process and created a haphazard list of potential leads. Some leads came from newsletters, others came from emails, suggestions from consumers, and some even came from Google, but my grants pipeline fell flat. The list was not comprehensive and didn't allow for much strategy or prioritizing based on project.

When I learned how to capitalize on the power of grant research databases, my entire grants strategy changed. I was able to seek out grants and grant-makers by specific programs or program elements. I was able to focus my search for topic-specific grants, and I was ultimately able to develop an annual strategy that would allow the organization to reach its funding goals. Once I harnessed the power of a grant research database, I was able to find dozens of grants and grant-makers that shared mission alignment, and whose funding priorities were an ideal match.

If your organization has the means to subscribe to a database, it is worth the investment. For smaller organizations, however, it may not be feasible. In this case, it is worth checking with your local library. Frequently libraries provide access to a grants database, free of charge. They may also supply a directory of local grants that are not always represented in online grants databases.

If you have tried all of the above and you still feel over-whelmed by the thought of research, call in a professional grant researcher—we exist! Good research is one of the most important steps in the grant-seeking process, and it is worth the investment.

#2 Research a *grant-maker's geographic focus*. Location, location, location! When I conduct grant research, geographic focus is my first point of research criteria. There is possibly no worse scenario than finding the perfect grant opportunity, only to realize that you fall out of the geographic scope of the grant-maker. Grant research databases will allow you to set geographic parameters in your search criteria, so use them! They will save you a lot of time, energy, and potential heartbreak.

#3 Research a grant-maker's *mission alignment* and funding priorities. As I've already mentioned, being awarded a grant has very little to do with how much a foundation has to give and everything to do with what the foundation gives *to*. Again, if you are the Beefeaters of America and you're seeking a grant from the Vegan Friends Family Foundation to support your beef-only initiative, it doesn't matter if the foundation has $1 to give, or $1,000,000—you won't be getting it. Save your time and resources by making it your goal to identify grant-makers whose funding priorities align with your mission and programs.

#4 Do your due diligence, read the *grant-makers' guidelines* . . . and follow them. Once you have identified a grant-maker, familiarize yourself with their guidelines, including all dead-lines. While some grant-makers may only require a grant application, others may require a pre-application phone call, a Letter of Inquiry, an in-person meeting, a site visit, or all of the above! Avoid disqualifying yourself by missing one of these steps.

Similarly, each grant-maker will have different criteria for the grant itself. Read the guidelines carefully and follow them. I cannot stress this enough. While some may be more forgiving than others, some grant-makers will not even look at your application if you have failed to follow the guidelines perfectly. When a grant-maker has 75 applications and can only provide funding to 5 candidates, they will look for ways to whittle down the applicant pool. Sadly, even something like incorrect font size is enough to land your application on the chopping block.

If you have questions about an application or guidelines, don't hesitate to ask. While grant-makers may seem mysterious and intimidating, they are real people. In my experience, they have always been happy to help clarify or answer any questions that I have.

Finally, when reading guidelines (and following them!), make sure you familiarize yourself with—and fully understand—what will be required of you once a grant is awarded. Documents may need to be signed and returned by specific dates, reports may need to be completed throughout the grant-period, etc. Make certain you have the capacity to manage the entire scope of the grant, including all post-award requirements.

*   *   *

As we began to wrap up, Dan asked if I would be open to meeting his client and at least talking them through some of these initial hurdles. I said I'd be happy to speak with them. At the very least, I hoped—perhaps naively—that I could save them the time and energy by directing their efforts away from grants. In parting, Dan left me with one final thought:

"One more thing they've decided, they're only interested in applying for grants that are six-figures, plus. They don't want to waste their time on anything smaller."

Wasting *their* time? What about wasting the time of the grant reviewers or trustees who will have to read through a sub-par grant application? I bit my tongue. One thing was certain, I had my work cut out for me with this would-be client.

MISTAKE #65

Setting Unrealistic Grant Expectations

Are there opportunities to apply for grants that are six-figures plus? Absolutely. Should all organizations apply for them? No, at least not exclusively. In addition to being a lofty goal for a new organization—particularly one with a limited funding history and no proven outcomes—this strategy of *only* applying for large grants is short-sighted. Limiting your applications exclusively to large grants can do an incredible disservice to your organization, because in doing so, you potentially exclude grant-makers right in the heart of your own community who are passionate about your cause.

Additionally, while a six-figure grant may be great in theory, an organization needs to ensure they have the capacity and resources necessary to meet the requirements of the grant. From the little Dan had told me, I was confident this organization had big goals, but insufficient capacity.

How to Avoid Mistake #65:

#1 **Consider the *full value* of a grant.** When determining the *full value* of a grant, it is important to consider that value extends beyond the actual dollars received. For some grant-makers an initial small or mid-sized grant may be a great opportunity to get to know your organization. It may also allow your organization to get its foot in the door and build a partnership with a grant-maker who has larger long-term potential.

For other grant-makers, an initial mid-sized grant may

lead to year-over-year support that develops into a long-term partnership, i.e., a dependable source of funding. As you continue to foster relationships with grant-makers, those year-over-year relationships can be of far greater value than a one-time grant of six figures.

#2 Don't underestimate the *impact* of small grants. On the surface, small grants may not seem worth it—but they can be. Frequently, smaller grants have abbreviated applications, minimal reporting, and can be less competitive, which means the resource expenditure to manage them can be minimal. While I wouldn't recommend bombarding your entire grants calendar with small grants, they do serve an important role for organizations of *all* sizes.

In my community, there is a local foundation that provides several $1,000 grants each summer. The goal is to support organizations that create opportunities for kids and teens throughout the city during the summer months. For an organization who has never received grant funding, this grant is a great first step. It is a low-risk opportunity that allows them to become familiar with the grant-seeking process. The application is straightforward and the reporting is minimal.

For some organizations, $1,000 may feel like a drop in the bucket. But if you consider the true impact of that grant—perhaps it underwrites a summer-long cooking class, a square-foot gardening project, or all the supplies needed for a summer art camp—all of a sudden that *small* grant packs a punch.

One other thing worth noting is that this particular foundation also provides numerous opportunities for substantial grant funding throughout the year. So, in addition to receiving $1,000 toward your mission, this *small* grant could lead to long-term impact as it can allow you to begin cultivating a relationship.

#3 Avoid the "Large Grants Only" Trap. Just as I recommend organizations avoid bombarding their calendar with small grants, I equally caution against exclusively pursuing large grants. While tempting, large grants tend to be less frequent, more competitive, and can require substantial commitments— which can be a strain on smaller organizations. When you limit yourself to *only* seeking grants of $100,000 plus, you are also effectively excluding lesser, yet no less substantial, long-term funding opportunities and partnerships with foundations that may be equally passionate and dedicated to your mission, but only offer mid-sized funding opportunities.

Limiting your applications to *only* large grants, even if you are successful, is not always beneficial. Take one of my current clients, for example. A few years ago, their annual goal was to bring in $350,000 in grants. Over the years they had developed relationships with three primary grant-makers who provided substantial funding, allowing them to reach this goal. Year-over-year the grants came in and the organization, which had a long legacy and was well respected in the community, grew comfortable and complacent. They stopped cultivating relationships with other grant-makers. The strategy worked well, until it didn't.

One day this client received a call from one of the foundations, stating that they had decided to go in a different direction. After 10 years, with a single phone call, the organization lost 33% of its grant funding. As true misfortune would have it, that organization was dealt another substantial blow two years later, just as they were gaining traction again. The second grant-maker announced that their funding would be reduced by at least half. Within a couple of years their once-dependable grant pool had been destroyed, reduced by nearly 60%.

Had they considered the full value of small and mid-sized

grants, they may have avoided falling into the Large Grants Only trap, which would have allowed them to weather the storm a little easier. It ultimately took them four years to recover, and the process is ongoing. But in that time, the loss sustained over multiple years ultimately led to numerous layoffs and a complete closure of an entire department.

While it may be tempting to only apply for large grants, the value of a diverse grant pool that includes mid-sized and small grants cannot be overstated. Before you fall into the Large Grants Only trap, it may be worth asking yourself if that is the most sustainable strategy for your organization.

*   *   *

If you're curious, I did go on to meet Dan's client, who was—as anticipated—not quite ready to begin applying for grants. However, over the past year they have worked diligently to hone their mission and develop solid programs with measurable outcomes. They have committed themselves to cultivating relationships with individual donors, stakeholders, and partners in the community, and have begun to see results of this work. Together we have completed comprehensive grant research and I am confident that they will be successful when they begin pursuing grant funding.

As for that other organization, they did receive their van—but it wasn't from the Ford Foundation.

MISTAKE #66

Not Investing in the Prep Work for Monthly Giving Success

By Erica Waasdorp

I see nonprofits make two major mistakes that really prevent them from growing their monthly giving program to its fullest potential. They go hand in hand.

The top mistake nonprofits make with monthly giving is NOT PREPARING!

Many nonprofits have little staff and they're spread very thin. Time is at a premium. I get that. That's why I recommend thinking through the various options and creating the basics. Then, you're ready to start asking.

Sadly, what happens a lot is this: organizations start promoting, then everything comes crashing down because they were not prepared! Often, the program comes to a screeching halt and you'll hear things like:

- Oops, we forgot to test the process first . . .

- Now what? The monthly donor clicked the button and . . . Shoot! We did not write the thank you letter. Drop everything because we have to do that.

- OMG! The monthly donation confirmation email is not showing the recurring giving option. We have to fix that.

- Help? . . . The donor calls and wants to join the monthly giving program, but the volunteer answering the phone has never heard of it so the donor hangs up.

- Yikes! This donor wants to give via AMEX, but we did not offer that on the form.

- Technical question . . . I've got them via the online donation page, but how do we process them every month? Is that automatic?

- The system spits out a monthly donation letter, but should we send that instead?

Perhaps the finance person calls because she does not know how to report these monthly donations. Or she's not reporting them at all and you can't find them in your reports.

And the list goes on and on.

Monthly giving knows many 'moving parts.' You have to pay attention to a mix of technical, system, financial, and promotional areas—probably more so than with any other type of fundraising program I know. So, think through the whole process and work through the donor base/online giving option, recognition, cultivation, and reactivation piece *before* you begin. **If you spend just a little bit of time in the beginning, you can eliminate so many of the *oops*, *help*, *yikes* moments later on. Trust me!**

Check out the free Monthly Giving Starter Kit which I wrote, available to you from DonorPerfect. It's important to have everything ready to go before you launch. While marketing and promotion still require a lot of work, it's not nearly as much as doing the start/stop/start/stop routine that's often so frustrating and makes it tough for organizations to really focus on it.

So, *prepare* first and then start asking.

The other major mistake I see nonprofits making is not asking for monthly gifts.

I still see way too many organizations that are not asking for monthly donations. Yes, they might have added the monthly donor option to their donation page. But that's where it ends.

They never include a monthly ask in their appeals, mail, or email. They're afraid to pick up the phone and have a conversation with the donor asking them to join the monthly donor program.

Monthly giving is no different from other fundraising. The number-one reason why donors join your monthly giving program is because you ask them. But here's the reality: monthly giving asks are not a once-a-year thing. You must really focus on it and make it easy for the donor to join. You must ask continuously, and you must honor the donor's preferred amounts, no matter how small.

Monthly donors are like little giants that are 'asleep' in your donor base. I believe this so much that I wrote a book about it, called *Monthly Giving. The Sleeping Giant*. You have to wake them up! You have to tell them how easy it is for them to make a difference to your organization. Share the benefits of giving monthly for them and you. Use every medium you have available to ask them. If you start asking early and often, you'll have an amazing monthly donor program pretty soon!

MISTAKE #67

Not Investing in Donor Acquisition

By Andrew Olsen, CFRE

If you've been in the nonprofit sector more than a minute, chances are you've heard an Executive Director, Chief Financial Officer, or Board Member say something like, "Why do we have to keep spending money on acquisition? Every year we lose money on it!"

First, let's acknowledge the elephant in the room. YES! Acquisition is wildly expensive. And yes, most (like 99.99%) organizations lose money up front to acquire new donors. Over time those donors—if you cultivate them correctly—will yield significant revenue. And up front, the numbers look very ugly.

BUT . . .

Not investing in acquisition is typically a much worse decision—one that will cost you significantly more in the long run.

That doesn't mean you should be constantly addicted to acquiring new donors and building the largest donor file possible. A lot of direct mail fundraising agencies hope you might get addicted—but trust me, a bigger file doesn't always mean more value for your organization.

An organization that has retention rates of 85%-95% can get away with (maybe) taking a year off of acquisition. But in that year off, they'd still need to generate considerably more revenue from existing donors in order to offset the revenue they'll lose from that 5%-15% of donors who stop giving. And that's just to maintain revenue at the current level. If they are hoping to grow, they'll need to increase revenue from existing supporters even more aggressively.

What I've seen at least three times in my career is the truly harmful impact of organizations stopping acquisition without having a plan to offset the revenue they lose from donors who stop giving in the years they aren't conducting donor acquisition. In each instance it took those organizations an average of three additional years just to get back to the level of revenue they were generating in the year they stopped acquisition. One of the three spent almost five years just getting back to "normal" revenue levels.

Here's the thing: If you want to cut your acquisition budget (either a significant cut, or stop completely), I'd recommend you not do so until you have the structure, staff, and plan in place to effectively pursue deeper, more meaningful relationships with donors who can give significantly to your organization. Once you have those pieces in place and you're able to raise much more through face-to-face relationships with donors and highly personalized asks, THEN you can dial back in acquisition. I still wouldn't recommend you stop acquisition completely—but I'm all for reducing that investment so you can spend more expanding your capacity to build personal relationships with top donors and dramatically growing your major gift revenue.

If you're not ready or willing to make that shift though, then you'll likely end up suffering for a few years after you cut or stop acquisition.

MISTAKES #68-#70

Missing Out on Federal Grants as a Revenue Source

By Brent Merchant and Mark McIntyre

"Knowledge will always govern ignorance."
—James Madison

Having helped colleges, universities, hospitals, health systems, social service agencies, international NGOs, and municipalities win significant federal funding since 1994, here are the three most common mistakes I see nonprofit leaders and local government officials make when pursuing those dollars:

MISTAKE #68

Ignoring Federal Funding Opportunities (Ignorance is not bliss, it's fatal)

The US government is by far the world's largest "major donor," investing hundreds of billions of dollars in nonprofits— from the largest and most prestigious research institutions to municipalities to rural hospitals to small, faith-based homeless shelters to international NGOs. Last year, the federal government invested well over $100 billion in nonprofits and municipalities.

Of course, this is more money than we can comprehend so here's a comparison—the Bill and Melinda Gates Foundation makes approximately $5 billion per year in grants. Meanwhile, last year's Labor, Health and Human Services Appropriations Bill—just one of 12 annual appropriations bills—provided $121 billion in funding.

The federal government relies on nonprofits to feed people, house people, educate people, cure diseases, conduct research, build infrastructure, deliver healthcare and provide other vital social services. (The federal government invests in for-profits for some of the same reasons. Just like nonprofits, select corporations can provide certain services better and more efficiently than the government.)

Therefore, if the mission of your nonprofit is aligned with the mission of particular federal agencies, you should be exploring how to tap into the $4.4 trillion annual federal budget. You just need to know where to look and how to apply.

In our experience, the vast majority of nonprofit leaders give up before ever actually applying for a federal grant because they're ignorant of the funding opportunities. They quit before they start.

MISTAKE #69

Not Building Relationships at the Federal Grant Level— Trying to Mail it in

If we had a mortal enemy, the assignment we would give him is to attempt to win federal grants remotely without ever visiting DC to ask federal program officers what they're looking for in award-worthy applications. That approach is akin to firing arrows against a fortress wall.

The first essential step in applying for federal grants is to have a crystal clear understanding of what the federal program officers are looking for in a winning submission.

President Truman famously said, "If you want a friend in Washington, buy a dog." Respectfully, he was wrong. The inner workings of our nation's capital are built on relationships— much like a small town. You've got to get to know the people who will be reading and judging your grant applications!

Winning federal grant dollars is major donor development. (The potential major donors are the federal program officers, and the dollars they have to "donate" are our tax dollars!) Can you imagine "making the ask" of a major potential donor without ever meeting her?

MISTAKE #70

Giving up Too Easily
on Federal Grants

Whoever said, *Perseverance is the root of every achievement* must have been a federal grants writer! We've never met a grants professional or nonprofit leader who has won every grant he's ever submitted. No one is undefeated in grantsmanship.

Identifying, writing, submitting, mobilizing congressional support for, winning, and complying with federal grants is a marathon—it's not a sprint or even a 10K.

The great *New York Times* sports writer Red Smith was once asked to describe the pressure of producing a column four times a week. "Writing is easy," he replied with a wry smile. "You just open a vein and bleed."

If you've ever applied for a federal grant, perhaps you've experienced the same feeling—with some sweat and tears thrown in for good measure.

Why, then, do otherwise sane fundraising professionals go through the sometimes-agonizing federal grants process? Because persistence pays.

Significant grant dollars can strengthen, expand, and even elevate the effectiveness of your organization (or a specific program) to an entirely new level. Further, once an organization earns the trust of federal agency decision-makers, it becomes easier to win grants on an ongoing basis.

Finally, when a nonprofit secures federal funding, it is a stamp of approval that can be leveraged and multiplied into greater private support. The rigor of federal grantsmanship is a blessing. If you can win a federal grant, you can win any type of grant.

Do you know of a major nonprofit doing great work and possessing a strong brand identity that is not receiving federal support on a regular—if not annual—basis? There is an obvious reason for that.

Pursuing federal support is akin to identifying and cultivating a major donor. It is time-consuming and labor-intensive, and the actual ask is merely one important step in a relatively long process. In fact, pursuing federal grants is a great activity for people who refuse to take "No" for an answer. More on that later in the chapter...

Fish Where the Fish Are

In the years ahead, the Administration and Congress will make major investments in healthcare, job training, workforce development, apprenticeships, recruitment and training of STEM students at non-research institutions, economic development, campus security, infrastructure, public safety and homeland security, and international development. If you are the leader of a nonprofit in any of these areas, it would be strategic to evaluate whether your institution's mission matches what the federal government is striving to accomplish.

Perhaps the most dramatic federal investment among nonprofits in the years ahead will be in healthcare. The government will spend trillions of dollars to expand access, improve care, and lower costs. For example, Congress has authorized $10 billion for the Center for Medicare and Medicaid Innovation (CMMI) for testing various payment and service delivery models that aim to achieve better care for patients, better health for our communities and lower costs through improvement for our healthcare system.

Does your healthcare institution fall into any of these

categories? Do you have a new model that CMMI should consider? If so, this is a large, new source of federal spending that has already been authorized. It's waiting to be taken.

Of course, that's just the beginning . . .

Through the Health Resources and Services Administration (HRSA), there is significant funding available for the expansion of primary care services, training, graduate medical education, telehealth, and workforce development. If you serve a unique patient population (rural, disadvantaged, high Medicare/Medicaid participation, etc.), there are specific opportunities dedicated for you.

Regardless of the political party in power, both the Administration and Congress are in heated agreement that the federal government must invest more in our nation's infrastructure. The only question is how much. BUILD (formerly TIGER) funding has increased from $500 million to $1 billion, and is expected to grow further. Does your municipality have a surface transportation project on the drawing boards or something shovel-ready? If so, you should consider applying for either a planning grant or a much larger ($10 million-$25 million) implementation grant. Significant BUILD funding is set aside for rural municipalities.

The Economic Development Administration (EDA) awards grants on a rolling basis to colleges and universities, municipalities, port commissions, development corporations, and other nonprofits for purposes as disparate as business incubators, economic development planning studies, public works projects, and disaster recovery.

The EDA grant application is unique, though. Rather than write a grant proposal in response to a solicitation, when you apply for EDA dollars you collaborate with regional EDA staff. We call it "co-create."

For example, the president of a private university came to

us and said, essentially, "You helped us get earmarks. Earmarks went away. Now what?"

"Every congressional earmark flowed through an Executive Branch agency," we responded. "Let's follow the earmark back to the agency, like a great running back following his lead blocker. Let's run to daylight."

We approached the federal EDA because the university president wanted to help address his region's high unemployment rate and low baccalaureate completion rate. We did our homework. We researched the EDA's mandate, and reviewed previous grant awardees. We built relationships with both the federal EDA program officers and the regional EDA decision-makers. We collaborated with local economic development agencies. Finally, we rallied bipartisan congressional support.

The result? EDA awarded the university a $2.5 million grant to build a business incubator that will provide the greatest single sustainable economic development engine in a tri-county area in rural Ohio.

The university president is still shaking his head: "When we began this process, I didn't even know a university could apply for an EDA grant, much less win one. Okay, what's next?"

Another example: On behalf of a healthcare system in Missouri suffering from a nursing shortage—sound familiar?—we approached the regional EDA representative with a workforce development project. His initial response was, "Your proposed project is ineligible . . ."

(*Did I mention that federal grantsmanship is a great process for people who don't easily take "No" for an answer . . . and that applying for EDA dollars is a co-creation?*)

Our response to our new friend at EDA was, "Gosh, we're in desperate need of nurses in your region. We have a proposed project that will create a pipeline of nurses for a generation. How do we make this project eligible?"

That was in July. After five months and significant collaboration, EDA made a $2.2 million award to our client. The award letter stated, "Your project is approved ... without caveats (revisions)." Merry Christmas!

One final EDA anecdote: A regional EDA representative once humorously told us, "We build roads and commodes." Then how does that square with EDA funding a nursing workforce development project? The nexus is J-O-B-S, the single most compelling rationale for federal investment.

In addition to the EDA, there are a variety of economic and community development opportunities available through the US Department of Health and Human Services (HHS) and the Rural Development Office at the US Department of Agriculture (USDA). These award numbers are typically very large, depending upon the project and the service area.

Another annual program open to a wide range of nonprofit organizations is the Administration for Children and Families' Community Economic Development (CED) grant. The CED awards approximately $800,000 to organizations focused on community development, economic development, or job creation, and encourages partnerships with local food and agriculture organizations to increase food security.

As an example, Merchant McIntyre recently submitted a $525,000 CED grant to help a Christ-centered rescue mission launch a social enterprise cafe and coffee house that will create 21 full-time jobs for low-income individuals who are experiencing homelessness.

The federal dollars will fund building renovations, the purchase of specialty equipment for the retail operation, job training, job coaching, and supportive services to facilitate the staffing needs of the initiative and prepare participants for sustainable employment. Further, the cafe and coffee house will help revitalize the surrounding community by ending homelessness partially through job training/placement/retention, and create greater self-sustainability with less reliance on charitable giving. Last but certainly not least, this social enterprise will create a new and sustainable revenue stream for the Mission that can be replicated in multiple locations in the future.

Pretty good, huh?

Is your nonprofit considering a revenue-generating social enterprise that would benefit from a one-time federal investment through a competitive grant?

The Administration for Children and Families and the Department of Justice offer grants to local, regional, and national organizations serving at-risk, underserved, and disadvantaged youth. These programs usually award between $100,000 and $800,000 per grant.

There is significant funding from the USDA and the US Agency for International Development (USAID) for international aid projects. These are massive programs, with awards reaching up to tens of millions of dollars for food aid, development activities, local business training, education, health, and public works projects. If you're the leader of an international NGO interested in securing major USAID dollars, it's often strategic to begin as a sub-award grantee.

I like to get paid to breathe, how about you? That's a provocative way of introducing this potential federal funding stream—if your college, university, or social service agency provides employment training, you could be getting reimbursed up to 50% for what you're already doing!

Nonprofits may receive up to 50 cents per dollar for these eligible activities. If this sounds too good to be true, it's because filling out the necessary SNAP E&T paperwork to get started is like reading Moby Dick backwards—twice. That's why nonprofits retain Merchant McIntyre—so we can suffer the brain damage instead.

However, if you're willing to wade through the icy waters, SNAP E&T dollars can be transformational. To wit, we helped a small nonprofit that provides job-skills training for opportunity youth of New Orleans go from zero SNAP E&T support to $500,000 annually to $970,000 . . . and growing. That's the other friendly fact about securing federal support through a program like SNAP E&T—once you're in, they have to sandblast you out.

By the way, did I mention that these federal reimbursement dollars are for programs you were going to provide anyway? Do you like getting paid to breathe?

These examples of funding programs are illustrative but not exhaustive, obviously. There are hundreds of federal grant programs. Is your organization or institution a natural match with the mission of selected government programs? Does your municipality need investment that will create new jobs and improve the quality of life for your citizens? Can you demonstrate that your nonprofit is a wise investment because it achieves results efficiently? If so, then the federal government is a major donor you should approach.

Ten Steps for Winning a Federal Grant

Never pursued a federal grant before? Tried and failed, but ready to try again? Here's how:

1. **Lay the foundation.** First, conduct an internal resource inventory with executive leadership, senior administrators, and key program people to identify your priority funding needs. Beyond your needs, determine your institutional strengths as they relate to pursuing federal support.

2. **Do your homework.** Research potential federal grants. Based on your research, determine the nexus between your major funding priorities and federal resources. Grants.gov is the official government site for information on federal grants. Another resource is the Assistance Listings website (temporarily located at beta.sam.gov/), which is the official US government website for people who make, receive, and manage federal awards. Again, reviewing this publicly available information is a modest beginning. If you want to know the "unwritten rules" of winning a particular grant, contact the federal program officer(s) who run the program(s) you're targeting.

3. **Ask the right threshold questions.** Everyone seems to have a horror story about federal grants. Typically, the horror story begins after winning the grant. That's because people often don't ask themselves the right questions before applying for the grant. At Merchant McIntyre we follow the wisdom of a legendary and beloved science teacher from Mark's high school, Helen C. Boyden, who routinely reminded her students, "The trouble you don't get into, you don't have to get out of."

Before ever putting pen to paper, we break down each federal grant solicitation into about 10 "threshold questions," all designed to enable our clients to assess whether they're willing to accept the conditions and reporting requirements of winning the big grant dollars! If the facts are friendly, we proceed with vigor. If not, we don't "borrow the trouble" and move on to the next grant target.

4. **Confirm you are competitive.** It's a low bar to be "eligible" for a federal grant. The essential question is: Are you, or can you become, truly competitive? How can you tell the difference? Carefully evaluate the grant's funding criteria. Will your proposal be strong where the most points are awarded? Perhaps the best way to assess competitiveness is to review previous winners and their proposals. (You may obtain these by filing Freedom of Information Act requests.)

5. **Develop a proposal management plan.** For internal management purposes, put in place a proposal management plan for all grant applications that establishes deadlines and deliverables from start to finish for each grant. This helps guarantee that you are able to produce a quality proposal on time.

   True story: The president of a small liberal arts university rallied his faculty and administrators to work for months to write a long, complex, multi-million-dollar Department of Education grant proposal. On the day of the deadline, it took his team longer than expected to submit the grant online. No one had thought to test drive the submission process. Moments after celebrating a seemingly successful submission, the team received an email reply. The Department rejected the application because it was four minutes late.

   The university president retained our agency the next day. "That was too painful," he said. "I can't allow it to happen again."

6. **Meet with federal agency program officers.** Call— or even better, meet with—the federal agency program people who are responsible for overseeing the grant program(s) that interest you. Typically, these program officers are seasoned professionals who are always on the lookout for new partners. Think of it from their perspective: Program officers want to deliver victories (effective programs) for their managers, departments, agencies—and for themselves! As a result, they are surprisingly forthcoming with invaluable information about their grants. If you simply try to "mail it in," you are likely at a fatal disadvantage. Think about it: Do you EVER simply mail an ask to major donors without first meeting with them?

Here's a brief example of the value of listening to federal program officers: We took a city manager to meet with the DOT staff in charge of BUILD (formerly TIGER). They provided honest feedback regarding our proposed project, and specific advice about the criteria they were seeking. They even suggested a specific dollar request ($8 million-$12 million).

Our client returned home and decided to ignore the advice of the DOT staff. We submitted the grant doing it his way. We lost. The next year we met again with the DOT staff. This time, we followed their advice. We won an $11.4 million award.

Most people think that the key to success in DC is talking. It's not. It's listening.

7. **Meet with members of Congress and their staff.** Much to the chagrin of rank-and-file members of Congress and their staff, the congressional leadership

placed a moratorium on line-item earmarks (legislatively directed grants) shortly after the 2010 elections. If anything, this has made congressionals even more motivated to help their nonprofit constituents secure federal dollars through the competitive grants process.

Schedule introductory meetings with members and staff in Washington, DC, or in their state or district office. (Simply look up a senator's or representative's name online for all contact information.) Use these meetings to highlight the important work of your organization. Provide them with background information about the grant programs you have targeted. Ask your senators and representatives to write a letter of support to the appropriate federal agency leaders, and then draft the letter for the staff to save them the work of writing it themselves. (This helps ensure you get a strong, accurate letter.)

8. **Apply with substance and attention to detail.** The first round of competition for $1 billion in Innovation Challenge grants from CMMI shows how essential it is to follow all of the instructions when applying for a federal grant. Approximately 3,000 institutions and organizations submitted applications. Of those, about 800 were disqualified for technicalities. Dot your i's and cross your t's. You must pay vigilant attention to detail to ensure your application is ultimately considered.

9. **Ensure compliance, build relationships.** After winning a federal grant, implement internal measures to ensure compliance. This includes outlining the

project plans for milestones and deliverables, ensuring you have templates for technical and financial reporting, ensuring continued communication with the relevant federal agency program officers to secure the release of dollars in a timely manner, and working with federal agency officials to obtain reviews of your performance under the grant. Build relationships with the federal agency personnel so it's easier to address performance issues, and position your organization for future funding opportunities.

10. **"No" means "not yet."** One of the keys to long-term, sustained federal funding success is being curious about why your application was not funded. Review the scoring of your application, then circle back to the federal agency decision-makers. Be authentically curious about why your application fell short. Again, the federal program people typically offer honest, thorough feedback. If you truly have ears to hear and are willing to process constructive criticism, then you can turn "no" into a winning application during the very next competition.

Here's a great example of turning a "No" into a "Yes" . . .

The VP for Institutional Advancement of a critical access hospital approached us after scoring 97 out of 100 on a federal grant . . . and not winning dollars because the program ran out of money before it could "fund down the slate" of worthy applicants.

He stated emphatically, "I already know my congressional delegation, so I certainly don't need access. My hospital has a great staff and great projects. The need is obvious. What am I missing?"

Put simply, he lacked an overall federal grants plan, with boots on the ground in Washington, DC, to implement it.

We extended the hospital's reach beyond its congressional personal staff to the Committee professional staff—the people with the power to ensure that federal agency programs are properly funded. We built new relationships with the Executive Branch program officers.

We asked them, "How can we do better on our next application? What are you looking for to help accomplish the mission of your agency?" We listened. We went back to the drawing board.

And then we started winning . . . First, a $650,000 grant for a new medical residency program . . . Then, $900,000 for rural physician residency training . . . Then, the game-changer—a $10.5 million Innovation Challenge grant from CMMI. Again, these federal dollars were flowing to a rural, 24-bed hospital.

"The harder we work, the luckier we get," the VP for Advancement chortled.

Are federal grants political?

We're talking about Washington, DC! Further, are foundation grants political? Corporate grants? Have you ever indulged any political whims to accommodate a major donor writing a big check?

Would you really be surprised if you discovered there is a political component to winning certain federal grants? That seems a bit like Captain Renault's raiding Rick's in the movie *Casablanca*—"I'm shocked . . . shocked to find that gambling is going on in here!"[1]

The messenger matters. Relationships matter. So build some relationships. The obvious way to build relationships with federal funders is to invest time with them. A more subtle and highly effective tactic is to volunteer to serve as a proposal evaluator, based on your expertise. This allows you to work closely with federal agency decision-makers, and enables you to learn about the proposal process from the inside out.

Remember that members of Congress and their staff take seriously the Legislative Branch's constitutional authority as "the sole power of the federal purse."[2] They work with the leadership of federal agencies to ensure that the applications of worthy organizations and institutions in their district/state are highlighted for thorough consideration. Therefore, if you plan to submit a grant proposal, ask your members of Congress to express support for your application.

Is "lobbying" a bad word?

Pursuing federal grants does not require registering to lobby. Still, we at Merchant McIntyre frequently choose to register because our agency culture emphasizes over-communication, honesty, and transparency.

We're bemused by the negative perception people have of lobbyists—especially among our conservative friends who pride themselves as strict constitutionalists. We understand it, of course. The media defines every profession by the "least among us," so to speak. The media highlights rascals and scandals, not hard-working folks who represent their clients with integrity and extraordinary strategic thinking. Further, politicians and elected leaders right up to the President of the United States have used lobbyists and the special interests they serve as a punching bag for decades. (Note to self—we're all special interests!)

The First Amendment to the US Constitution guarantees the right of every citizen "to petition the Congress."[3] Nowhere in that august document does it state that citizens get extra style points for going it alone. That's why nonprofit leaders retain the services of our agency. We're experts at petitioning Congress and the Executive Branch agencies to win federal funding for our clients.

It's knowledge like this that governs ignorance. James Madison could relate.

[1] Curtiz, Michael, Humphrey Bogart, Ingrid Bergman, and Claude Rains. Casablanca. S.l.: Warner Bros, 1942.

[2] *U.S. Constitution.* Article I, Section 9, Clause 7.

[3] *U.S. Constitution.* Amendment I.

MISTAKE #71

Thinking Donors can be Successfully Acquired Without Professional Help

By Andrew Olsen, CFRE

As the cost of fundraising continues to rise, many nonprofits are taking as much of their marketing and fundraising in-house as possible to save on costs.

The thinking often goes something like this . . .

Even if we don't do as well as before, we've cut the cost so significantly that it'll almost be a wash!

However, one of the biggest mistakes nonprofits make is assuming they can make this switch with their donor acquisition efforts.

Several years ago I was consulting with a Catholic Charities agency in the Midwest. They had taken their acquisition program in-house a few years prior. On the surface their program looked successful. Taking it in-house helped them save almost $45,000 per year. That's enough to fund an entire additional position for their organization, which is huge!

But once we got under the hood and looked at the key metrics in their in-house acquisition program it was pretty clear their program wasn't as successful as everyone thought.

Their total annual investment in donor acquisition was $175,000. For that investment, they had steadily acquired ~500 donors per year. That's a cost per donor of $350. The problem with that number is that their five-year long-term value for those donors they were acquiring was only $158. That means after five years, they were still upside down on that investment to the tune of nearly -$200 per donor. At that rate, those donors would NEVER generate net income for their ministry programs.

After seeing these numbers they agreed to let me run their acquisition program.

Keeping their total budget the same ($175,000), we acquired 5,300 donors for them in the following year. Their cost per donor decreased from $158 to $33, meaning they'd net +$125 per donor instead of losing $200 per donor!

Sometimes, the money you save by taking work in-house actually ends up costing you in the long run.

MISTAKE #72

Using Vague Words in Fundraising Communication

By Jeremy Reis

Supporting our programs will provide hope. Supporting us will help hire the staff we need to empower people and accomplish the good work we're doing. We provide sustainable solutions to solve inequality and help the financially disempowered.

I enjoy a great fundraising appeal. As my wife and I sat at a fundraising dinner for an organization whose work we value, I got excited to hear the appeal. The agenda for the night was well-constructed. The event featured two entertaining co-hosts and music by a local group. We heard two stories about people whose lives were transformed from the work of the organization. The second story was about a project my wife and I donated to, so I was excited to see the fruits of our gift.

The Executive Director, a middle-aged gentleman with thin, wiry glasses, took the stage. He was new to the organization—having taken the job just a few short months before the event—and this was the first time we were introduced to him.

It was time for the appeal.

He thanked the hosts and the audience for attending the event, then said the words many of us in fundraising know all too well: *Hope. Support. Hire staff. Empower. The good work we're doing. Sustainable solutions. Inequality. Financially disempowered.*

The dinner had the right elements for a successful fundraising event: emotional stories of impact, enjoyable music, engaging co-hosts, and well-shot videos. At the culmination of each of these elements building upon the previous one—instead of a crescendo—the event ended with a vague ask to provide hope. Needless to say, few commitment forms were completed and the evening ended in a whimper.

I reached for a pen and a slip of paper to write down what happened. As I stared at the words the Executive Director used, I realized how often the fundraising team in my organization does the same thing.

It's not just in major donor or event fundraising—nonprofit fundraisers often use vague phrases in all forms of communication. We talk about providing "hope" instead of "a meal to someone who is hungry." We describe someone using the word "impoverished" because we don't want to offend by saying "poor." We say "You can make an impact," when that phrase ultimately has many open-ended meanings. We say "food security" when we really mean someone has nothing to eat. We use vague words to make ourselves feel better, rather than addressing the real problems people face.

William Zinsser writes in his classic book, *On Writing Well*:

Our national tendency is to inflate and thereby sound important. The airline pilot who announces that he is presently anticipating experiencing considerable precipitation wouldn't think of saying it may rain. The sentence is too simple—there must be something wrong with it.[1]

Though no industry is immune to jargon, nonprofit communicators often fall into the trap of using these words in order to sound intelligent about an issue—or to protect the dignity of their beneficiaries. Unfortunately, using words that aren't clear results in a muddled message that ultimately doesn't convert.

So, why do we use jargon or more-complex words when simpler words are clearer?

First, many communicators aren't intending to sound intellectual, but are simply writing at the level they are trained. Someone who earns a PhD often has a difficult time writing clearly and succinctly. The Executive Director might think, "With so much information to educate the donor about, I need to make sure she understands everything we do so she can see the breadth of services we offer constituents." As a fundraiser, your job is to concentrate this information down to a sixth-grade reading level. This writing technique can be difficult to understand for those with a high level of education. There is a belief that by writing at a sixth-grade level, the writer is perceived to be a poor communicator. *The opposite is true—being able to communicate a complex topic using simple words is a sign of an excellent communicator.*

Second, some nonprofit communicators believe some words have a negative connotation, and they don't want a beneficiary to feel undignified. This is a valid concern. As a nonprofit communications professional, you don't want to create content that negatively affects the dignity of the people your organization serves. Most nonprofit staff are more cautious about certain words than donors are, or the people you serve. However, don't let words scare you off when they are both effective conversion tools and not likely to offend the people you support.

Third, nonprofit fundraising professionals often get bored with repetitive communications. It's easy to tire of seeing similar content each week. However, donors don't get bored reading your content, as they aren't reading every word of every appeal you send them. Instead, they appreciate repetitive and direct messaging that reinforces a theme. Faced with following convention and delivering the same message in a repetitive fashion, many nonprofit communicators will choose to do something new and different, even if it loses clarity and impact.

Fourth, fundraisers often use vague words when they don't have the confidence to ask for money. Fear drives them to ask in an indirect and vague manner instead of being clear and to the point. By saying the phrase, "We'd love your support," they escape having to say "Your immediate donation will help." An indirect ask often confuses the audience.

At a recent fundraising event, a friend—who is not a professional fundraiser—delivered the appeal. Before the event, he asked me for coaching on what to say. I explained the format for a good story and how to present a strong call-to-action in order to successfully close the appeal. When he got in front of the crowd, all of the tips I had given him were thrown out the window as his nerves took over. He ended his appeal with, "Our staff would really covet your prayers and support."

Unfortunately, when using words that don't have a clear meaning without context, such as "support," you run the risk of confusing the audience. For example, at this event, by hearing "your prayers and support," the audience was most likely unclear about the desired action and didn't understand the organization desired a significant financial donation. Some people donated, but not nearly enough to meet the financial goal for the event.

So how can we avoid these fundraising communication pitfalls?

Language testing shows how using plain language positively impacts conversion rates. NextAfter, a leading digital agency for nonprofits, investigated how using simple and straightforward language impacts conversion. NextAfter tested need-based, more-common language for CaringBridge.[1] Using simple and straightforward language resulted in a 63.9% increase in CaringBridge's conversion rate.

What does this research ultimately tell us? Using vague words is hurting our fundraising.

We're losing donors, as they equate our ambiguity with deception and they stop giving. The Association of Fundraising Professionals' (AFP) *2018 Fundraising Effectiveness Survey* found that overall donor retention was only 45.5%. The average nonprofit is losing 54.5% of their donors each year. Unfortunately, the trend for the past decade has been a decreasing rate each year.[2]

One of the primary reasons for donors losing interest is the sterile language we use. Instead of language like, "George, a homeless veteran, had a hard time adjusting to society. He spent most nights under a bridge trying to sleep through the hunger pains," we write, "George, an unhoused client, struggled while being unsheltered and suffering from food insecurity." Donors find this language confusing and not compelling. Most of your donors will never meet a homeless man, an inner-city child needing an education, or a starving child. Your vivid description and engaging story help the donor understand the plight of the beneficiary and the resulting impact of their donation.

How do we identify vague phrases we're using in our communications? Here are five types of words or phrases we use that you can edit, change, or eliminate.

1. **A sanitized word or phrase** is one that is selected to stand in for a clearer word that may have a negative connotation. For example, a writer may choose to

say a family is "impoverished" instead of "poor." Sanitized words lead to confusion as the reader may be unfamiliar with the term, or it may not make immediate sense. Sanitized words often lose the impact of the original term. For example, if we write a story about a child suffering from "food insecurity," instead of saying she's hungry, the image painted in the reader's mind has less impact and our choice of words will reduce donations. As you're reviewing donor communications, look for terms that reduce the impact and vivid nature that a more realistic term provides.

2. **We love our acronyms in the nonprofit industry.**

   On your last DM appeal, do you know the ROI impact the A/B test had for the change on the RD and the BRE? If you give now, your donation will be matched due to generous gifts from USAID and WFP!

   Even at Food for the Hungry, we often shorten our name to the acronym FH. A good rule of thumb is to look for acronyms in fundraising copy and determine if the public would understand its use. If it isn't a commonly used acronym, consider replacing it with the full term.

3. **Every industry has insider words that are called "terms of art."** If a word or phrase isn't widely understood in the public realm, but has a specific meaning in the nonprofit industry, it is likely a term of art. We use these words both in our fundraising departments—such as lapsed donor, donor cultivation, or development—and in our programs area—such as monitoring and evaluation, sustainability, or

collective impact. We use terms of art so frequently inside the nonprofit industry that it becomes difficult to not use them when we write donor communications. When you review copy for terms of art, consider whether your spouse, brother-in-law, or mother would understand the definition of the word or phrase you're using.

George Eliot once said, "The finest language is mostly made up of simple unimposing words." Donor communications should be written in a simple, conversational style. It's easy to fall into the trap of using complex words when a simpler one would produce better results. An easy rule to follow is to write at a sixth-grade reading level. This simplifies your content to appeal to the widest audience in a way that is easy to understand. The tool I use to help me produce this style of writing is the Hemingway App, a free web-based tool at hemingwayapp.com. Hemingway App grades the content and then identifies sentences that are too complex. Simple words increase clarity in your communications.

4. **Unfortunately, sometimes we use meaningless words in our communications.** Words such as "marginalize," "disenfranchised," "innovative," "solutions," and "mechanisms" lose their meaning (or never had one to begin with) when we overuse them in our communications. As with terms of art, look for phrases or words that your spouse, sister-in-law, grandmother, or aunt wouldn't easily understand. Replace meaningless words with words that have a clear meaning.

5. **Vague words are negatively impacting our fund-raising.**

Challenge yourself to identify and change phrases that lack the punch necessary for successful donor communications. When your communications become simpler and clearer, your donor trusts your organization more and he or she is more likely to engage in a long-term relationship. I close this chapter by identifying commonly used vague phrases and what we really mean. Add to this list and suggest your own on Twitter by using #npjargon.

Vague Phrase	What We Mean
At-risk	On the verge of trouble
Clients	People we serve
Core competency	What we do really well
Disenfranchised	Lost access to rights
Disincent	To drive away from something
Empowerment	Give people control over their situation
Engagement	Work with
Food insecurity	Hungry or starving
Generational poverty	Poor for many generations
Give hope	A tangible outcome for the person
Global south	Developing nations
Grassroots/Grasstops	People at a local level
Impoverished	Poor
Incentivize	Encourage an action
Initiatives	Activities or projects

Learnings	Knowledge or information
Marginalized	Target populations
Mechanisms	Ways
Outcomes	What is accomplished
Programs and services	Describe what you actually do
Resourced	Provided the necessary materials
Stakeholders	People who are actively involved
Sustainable	Ongoing results
Systemic	Multiple solutions to a problem required
Underserved	Needy or desperate
Under-resourced	Poor
Vulnerable	In trouble or on the verge of trouble

[1] Giddens, Jeff. "How Straightforward Copy and a Quantified Ask Affects Donor Conversion ." *NextAfter.com*, www.nextafter.com/research/2017/03/how-straightforward-copy-and-a-quantified-ask-affects-donor-conversion/. Study duration 3/16/2017—3/21/2017

[2] Levis, Bill, et al. *2018 Fundraising Effectiveness Survey Report.* The Growth in Giving Initiative, 2018. pp 17-18

MISTAKE #73

Ignoring Donor Migration and Middle Donors

By Roy C. Jones, CFRE

Climbing the Ladder: Does Your Direct-Response Fundraising Program Feed Your Major Gift Officers?

Donor migration is one of the most critical processes in fundraising today, and the sad fact is that most development professionals often ignore it entirely. Make no mistake about it, thousands of nonprofits treat their major gift programs separate and apart from their direct response program. Direct response programs that do not feed donor prospects from the middle donor segment to the major giving level can cripple fundraising programs. There is a donor migration crisis being overlooked by the majority of charities and nonprofits in the United States.

NextAfter recently completed a study called *The Mid-Level Donor Crisis*. For their research, NextAfter made gifts between $1,000 and $5,000 to 37 different charities. Now as mid-level donors, they tracked the communication from those charities for 90 days after the gift was made. Jeff Nickel and Steven Bushie of TrueSense reported the study's findings last year, and they were shocking:

- Only 8% of the charities made a personal thank-you call to middle donors.

- Only 31% of communication received came from a real person.

- Almost half (49%) of organizations sent nothing at all or stopped communicating after one month.[1]

Prioritizing mid-level donor development should be job #1 at your charity or nonprofit. Determining the size of your middle donor pool should be calibrated based upon how many new major donors need to be harvested from the middle donor pool each year. People are not major donors for life. Understanding attrition is critical to understanding how to design your regular donor, middle donor, as well as your major donor initiatives.

The first step of any successful program is looking at how many major donors gave this year that also gave in the previous year. Of course, when you know your major gift renewal rate you then have defined the real problem . . . *how many major donors have fallen into the LYBUNT category?*

LYBUNT??? A term you are not familiar with in your major gift program? *Last Year, But Unfortunately Not This Year.* You have to begin each year with a clear understanding of not only how many major donors you have lost, but how much lost money you need to replace just to get back to where you were a year ago. Determining your break-even benchmark for the number of donors in your major gift pool is critical. You cannot grow until you get back to the benchmark from the previous year.

Many development professionals falsely assume that once someone is a major donor, they will always be a major donor. They are working caseloads or donor assignments that have been categorized as "major donors for life." Huge mistake. Huge!

Nothing can be further from the truth. Wealth changes every day. Donor capacity is a moving target. A person who was a major donor a year ago can quickly move back to regular donor, middle donor, or lapsed donor status for a myriad of reasons. Most donors tell you this by self-qualifying with the size of their most recent donation or lack of one. Donors just don't climb up the ladder. They can climb down the ladder, and sadly, many donors fall off the ladder (lapse). It is our job to address these migration trends as quickly as possible.

A divorce, a business loss, kid(s) in college, or simply because of age of the donor, (maybe they are moving to a fixed income)—there are many reasons donors can move down the ladder or fall off. The vast majority of the time, the former major donor still loves the charity, but they have just grown older. As people age and approach their mid-to-late 70s (certainly in their 80s), they often cap what they give to charity. And of course, there are some donors whose advanced age brings health and mental complications that drastically change their priorities in life. Age is most often the reason most major donors lapse.

Every donor file is different. The demographics vary from file to file. Offsetting attrition—especially in the major donor segment—is one of the most important strategic fundraising considerations in the business.

Again, once you know how many donors you have to upgrade to offset attrition in your assigned major donor case-loads, you are then able to calibrate your direct response program to upgrade donors to the appropriate levels.

Set up a Process for Donors to Climb the Ladder

As touched on previously, I like to compare major donor development to the rungs on a ladder. The best fundraisers always use the donor's giving history as the basis for determining how much that next ask should be. Those who fail usually make the mistake of asking for too much or asking for too little.

The donor's most recent contribution (MRC) and highest previous contribution (HPC) are the two best indicators for determining the next level they should be upgraded to . . . . aka, the next rung on the ladder.

It is very difficult to take a donor who has been giving $1,000 and upgrade them to $25,000, even if you know they have the money. You have to move donors to higher giving levels incrementally, *one rung at a time*. Remember, major donors do not make gifts, they make investments. A good investor will make a gift and based upon the results they see . . . they will give a little more next time. The major donor wants to see how quickly they are thanked; did the gift they gave get used as you said it would? Did their gift have a measurable impact? In short, they want to confirm that your ministry or organization is a good steward of their money.

A $1,000 donor can be successfully asked for $50,000, $100,000, or more, but a response in the affirmative will be the exception, not the rule. The best option would be to take the time to build and cultivate the relationship. Explain the bigger need, but ask the $1,000 donor to consider a gift of $5,000 or $10,000.

Some organizations get frustrated because they only have two rungs on their giving ladder: the low-dollar $25 donors, and the high-dollar bequest or six-figure major gift donors. With no rungs or levels between entry-level giving and major gifts, it is almost impossible to take donors to the top of the giving pyramid.

Offer Development is Critical

You have to take your program needs and create price points that can be translated and presented to donors at each rung on the giving ladder. This is very different than how an accountant or finance department presents a budget or annual report. Fundraisers must create a needs list with variable dollar amounts—as well as giving recognition levels, which are natural benchmarks (giving levels) for your donor file and organization. Of course, this also gives you a process for prioritizing your donor visits and event strategies.

Here are a few tips for improving segmentation and moving donors up the giving ladder:

1. **Set your giving levels so that they challenge your donors to increase their financial support:** for example, $1,000, $5,000, $10,000, $50,000, $100,000.

2. **Develop your needs list** with specific needs or projects at each giving level (be sure to build overhead or admin costs into each project price point).

3. **Plan to establish at least three levels of giving recognition** so donors see the progression in size of gifts, and thus upgrade their contributions. For example, $5000—$10,000—$25,000

4. **Select a name for identity giving recognition levels.** Conventional names include Century Club, President's Society, Founder's Club, and Director's Roundtable. Consider, however, names unique to your organization: the name of your founder, a famous member, a historical figure embodying your organization's mission, or a concept important to your organization.

5. **Determine the donor's benefits at each level:** plaques or certificates, autographed book, listing of their name in a program or annual report, access to key staff, invitations to special events.

6. **Decide how and where you will recognize and publicize giving by donors at each level:** newsletter, plaque, annual report, program, and special brochure.

7. **Identify board members and key donors who can "seed" each giving level with their contributions.** Contact them personally to ask them to serve as charter members.

8. **Prepare a brochure for each level:** Describe how the giving at each level works, stipulating an annual contribution of at least $ _____ for (usually) unrestricted support.

9. **State whether a gift can be made in several payments**—and whether deferred gifts will be counted (some organizations have a giving club just for those who've remembered the organization in their wills).

10. **Identify and illustrate the benefits of membership.** List charter members.

11. **For higher-level giving, plan an annual special event** such as a luncheon, dinner, or seminar. The president or executive director must be on hand for these events. Consider also inviting a prominent person or special speaker. These events will encourage renewal of contributions.

12. **At least once each year, list donors and giving levels** (rungs on the ladder) in your newsletter, annual report, or (preferably) a special publication. (*Be careful about posting this information on your website. Web-crawler technology will capture this information and make your donors targets to other charities.*)

Build Out Your Middle Donor Team First

Direct mail and digital campaigns are not enough to get donors from the middle donor segments to the major donor segment. Taking donors from $1,000 to $5,000 and then from $5,000 to $10,000 with just direct response can happen, but it takes a lot of time: direct-response-driven middle donor programs can take three to five years to upgrade donors to the five-figure or six-figure major gift threshold.

The math adds up over time ... 14-18 appeals per year to generate about three gifts per year. Through the use of gift arrays (suggested gift amounts), *donors with capacity* who give three times per year can often double their giving annually:

- Year 1—$100 donor becomes a $200 donor

- Year 2—$200 donor becomes a $400 donor

- Year 3—$400 donor becomes an $800 donor

- Year 4—$800 donor becomes a $1,600 donor

- Year 5—They finally get approached by a major gift officer for a five-figure gift

The process is time consuming and expensive. Far worse, many high-net-worth donors just stop giving long before year five. High-net-worth donors—regardless of their current giving amount—will often leave a charity if the charity cannot seem to figure out who they are as a donor and start treating them like a high-capacity, high-net-worth supporter.

The solution: beef up your middle donor representative (MDR) pool. These are the people in your donor services department who call donors to say thank you, send out hand-written thank you notes, answer questions, and support the donor. For every two major gift officers (MGO) in the field managing 100 to 150 major donor relationships each, there

MGO = Major Gift officer

should be one middle donor rep in house cultivating 750 to 1,000 middle donors to become major donors. The middle donor reps are the inside sales force, and the major donor reps are your outside sales pros in the field, doing frontline or face-to-face fundraising with your donors.

How does that break down? If you have 10 major gift officers in the field working face to face with 1,000 major donors (100 donors per MGO), you should have a minimum of 5 middle donor reps in-house working with 3,000 to 5,000 middle donors (750 to 1,000 donors assigned to each MDR). Their objective is to identify wealth and capacity—but most importantly, philanthropic intent. The ultimate goal is to set up meetings and introductions for the major gift officers in the field.

When a donor meets with a major gift officer and upgrades their giving, a real celebration should happen. Middle donor reps are the most critical people in the fundraising process. They are the backbone of the development operation. Many charities fail because they refuse to invest in their middle donor programs. They believe they can work middle donors with just mail or paid telemarketers, and this just isn't the case.

The ratios stay the same for smaller organizations. Let's say that you only have two major gift officers who each manage about 150 major donors. Then you will need at least one middle donor rep working with about 1,500 middle donors. Of that pool of 1,500 middle donors, this rep will need to upgrade and refer 5%-10% annually to the major gift officer team.

Depending on the age of your major donors, attrition can be as high as 25%-50%. So your middle donor representatives need to be feeding and referring enough donors to the MGOs in the field to offset attrition.

Don't Forget that Some People are Middle Donors for Life   *MDR - middle Donor Rep*

The goal of the MDR (middle donor rep) is to align philanthropic intent with capacity. There are people who love the charity and would gladly take a meeting. However, they do not and will likely never have the capacity to make a five-figure or six-figure gift in a single calendar year.

The worst thing you can do is to upgrade true middle donors (without capacity) to a major donor officer's caseload. The donor will be ultimately embarrassed when asked for a $10,000+ gift that they will never have the resource to give. Often, middle donors who are prematurely asked for a big gift are pushed off the ladder, not up it. They literally lapse due to the embarrassment of the big ask, or the feeling of being not important enough to the charity.

More often than not, the person who makes a $1,000 gift did not give you their last $1,000. Most who give at that level do have capacity. The challenge is cultivating the relationship and igniting their passion about meeting with a donor advocate in their region or area to help them with their philanthropy. It truly is an art, not a science. Good middle donor reps develop an instinct and know how to read the signals that a donor is ready to do something more.

Some of the signals that a middle donor is ready for a meeting with a major gift officer may include:

- The donor wants to attend an event

- The donor wants to meet other supporters in their area

- The donor has questions about their designated giving last year

- The donor asks for an impact report on their previous giving
- The donor has sold a business or shares about an inheritance or windfall
- The donor asks if your organization has any special needs right now
- The donor asks questions about giving vehicles (or stocks, real estate, gold, or other appreciated assets)
- The donor asks to tour the charity or see the work firsthand

I could go on and on, but you get the picture. Good middle donor representatives know how to read the tea leaves and when to suggest a donor meet with a charity representative in their area.

Don't Forget About Your Sustainers and Monthly Donors

The rules are certainly different for cultivating sustainers for a major gift. A donor who is giving $100 per month to cross the $1,000 threshold annually should not be automatically thrown into the middle or major donor program. However, the person who is giving $500 per month ($6,000 per year or more) should be cultivated as a middle donor and solicited at year end for a special one-time gift of $5,000 or more.

I recommend not moving sustainers into a major gift officer's caseload until: 1.) the sustainer or monthly donor engages with the middle donor rep and 2.) expresses an interest in meeting with a major gift officer in their area or 3.) makes a single gift of $5,000 or more and 4.) has verified high net worth that qualifies them to be cultivated as a major donor. You do have to be careful about putting these donors into the middle donor mail stream—they should receive limited mail for sure. However, this should not prevent building a one-to-one relationship with the middle donor rep or major gift officer. Of course, take into consideration that these contributions would be in addition to their monthly support.

Ignoring high-net-worth donors because they are plugged into formal sustainer initiatives is a mistake. Doing so can inadvertently downgrade their giving—and far worse, high-net-worth donors may begin to wonder why no one is reaching out to meet and work with them like the other charities they support. If you are not careful, you can spike attrition by not moving high-net-worth sustainers to your middle and major donor programs.

Remember, Middle Donor Reps can Reactivate Lapsed Major Donors Too

Donors must be able to climb up the ladder, but it is just as important for them to have the option to climb down the ladder. If they cannot downgrade when their financial situation changes, many will lapse out of embarrassment. Having the option to climb down the ladder is critical. Middle donor programs can be a safety net for major donors who need to take a break.

Leaving major donors in a major gift officer's caseload when the donor's financial situation or interests have shifted is a huge mistake.

Stop Competing for Donor Assignments—do what is Right for the Donor

Breaking down management silos is critical to making the fundraising program work. Major gift development is simply adding an additional layer on top of the regular donor and direct response initiatives. Major giving is an extension of good direct mail and digital fundraising.

It must be a team effort. The direct mail team should understand that their goal is to feed donors to the giving ladder to upgrade them to the middle and major donor programs. In addition, major gift officers should not view it as a failure if a donor needs to downgrade to the middle or regular giving program. Allowing donors the freedom to climb up or down the ladder is critical to offsetting attrition.

Barbara O'Reilly of Network for Good outlined the importance of successful middle donor and major donor collaboration in her article titled "3 Reasons to Develop a Middle Donor Program."[2]

1. **Today's Middle Donors = Tomorrow's Major Donors.** This group of donors is your pipeline to your future major gift donors. If you don't have a donor-giving circle, this is a good place to start. And if you do have some higher annual fund giving society, you are on the right track! A giving circle recognizes the higher annual investment of these donors by allowing them special access to your work through invitation-only events or special publications. Building those relationships now could lead to bigger donations in the future.

2. **They are a Valuable Source of Regular Revenue.** While every middle donor is not going to become a major gift prospect or donor, these donors have self-selected a higher-level annual gift to your organization with relatively little effort. Retention rates among this donor group are usually higher than with smaller donors. So, just think about what potential may

exist for increased annual revenue with a little more personalized level of communication about your work and special opportunities that deepen their connection.

3. **Inspire Others to Give More.** Developing and promoting a middle donor program also gives smaller donors an incentive to upgrade their own giving. For some donors, knowing that they will get a distinct set of "benefits" and recognition in your annual report, on your website, and in other ways with a slightly bigger annual gift may be just the incentive they need to commit to a larger level of support.

Conclusions

The end result of an effective donor migration process is calibrating and reformatting the donor treatment by segment to align with where the donor is in their journey to support your charity. It is not just a special club or logo that defines the mid-level giving program. It is one-to-one relationships with donors. Taking the time to find out what they want, not just pitching what the charity's needs are.

In the end it is about tailoring communications and actual interactions with a real person in a manner that is comfortable to the donor. It is about identifying the donor's passion and the issues they are concerned about, and then delivering programs and giving opportunities around the donor's heart and desires.

It is not about the charity or the causes it serves. It is about the donor. The donor—period, nothing more and nothing less. Meet their philanthropic needs and you will raise more money for your charity than you can count.

Meeting donors where they are and ministering or caring for

their needs and desires is what makes effective donor migration work. It is truly what keeps donors climbing the giving ladder, giving more and more each and every year.

I have said it often, almost to the point of being preachy, but money always follows ministry. Are you caring for the heart of your donors?

[1] Kachuriak, Tim. *The Mid-Level Donor Crisis*. NextAfter, 2017.

[2] O'Reilly, Barbara. "3 Reasons to Develop a Middle Donor Program." *Networkforgood.com*, 14 Dec. 2015, www.networkforgood.com/ nonprofitblog/3-reasons-to-develop-a-middle-donor-program/.

MISTAKE #74

Making Short-Sighted Decisions About Digital Fundraising

By Jeff Kliewer, CFRE

The next Wild West, The Last Frontier. This is how the digital fundraising frenzy has been described in countless "How to" digital fundraising sessions at AFP, DMA, NTEN, BBCON, and various other conferences. Now, I'm sure there will be future frontiers and new territories to explore, but let's pause for a minute and reflect on this.

Stop and picture settlers bouncing along on horseback and in their covered wagons, exploring miles and miles of road-less terrain. I'm guessing it was messy, exhausting, and even scary, but the hope of a better future drove them on. Many of them reached their destination. Covered in dirt, weary, but they arrived.

But some never made it. They lost sight of their objective, became distracted by interesting yet unimportant aspects of their travels, only to find themselves completely off track and unable to find their way back to their intended destination.

I see the same distractions derail fundraisers and nonprofit leaders when it comes to navigating the digital fundraising landscape.

It's interesting what we hear these days in our fundraising space. A fundraiser recently told me that their number-one goal was to have every one of their donors neatly organized into one database. If they found a great third-party platform but it didn't completely integrate with that database, it wouldn't even be considered. Another fundraiser commented that they would only use platforms and products that completely matched their coveted brand book. My guess is that when organizations started raising money on social media, these two fundraisers weren't in that covered wagon exploring the new frontier.

Fundraising can be a grind. Frontiers are messy. In this day and age, we need to pull out every stop and leverage every possibility to increase revenue, even if it's messy. If you're reading this chapter, it's safe to assume you are an open-minded and aggressive fundraiser, hungry to find a way to increase revenue.

As you explore the digital frontier, may I suggest a few perspectives to adopt to help you successfully navigate uncharted lands?

1. The Fluid Goal. You know what you need. You know what you're looking for—new donors, retention, monthly giving, larger gifts, etc. You're a fundraiser and your number one goal is to raise funds to help your organization do more of the important work it set out to do. You have goals and measurables to steer you in the right direction and evaluate success. As you engage new technology, keep these goals fluid.

Think of this as a train in motion. The train needs to get to the destination and needs to keep moving. Every once in a while, leadership parachutes in to evaluate the progress of the train. Is it going fast enough? Does it have the resources it needs to keep going? And most importantly, is it still moving in a worthwhile direction? Slight shifts and changes might help it reach a new but more desirable destination.

What does this look like in fundraising? You might find yourself utilizing a new technology strategy to engage middle donors and, after several months, you realize that it's actually a better strategy or tool for major donor engagement. Make the shift and move on. Don't be stubborn and try to make something work, simply because that was your original goal.

I remember conversations with my colleagues in the early days of launching my company, ViewSpark. All of us had been in fundraising for decades and were so challenged with the lack of good, fundraising-centric technology available in the nonprofit space. We'd see lots of giving-page gimmicks and "total funds raised" thermometers, but nothing designed by fundraisers that was really pushing the needle forward and helping them raise more money.

We set out to build an app-creation-based platform, but quickly realized that wasn't the answer the industry was looking for. We identified a much more significant need—a simple way for fundraisers to create and send real-time updates, delivered within seconds to a segmented portion of a donor file in a mobile-optimized format. For the first time, donors would actually be able to see their giving in action, which would encourage them to give more and give again, year after year.

We accomplished this goal, but the roadmap that got us to success was drastically different than the one we envisioned when we set out on this journey. Had we been stubbornly stuck to our original plan, we would have invested a large amount of time and money to develop some really fancy technology that would have been basically useless in the industry.

2. The Hassle Factor. Earlier I mentioned the fundraiser whose goal was to organize all donors neatly into one database. Now, this sounds dreamy, but this goal falls into the "nice-to-have" category, not the "must-have." Engaging new technology that doesn't integrate—or might cause additional back-end work for the gift processing team—should not have a final vote in the decision-making process.

What if I told you I would make a million-dollar donation, but I was going to pay in one-dollar bills and you had to drive a U-Haul to San Diego to pick it up? Most of you would take me up on that offer. You might not make the drive yourself, but I'm sure you could find a team member to make the drive (may I suggest a Major Donor Officer?). It would be a hassle and would take a lot of time, but worth the investment. Now, if I said I *might* make a million-dollar gift, consider there's a bit more homework to explore the probability of the gift and weigh the hassle factor, but don't let it drive your decisions.

As you evaluate new technology opportunities, focus on what they might be able to accomplish for your organization first—and then work backwards to fill in details of time and effort.

3. What About Failure? So, your new technology strategy is a total flop. You invested time and money but nothing came of it. Pick yourself up, dust yourself off and keep moving forward. Pat yourself on the back and say "Well, that didn't work." The key is you tried something new, and eventually, one of the things you try will, in fact, work. It could even be a significant breakthrough for your organization.

Years ago I worked at a fundraising agency that had a pretty simple new business strategy—wait for potential clients to approach us. Well, my colleague and I really enjoyed selling, but the thought of a new business team was unheard of. "How can we pay salaries to employees who don't have guaranteed income from existing clients?" We weren't going to be deterred so we started to tack on an extra day or even just a half-day to our client visit trips in order to meet with prospective clients. Pretty soon, my client load was cut in half to make more time for new business efforts, and within a year, I was managing a team of three with all of us 100% focused on new business.

The agency was willing to try something new. They made a calculated decision that was tested at several points, and they continued to reevaluate the risk factors. We made many mistakes along the way, but they were fractional compared to the increased income from this new approach to income generation.

MISTAKE #75

Asking at the Wrong Time

By Andrew Olsen, CFRE

I worked on a capital campaign for a large hospital several years ago. It came about because the hospital CEO and Medical Director discerned that there was a need in the community for a specific type of treatment and no other hospital in the community was providing it at that time. Since no one else was providing this particular service, they also assessed that adding this service line would create significant opportunity for growth for the hospital.

And just like that, a campaign to expand facility, purchase equipment, and launch this service line was hastily brought to market. No feasibility study was conducted. No one reviewed the donor base to understand whether it could produce the $8 million needed. They just launched the campaign. And pretty soon, there was a prospect list. And then a short list of potential lead donors. Only problem was, the lead donors had no idea they were on the short list, and probably didn't even know that a campaign was taking place!

After a prospect management meeting the following week, it was decided that one donor who had given $50K per year for the prior three years would be the lead donor. This donor had upwards of $50 million of philanthropic capacity, and it was decided that they'd ask this donor for a lead gift of $2.5 million for the campaign. A lunch was scheduled. A campaign packet was created, with a list of naming opportunities for the donor. And off went the VP of Development to make the ask.

It was clear upon his return that the meeting didn't go well. Not only did this donor not give the $2.5 million, but she actually cut her $50K annual gift down to $10K per year.

Why?

This happened because the organization didn't listen to the donor. They didn't invest the time to understand what her goals and priorities were, or how she wanted to engage with them. They rushed a massive ask on her, and as a result she recoiled.

This is the kind of story that should remind us all that no matter what we think we need or when we want it . . . philanthropy happens on the donor's timeline, not on ours.

Instead of forcing an ask too early because that's what your organization's plan called for, you (and I don't just mean you personally—I'm referring here to the "corporate" you) need to reset expectations. It's ok to push a donor, to a degree. But pushing too hard simply for your own wants and needs will cost you in foregone gifts and damaged relationships.

MISTAKE #76

Not Paying Attention to Donor-Advised Funds

By Andrew Olsen, CFRE

There's been a lot of noise in the last few years about Donor-Advised Funds (DAFs). I first heard about them in any significant way from my good friend Greg Warner, CEO of MarketSmart. Since then, I've been shocked when I talk to nonprofits and they seem not to have any interest in even talking about how to engage DAF donors.

I've heard smart nonprofit leaders say things like, "It's too much work." "Our fundraising agency said it doesn't fit their strategy." "We can't put the DAF widget on our website because it hurts the user experience and we might get fewer online gifts."

Maybe you've had similar conversations in your organization.

Let me give you two examples of why it makes sense to intentionally focus on Donor-Advised Funds and the donors who use them.

In November of 2017 my team created a direct mail package

for one of our clients. These packages hadn't engaged donors well in the past, so we took a broad approach to the audience we included in our appeal. We opened the segmentation to pull in high-value donors who had lapsed—including several who had given gifts of up to $20,000 in the past, but hadn't given anything in 4-8 years. This appeal resonated with one of those very donors, a gentleman who had stopped giving years ago. In the past his gifts tended to be in the $5,000 range. However, after receiving this appeal with the specific suggestion to give through his Donor-Advised Fund, he made a $100,000 DAF contribution to the campaign. Had we not paid attention and had a plan to engage DAF donors, our client wouldn't have had the opportunity to benefit from this amazing gift.

Then there's the example from another organization that placed the DAF widget on their organization's homepage. This widget allows donors to make a Donor-Advised Fund gift directly within the widget on the nonprofit's site. The organization's average website gift ranged from $80-$200. What they found after adding the DAF widget was that only a small percentage of donors used it. But when they did, the average gift from these donors ranged from $1,000-$3,000. While adding the widget might decrease overall conversion slightly (though there is no empirical evidence of this from this organization's work), the tradeoff of securing significantly larger gifts from committed donors is likely worthwhile.

If you're not intentionally pursuing DAF gifts and the donors who make them, you should. Furthermore, if you don't have the DAF widget on your website, consider adding it. You can download it at dafdirect.org.

MISTAKE #77

Believing Your Job is
All About Money

By Andrew Olsen, CFRE

You can usually tell if a development officer thinks his job is all about the money. It's easy, because he'll almost always use crass language to talk about the work. Instead of investors, partners, or donors, they might be *targets, suspects,* or simply *prospects.* While it's ok to have a *prospect list,* it's not ok not to recognize the humanity of those who support and invest in your cause. Similarly, instead of inviting supporters to participate in your mission, someone who thinks their job is all about the money will instead talk about *hitting up* donors, *chasing after a gift,* or *going back to the well.*

One might argue that that's just shop talk, and that development officers who speak in this manner don't really mean it. I don't buy that. If they don't mean it (at least at some level), they simply wouldn't use the language.

We also see that people who believe their work is all about money tend to be the same people who push donors too early and too often just so they can "hit their goals." In fact, several years ago a colleague of mine was conducting a major gift consultation at a hunger-relief organization. They were behind significantly in their major gift revenue, and couldn't figure out why. As my colleague interviewed their lead gift officer, she recounted a horrifying conversation she'd had with a donor. While it will sound too insane to be true, I promise you this is how the actual ask went:

"Jim, if you could just see in your heart to make a $250,000 gift today, that would be amazing. It would help me hit my goal for the year, and I'm really struggling—your gift would mean a lot."

Can you imagine being the donor on the other end of that ask? If it were me, I think I'd be envisioning my face emblazoned on a bank ATM. That's clearly all this gift officer saw her donor as—an institutional (and almost personal) ATM.

When someone thinks their job is all about the money they are less likely to offer restricted gift opportunities to their donors, and more likely to continually push donors to give more and more frequently, instead of respecting the comprehensive value of donor relationships.

This mentality is easy for savvy donors to spot, and when they do, they'll run far and fast.

Instead of focusing on the money, focus on developing the deepest, most meaningful donor relationships that you can. When you do this successfully, donors will naturally come to understand that the unique role they can play in the organization is to provide the funding that allows you to achieve your mission.

MISTAKE #78

Not Understanding Your Competition

By Andrew Olsen, CFRE

Understanding the competition is an interesting thing. Some organizations completely disregard the competition. Others focus so intently on their competition that they get paralyzed with fear. I'm not suggesting you preoccupy yourself with the competition—that's a recipe for disaster. You shouldn't waste a ton of time following everything your competitors do. Nor should you completely ignore competitors.

As Friedrich Max Müller said, "He who knows one, knows none." The reason it's important to understand your competition isn't so much about any specific competitor. The value to you is really more in understanding your overall competitive landscape, and where your organization fits in comparison to other organizations that provide similar services. Understanding the specific value that your competitors provide will help you better identify and articulate your own unique value proposition, both to those you serve and to your charitable supporters. If you aren't able to do this, you'll just be one organization among many that provide essentially the same services.

However, if you can articulate your unique value proposition relative to all of your competitors, you'll stand out above the rest. You'll create differentiation, and become memorable in the mind of your donors. When you successfully differentiate yourself from the rest of the pack, that's when donors begin to seek you out. You become attractive to new audiences because of what you uniquely stand for and accomplish. And your existing donors see you in a new light as well, often identifying you as not just one of many nonprofits they support, but as their preferred charity.

MISTAKE #79

Thinking You Belong at Your Desk All Day

By Andrew Olsen, CFRE

Whenever I walk into a development office and see gift officers sitting at their desks I know there's a problem. The goal of every development officer should be to be out in the community visiting with donors, building and enhancing relationships, and advancing those relationships for the benefit of their organization.

However, some organizations place other unnecessary burdens on their Major Gift Officers—like managing events, filling out excessive paperwork on each donor, promoting the organization's social media campaigns, etc. This is the absolute worst kind of waste of talent and opportunity.

Think about it this way: In a single eight-hour day, a Major Gift Officer can likely make two or three in-person contacts, and another two or three contacts via phone. On the low end, each of those donors they're engaging might give anywhere from $2,500-$5,000, whereas on the high end of the spectrum, they might be talking to donors who can each give $50,000, $100,000, or even seven-figure gifts. The return on investment for the time spent with those donors will be anywhere from 10:1 to 100:1. That is a *huge* impact.

Now contrast that with asking that same Major Gift Officer to spend half her day in the office with non-essential, non-donor-focused tasks. The return on investment for that time is going to be less than 1:1. That's direct mail new donor acquisition ROI—and it's a terrible use of your top talent!

Roy Jones at Mercy Ships told me recently that he's restructured the way his entire major gift team logs their donor contact reports. Instead of asking each gift officer to fill out a lengthy document of their contacts, he's shifted to a very quick and easy reporting mechanism that they are only asked to complete once per week, on Fridays. That, among other changes, has freed his team up to spend more time out in the field with donors. The result is that Mercy Ships is raising more major gift money than they ever have before—and they are experiencing double-digit major gift revenue growth year-over-year.

MISTAKE #80

Assuming You Know What Your Donors Want

By Andrew Olsen, CFRE

One of the most costly mistakes an organization can make is to assume they know what their donors want. This often manifests in nonprofit staff deciding that certain donors or certain types of donors should or shouldn't receive specific communications from an organization, or that once a donor passes a specific milestone (i.e., a single largest gift amount, cumulative giving amount, or consecutive years of giving), they need to start receiving a significantly different kind of engagement from the organization. Often the type of communication donors are transitioned to is vastly different from those communications that have kept the donor engaged and giving since they first became a supporter.

I recall a story of one donor who was a significant investor in the children's hospital where I worked a decade ago. He had giving nearly $1 million to this organization over his lifetime. And he had been a patient at the hospital when he was a child. He was clearly deeply committed to the organization.

At some point during the year, this gentleman gave another significant gift—a six-figure contribution. Immediately after that, someone in the organization's gift processing/data management team decided that this gift was so large he should now be removed from all organizational communications. She was certain that because of his status, he would never want to receive communications from the organization. Unfortunately, she had the authority to make changes like this to donor records.

Several months passed and the donor finally called our office to ask if he'd done something wrong. You see, from his perspective, immediately after he gave a huge gift to our organization, he stopped receiving all communications. He was particularly concerned because the newsletter he loved reading hadn't shown up in two months. After speaking with him it was clear that he never intended for the organization to stop communicating with him through regular print updates, emails, and newsletters. While we were ultimately able to resolve this problem, it's only because the donor reached out to correct our mistake. If he hadn't called, we would have moved on, assuming that he was pleased with this change, and potentially never connected with him again.

In another instance, a development officer at a large homeless service organization arbitrarily decided that any donor who had given $1,000 or more should be removed from all direct mail communication. They had reached, in her mind, a "major gift" level, and her belief was that major donors hate direct mail. She believed instead that these donors should only be engaged in personal, 1-to-1 relationships moving forward. Her instinct wasn't wrong. Donors giving at significant levels—and I'd argue that a donor who can write a $1,000+ check is giving at significant levels—should absolutely be engaged personally by a nonprofit. However, you also need to honor what brought them to you, and what has kept them engaged. That doesn't mean they should get the exact same treatment that a donor giving $10 gets, or that they should get all 12, 15, or 20+ solicitations you send each year. In fact, it's likely they should get far fewer solicitations, more meaningful impact reporting, AND personal contact.

Unfortunately, because many of these donors weren't ready for a 1-on-1 relationship with the nonprofit (they simply didn't view their giving as "that significant" to warrant personal engagement), very few were open to regular face-to-face contact, or even telephone contact, with the organization. And because they had been removed from the direct mail program, they were effectively not being contacted by the organization. This resulted in a $1 million loss of revenue to this organization in the two years following this decision.

As you can see, making assumptions about what your donors want and need from your organization is a dangerous way to go. Instead, follow donor behavior, and only make significant changes in engagement when a) donor behavior warrants it, or b) the donor specifically asks for you to make a change.

MISTAKE #81

Investing in a Direct Marketing Program but Refusing to Follow the Most Effective Practices

By Andrew Olsen, CFRE

Last year a good friend and former client of mine called me in to help advise her hospital foundation's leadership team on their direct mail fundraising program. They had three staff members assigned to this program, and spent a significant amount of money running the program every year. They were mailing existing supporters but losing money each time they mailed!

What was the problem?

They were spending the money to fundraise in the mail, but they refused to apply the most basic of successful direct-response fundraising principles to their program.

1. Their foundation Executive Director and Chief Marketing Officer both had come from public relations agency backgrounds. They had become wildly successful in their careers by helping brands tell positive, happy stories about themselves—and by helping companies convince consumers that they were amazing. Given that this is what they knew, it's no surprise that they mandated the hospital foundation's direct mail program look and feel the same way. This meant there was no emotional tug. No urgency. No real

need. And no opportunity for the donor to intervene and solve a problem.

2. They didn't want the organization to "sound desperate," so they never actually included a direct ask in their appeal letters. Sure, in about the 10th paragraph, at the bottom of the back page of the letter they had a sentence that read something like, *If you're so inclined, we do appreciate your support.* As I told their Executive Director, they might as well have said, *Actually, we don't really need you. Save your money, and have a nice day.*

3. To save money, they didn't personalize any of their fundraising letters. Think about that. They were mailing to existing donors—many of whom were also current patients in their healthcare system—and they didn't even have the common sense (or decency) to call them by name. Instead, these donors all received letters that acknowledged them as *Dear Friend,* regardless of how long they had been giving, how much they had given, or how recently/frequently they had used the hospital's services.

After convincing this foundation's leadership that they were making some major mistakes in their mail program—and likely doing real damage to their ability to engage donors and raise money—they agreed to make some simple, but impactful changes. We went about fixing all three of the issues I listed above.

The result?

In the first quarter after they made these changes, response to their appeals increased by 86%.

It's amazing what happens when you apply the practices that are most effective at creating connection and bringing in revenue for nonprofits.

Don't let your own preferences or desire to save money keep you from applying proven direct-response fundraising principles to your program. If you're going to spend the money necessary to do something like direct mail, the least you can do is do it well. Otherwise, you might as well just burn the money you were going to spend on printing and postage, because you'll get about the same result either way.

MISTAKE #82

Not Sending a Paper Thank You Letter to Online Donors

By Andrew Olsen, CFRE

This is such a frequent mistake among nonprofits. In fact, it happens in nearly 50% of all nonprofits I've engaged with in the last 15 years (which is close to 1,000). In my experience, there are typically two reasons nonprofits make the decision not to send paper thank you letters to donors for gifts made online.

The reason most frequently given is the belief that when a donor gives online they are indicating a communication preference, and therefore should only receive an online thank you receipt.

The second-most-frequent reason offered is that the organization is looking for ways to reduce costs, so if a donor gives online they are only receipted online. That way, the organization can claim a cost reduction by not paying for the print and postage for those gifts.

Here's the reality check you need . . .

Three years ago I was working with one of the largest hunger-relief organizations in California. They called me in to help them figure out why their retention and second gift rates—and income—were down significantly year-over-year. In total, this organization had lost close to $300,000 in retained donor revenue in a year. We looked at every aspect of their solicitation strategy and their stewardship program, and couldn't find a smoking gun.

After a few hours of discussion one of the members of their staff mentioned that they'd made a change to their thank you receipt process the year prior. They had instituted a process where donors who gave online no longer received a paper thank you letter. After some discussion and results analysis, we concluded that this single change to the organization's thank you process indeed had an outsized impact on the organization's retention and revenue.

The organization mistakenly believed that because their donors were completing their transactions online, that their preference was to receive their acknowledgment letters online only. However, what we know about retention is that one of the most effective ways to promote retention (and value) is to encourage donors to give across channels. When you engage with donors across multiple channels, even—and sometimes especially—with their thank you letters, you are increasing the likelihood that those donors will give again.

MISTAKE #83

Not Talking to Donors Frequently Enough

By Andrew Olsen, CFRE

Notice I didn't say "not asking enough" here. Though there's probably truth to that statement as well, what I'm really talking about here is engagement. Dialogue. Building relationship. If you're committed to real relationships with your donors, you've got to act like it. Your best donors will expect it. When you don't stay in regular contact, they'll notice—especially if they're giving at similar levels to other organizations where they *do* receive regular engagement. If they're comparing that with your organization, and you don't make it a priority to engage with them to share updates, seek their advice, and build the relationship, they'll see a distinct difference.

I was with a hospital recently, discussing the fact that they'd lost $5 million in major gift revenue over the last three years. When I asked the brand-new Chief Development Officer about this, he shook his head—in what was either disbelief or disgust. Then he relayed a story of calling one of their largest prior donors, only to be told, "You asked me for a big gift three years ago. I gave you the gift, and this call we're having right now is the first time I've heard from your organization since you cashed my check." Whether due just to poor follow-up, staff turnover, or whatever else, this organization allowed their single largest individual donor to go THREE YEARS without so much as a thank you call, a follow-up meeting to discuss

MISTAKE #84

Not Inviting Donors to Make Restricted Gifts

By Andrew Olsen, CFRE

The most compelling ask you can make to a donor is one that is focused on a specific program, a specific project, or area of focus within your organization, about which your donor is passionate. In fact, when you make a specific ask to a donor to fund a specific project or program they have expressed interest in, you're not only more likely to get that gift, but you're more likely to receive a gift at or above the level you're seeking.

The only problem with that? The gift won't be unrestricted, general operating funding.

If your organization budgets "program" and "overhead" separately, then restricted gifts often put a strain on the overall organization because no portion of those gifts can be used to fund the overhead costs that keep the organization running and deliver those various programs.

This is why my strong preference and ongoing recommendation to organizations is that rather than budgeting those costs separately, they should allocate a percentage of overhead across each program budget to reflect the true cost of delivering that program (including all staff, rent, insurance, benefits, etc.), so that when a donor makes a restricted gift toward their favorite program, the gift would actually fund that program—and all of the costs associated with delivering the program.

MISTAKE #85

Thinking You Need an Expert in Planned Giving on Your Staff

By Andrew Olsen, CFRE

Legacy gifts (or planned gifts, as they're often referred to in the industry) are often the largest single gift that a donor will ever give to an organization. Some donors—typically those of significant net worth—may use complicated estate giving vehicles to make a legacy gift that also provides a tangible tax benefit to the donor. However, that's fairly rare for most nonprofits. In fact, the majority of legacy gifts come by way of simple bequests.

What's interesting to me is that so many organizations shy away from developing a legacy giving pipeline because they are afraid that a donor will come to them with a complex legacy gift opportunity, and they won't have the in-house legal expertise to help facilitate that gift.

I see two issues with that thinking.

First, knowing that the majority of legacy gifts come as simple bequests (which don't require significant legal expertise on the part of the charity), the smart move would be to launch a legacy giving program and only worry about a complex gift when that situation actually arises (which, for most nonprofits, is likely never).

The second issue I have with this limiting thinking is, if a donor of significant wealth and capacity wants to give my non-profit a complex legacy gift, I see that as a HUGE opportunity and win! If and when that happens, seek wise counsel to help your organization and the donor complete the gift transaction—and be thrilled that your donor loves your cause and organization enough to entrust you with such a gift.

You can start simple by adding a checkbox to your direct mail and newsletters to invite donors to request information about including your organization in their legacy plans. Several of my firm's clients send a simple notecard a few times each year inviting donors to inform them if they've already been included in an estate plan, or to let the charity know they'd like to find out more about including the organization in their estate plan. Those two tactics surprisingly deliver a consistent volume of legacy gift leads for many nonprofits.

MISTAKE #86

Believing it's all About You

By Andrew Olsen, CFRE

In fundraising, it's NEVER about you. That's right—NEVER. Successful fundraisers know that the process and the experience are always about bringing the donor as close as possible to the people your organization serves, and to the greatest extent possible, removing your organization from the equation.

BUT . . . it's so difficult to actually do this. That's because often organizations employ well-meaning people who simply don't understand or maybe don't agree with this.

Here's what happens when you make fundraising about you instead of the donor:

1. Your language becomes internally focused

2. You talk about all the great things you do for the people you serve or the cause you champion

3. You subtly (and sometimes not-so-subtly) exclude the donor from the incredible impact that she's making possible for those you serve

You'll have much greater success if you remember that we are in the service business. Our job is to help donors navigate the complex philanthropic landscape and find the programs and projects that are most interesting to them and most in need of funding within our organizations. Ultimately, our role is to bring the two together in a way that adds value and meaning to the donor's life, and positively impacts our organization's ability to achieve mission objectives. When we do this well, we'll be successful.

MISTAKE #87

Letting "Who Gets the Credit" Dictate Your Fundraising Approach

By Andrew Olsen, CFRE

Picture this. You're sitting in the boardroom of a major US nonprofit, invited by the Annual Giving team to help them brainstorm ideas to increase revenue.

The conversation goes something like this:

We're behind goal for the year and need to make up $500,000 by the end of our fiscal year. What ideas do you have to help us close this gap?

After exhausting a number of ideas and recommendations, you propose three more:

1. **Promote Donor-Advised Fund giving**, because we know that when donors give through their DAFs, they give gifts that are anywhere from 2X-5X more than when they give from a cash account.

2. **Promote stock or asset giving**, again because we know when donors give appreciated assets, the value of those gifts tends to be significantly more than when those same donors make a cash contribution.

3. **Promote employer matching contributions** because a donor who gives you $100 and then gets their

employer to match their gift with another $100 has effectively doubled their impact for you.

All three of these ideas are about maximizing impact and creating additional value for your organization.

These three great (and strategically sound) ideas are met with the following response:

> *Those are good ideas, and we know they'd work. BUT...*
> *Our Finance Department rules mandate that those types*
> *of gifts would all get credited to a different team. Since that*
> *doesn't help our team with our goal this year, we don't*
> *want to spend the time or effort to do any of them. What*
> *other ideas do you have?*

This. Is. Pure. Insanity.

The blame for this flawed logic falls squarely at the feet of an organization's Executive leadership—Chief Executive Officer, Chief Financial Officer, Chief Development Officer. Allowing silly budget allocation rules to dictate what fundraising activities your people do or don't undertake—because you've set up a system of "credit" for activities that doesn't align incentives with desired behaviors is fully a leadership issue. It's not the fault of your fundraisers. They're just following the rules that were set by the organization's leadership.

In this particular case, given the size and value of this organization's donor base, these tactics could have delivered anywhere from $50,000 to $250,000 of additional revenue.

And yes. This is a real world example.

But because another team gets the credit for these types of gifts, the overall organization and the millions of people they serve all lose out.

You can overcome this kind of mistake by more effectively

aligning your incentives with the behaviors you want more of. If you want your people to raise more money, and to do it in the most effective ways possible, stop handcuffing them with silly rules around credit.

MISTAKE #88

Maintaining Multiple Databases

By Andrew Olsen, CFRE

Do you have your donor list in a CRM system, but maybe your volunteers, gift-in-kind donors, advocates, or some other audiences is stashed in a separate system somewhere else? This is a common challenge for nonprofits, because very few CRM systems are easily and cost-effectively customizable for various different audience types.

Let me give you just one example of why maintaining multiple databases or contact lists is a bad idea.

A few years ago I was sitting in the development department of a Food Bank with whom I was consulting. We were talking about a recent large gift from a major donor. One of the gift officers called the donor's home to thank him, and reached his wife. It was a Tuesday morning. When the development officer got the wife on the line, she thanked her, and asked her to convey their gratitude to her husband, the donor of record. The donor's wife swiftly replied, "Why don't you thank him yourself? It's Tuesday. He's in your warehouse sorting donated food, just like he does every Tuesday morning."

The development staff had no clue that this donor was

also a volunteer, because volunteer data (at the time) didn't sit inside their CRM system. They had no way to relate the donor and volunteer record together to get a 360-degree view of this donor's behavior. This was slightly embarrassing, but didn't ultimately hurt the donor relationship. However, that's not always the case. Missteps like this can easily lead to hurt feelings on the part of a donor who believes they are "part of the family," but who doesn't feel that way when their favorite nonprofit doesn't seem to know them as they think they should.

If you maintain multiple databases it's only a matter of time until you make a mistake. If you're lucky it won't be catastrophic. But some of you won't be so lucky. Now is the time to step back and assess the various data sets you have distributed throughout your organization, and develop a plan to consolidate them. It'll take time and effort. It might even take some additional money. But ultimately, it's well worth it if it helps you protect and improve your donor relationships.

MISTAKE #89

Insisting All Fundraising and Communications are Highly Branded

By Andrew Olsen, CFRE

Our brand is super positive. We're all about happy stories and positive outcomes. We don't want to depress people or make them think we're needy. We can't show "sad" photos or talk about our program participants in ways that make them seem like they can't help themselves. Our brand includes a 4-color logo. Everything we produce must be 4-color to adhere to our brand standards.

If I had a dollar for every time a nonprofit marketing director, fundraiser, board member, or executive director said these words to me, I'd be retired and sitting on a beach in Fiji somewhere right now.

Good branding is critical to fundraising success. But it's important to remember what the role of brand is. In the commercial world, the goal of branding is to create preference for your product or service, and to support the organization's sales efforts. If branding doesn't drive sales, it gets changed.

The same paradigm exists in the nonprofit sector, whether you want to admit it or not. The role of branding in the nonprofit space is to create preference for your organization among the millions of other nonprofits (and for-profits) where donors could otherwise spend their money, and to help inspire those donors to action in support of your cause.

Branding is not a goal unto itself—it is a tool that needs to live in service to your organization's sales efforts (i.e., your fundraising). If your branding negatively impacts fundraising, you don't change the fundraising. You change the branding. To do the opposite is simply stupid, and will result in less revenue for your organization and your cause.

Let's unpack the examples I listed at the start of this chapter . . .

Many organizations only want to tell happy stories. They want to focus on the solutions their programming creates, rather than the needs their organization is meeting. However, to inspire donors to give to your cause or organization, they need to feel compelled by an urgent need that they can solve. And they need to be allowed to be the hero in that story. If your brand is only positive and you never tell those stories of need, donors will assume you don't need their help, and they'll move on to the next organization that tells them very clearly how they can step in to meet a need and solve a problem. This is not to suggest that you should be dishonest, overstate needs, or behave in deceptive ways. But when you only show and tell the positive side of an issue, you remove the impetus for donors to act on your behalf.

The other thing I run into a lot is organizations that want to use 4-color on all of their fundraising materials. Often this comes from a desire not to look "cheap" or "old." And for some organizations in certain nonprofit sectors (i.e., international relief, healthcare, animal welfare, environmental), 4-color packages work very well. They also might work well with certain audiences (i.e., younger donors, major donors, event participants). However, most donors who are giving to nonprofits through the mail tend to skew older. Those donors, especially if they are giving to any cause that is related to social services, largely respond better to 2-color packages.

This 2- versus 4-color issue is something I've tested for clients on at least six occasions in the last five years. What we've found is that 2-color direct mail consistently wins out (both through higher response rates and lower costs). When it comes to newsletters, annual reports, and things of that nature, 4-color tends to do better. The moral of the story on this point, however, is that just because your brand might call for 4-color treatment, if that is going to negatively impact your fundraising performance you shouldn't force it.

MISTAKE #90

Refusing to use a Fundraising Tactic Because You Don't Like it

By Andrew Olsen, CFRE

Nowhere is this more true than in the field of telemarketing. I'll bet you just cringed when you read that word, didn't you? Right? I mean, who of us actually looks forward to getting that dreaded telemarketing call right as we sit down to enjoy dinner with our family? Not me. I can't stand getting calls from telemarketers (except when I get a great one and can learn something from it for my clients). And I'm sure you don't like getting them, either. Your board really hates them, because each of your board members has that one friend who got a call from another charity once and won't stop telling them about how horrible the experience was.

Here's the thing: If your goal as an organization is to solve a big problem in our world—something like childhood hunger, sex trafficking, or homelessness—if you've signed on to help change and save lives from devastating issues like this, *you don't have the luxury of only using fundraising tactics you personally like.*

Whether you and I like getting telemarketing calls or not, we both need to realize that we're not likely the target donor audience, and what we like doesn't matter. What *does* matter is that things like telemarketing actually work to engage donors and raise revenue for nonprofits. The benchmark of channel selection should never be, "Do I approve of it?". It should be, "Does this channel deliver revenue at an acceptable ROI, will it help us reach our goals, and will it help us retain and grow our donor relationships?".

If a fundraising channel or tactic can accomplish those things, it shouldn't matter if you like it or not. And if you make decisions about a channel based on your personal preference—and as a result withhold critical funding growth from your organization and those you serve—you probably ought to rethink the line of work you're in.

This is another one of those times where we all need to remember, it's not about us!

MISTAKE #91

Allowing a Handful of Donor Complaints to Control Your Revenue Production Strategies

By Andrew Olsen, CFRE

I was once forced to stop a highly successful telephone fundraising program because 13 people complained. During that same campaign, we raised over $50K, and generated over 900 gifts. I'm not defending telephone fundraising as a medium, though I can tell you that in my 20 years of fundraising experience, I've seen a lot of positive impact come from phone fundraising (and also a lot of problems from disreputable phone firms).

Similarly, I worked with one organization that changed a long-standing email creative strategy because they received a number of complaints. When they changed that creative strategy, revenue declined by 50%.

In both of these instances, the organizations responded to a handful of donor complaints by changing their entire fundraising strategy. Those changes had significant negative impacts on their revenue, which has a direct impact on their ability to deliver programming for the people they serve.

It's important to honor the wishes that your donors express. However, reacting to a few donor complaints by completely changing strategy and negatively impacting revenue is a dangerous proposition. Instead, I'd recommend you make changes for those specific donors rather than for your entire base of supporters.

MISTAKE #92

Apologizing for Soliciting Gifts

By Andrew Olsen, CFRE

Can we be really honest with each other? I mean, can I be real with you without causing you to light fire to this book and miss the rest of the great content that follows this mistake?

Ok, here goes . . .

If you feel like you need to apologize for soliciting a gift—any gift—then there's something significantly wrong.

Maybe you feel like you have to apologize because the organization you work for doesn't actually need—or deserve—

the philanthropic support of donors. If that's the case, you need to quit now and find another organization that is deserving of the support you're seeking, so that you can feel good about soliciting donors and do so in a way that doesn't cause you to be conflicted.

Or maybe the role of fundraiser isn't really what you're designed for. If this is the case, that's ok too. Very few people today (though this is changing) started their careers thinking they would be a fundraiser. Most started in other roles within nonprofits, or even somewhere else in the corporate world. And the life of a fundraiser isn't for everyone. If this is the challenge you are facing that is causing you to feel that you have to apologize for making asks, then I would urge you to move on from this work and find something meaningful that you can pour yourself and your energy into and feel good about. You deserve better—and honestly, so do your donors and those served by your organization (that's not me taking a jab at you, it's just me stating fact). Life is too short to invest 8+ hours a day feeling like you can't be who you really are.

MISTAKE #93

Not Focusing on Net Revenue

By Andrew Olsen, CFRE

If your organization focuses exclusively (or even significantly) on gross revenue instead of net revenue, you're at risk. Often when I talk to nonprofit leaders who are focused on gross revenue, they say something like, "I focus on gross revenue

because it's an indicator of growth—and I'm growth focused."
Or, "If I grow my gross revenue and just control expenses, then
we'll be better off."

In theory, that's all true. However, if you don't put equal
weight on managing to your net revenue, you open yourself
up to big problems down the line. For example, if you double
your gross revenue in a given year, but it requires you to triple
your expenses to achieve that, you could be facing a shortfall
on dollars that you can spend on program. And at the end
of the day, you can only spend net revenue on your program
initiatives.

The same holds true for focusing on return on investment
(ROI) rather than net revenue. You might think that ROI is
more important because it tells you how efficient you're being
with your investments. However, consider this scenario . . .

Option A: You raise $100,000 at a 10:1 ROI. That means
you brought in $10 for every $1 you spent. That's
spectacular ROI.

Option B: You raise $1,000,000 at a 5:1 ROI. That means
you brought in $5 for every $1 you spent. BUT . . . you
raised $900,000 more dollars, so you have a ton more net
revenue to spend on program.

I'm not suggesting you shouldn't monitor gross revenue—
but I am suggesting that it's net revenue that should be your
financial success measure.

MISTAKE #94

Worrying Too Much About Nonprofit Watchdog Organizations

By Andrew Olsen, CFRE

This is another mistake that often impacts a nonprofit's potential for growth and impact.

If you are most concerned about maintaining your 4-star charity watchdog rating, I'd argue that you're focused on the wrong things.

Here's the deal. Watchdog orgs set arbitrary expectations that don't account for the real-world issues you have to deal with on a daily basis.

Let's say the expectation is that you spend no more than 25% of your budget on administration and fundraising. However, your organization needs to grow in order to deliver a greater impact in your community, and you have the opportunity to double your capacity by spending 30% on admin/fundraising over the next three years. That's not failure—that's sound strategy and planning. But the watchdog orgs would say you missed the mark because your expense ratios are out of alignment.

Or maybe you want to hire two seasoned experts in your field so you can increase your ability to deliver quality programs and improved outcomes for the people you serve—but making those hires increases your overhead percentage slightly above the "established" goals that the watchdog orgs have set.

I'd argue that you should forget about the watchdog orgs and focus on raising the greatest amount of net revenue possible so that you can fund the most effective programs and deliver the greatest outcomes possible for your cause.

Impact is what matters. Not expense ratios.

MISTAKE #95

Sanitizing Your Mission

By Andrew Olsen, CFRE

At your organization you might not refer to this as "sanitizing your mission." Instead, you might call it "focusing on the positive" or something like that.

You know what I mean. Instead of showing the picture of a severely malnourished child suffering in a refugee camp, you only want to show photos of other children smiling and playing in that same refugee camp. It's an attempt to show *hope* instead of *need*.

Instead of talking about a child whose body is wracked with cancer that threatens to take her life before she's even old enough to understand, your hospital marketing team simply says she's *experiencing the effects of cancer,* because you've decided your brand is about hope—and telling that story just isn't hopeful.

This is one of the most devastating mistakes a nonprofit can make.

Here's why . . .

Donors tell us time and again that what motivates them

to give is the idea that there is some problem (or *need)* in the world about which they are passionate, and they are excited by the idea that they can intervene (through giving) to solve that problem.

When an organization sanitizes their mission and message, only focusing on positive stories, they rob their donors of the opportunity to solve the problem that motivated them in the first place. And when that happens, donors often choose to give elsewhere, where they can more easily see how their giving will make a difference in the world.

In head-to-head testing we have seen need-based stories and images deliver anywhere from 20%-40% more response than more positive, success-based content. Just last year I helped a hospital make this transition in their fundraising and the result was an astonishing 63% increase in giving from their existing donors!

Organizations like Operation Smile and The Smile Train have mastered the balance between need and success, often showing "before" and "after" images, and telling highly compelling stories of need that position the donor as the central figure that helps a child in need receive the healing care they need. This is a model that I would recommend you experiment with if you feel that focusing too much on need isn't comfortable for your organization.

MISTAKE #96

Chasing Every New Idea that Comes Along

By Andrew Olsen, CFRE

QR codes. Text to Give. An app. Social media challenges. Promoting a 3rd party's products in order to get a percentage of the revenue for your cause. Amazon Smile. The list could go on and on.

At some point, each of these was a new, shiny object in fundraising. Thousands of nonprofits invested tons of hours and dollars figuring them out, testing them, and in some cases, making huge bets that they'd be "the next big thing."

Most never really materialized in any significant way for 99% of organizations.

In my opinion, these kind of things all fall into the category of what my good friend Jason Lewis, CFRE, author of *The War For Fundraising Talent* calls "arm's length fundraising."

Many organizations are willing to spend so much effort and valuable resources to try these new things—but are at the same time so reluctant to invest in proven, highly productive activities like building individual relationships with donors and developing major gift programs. They're all too pleased to focus on these efforts that, if they're lucky, might return 1.5:1 ROI and raise a few thousand dollars. But they fully disregard the opportunity to deeply engage their best donors, and raise tens of thousands, hundreds of thousands, or even millions of dollars and an ROI of 5:1 or better.

Stop wasting your precious resources chasing the next new

idea that comes along, and instead focus on the tried and true elements that create meaningful donor relationships and unlock transformational giving opportunities for your organization.

MISTAKE #97

Ignoring the Amazon User Experience

By Beth Cathey & Ben Taylor

Have you ever purchased something from Amazon.com? If not, I'd be willing to go out on a limb and say that you've probably been living under a rock. ;) No matter if you believe in Amazon's politics or social stances, you can't deny the impact they've had on the online space and frankly, our lifestyles.

One of the biggest mistakes we see in the nonprofit sector is simply ignoring how Amazon's business model and approach have dramatically changed the landscape of digital user experience. Failing to embrace an Amazon-like model costs organizations both short and long-term revenue opportunities.

Let's look at some of the facts:

- As of the last reported period, Amazon had **310 million active customers.** If it were a country, it would be the fourth-largest in the world—quickly closing in on the United States, which currently holds third place.

- According to a July 2018 eMarketer report, **Amazon owns nearly 42% of retail market share in e-commerce**[1]

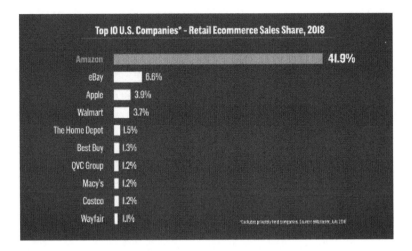

- New research suggests that consumers convert on Amazon.com at a rate that's 22 times higher than the average conversion rate of the largest online merchants in North America ranked in the Internet Retailer Top 500 Guide.[2]

- Amazon Prime members convert 74% of the time.

- Amazon focuses on particular niches of people within each of their different services.[3]

- On average, US Amazon Prime members shop at Amazon.com 25 times per year. In contrast, customers without Amazon Prime shop at Amazon.com an average of 14 times per year.[4]

- **The "Empty Chair"—the Most Important Person in the Room:** This is a Jeff Bezos/Amazon cultural reality, that the most important person in the room is a chair occupied by their imaginary customer. The empty chair is present in all of their meetings.[5]

None of these facts should be super shocking to anyone living in America, but this chapter is focused on helping you— our friends in the nonprofit space—learn some important lessons that can translate into your own communications and fundraising strategies for your nonprofit organization. And while you might not begin to see 74% conversion rates, moving the needle just a few additional percentage points can make a significant difference in the amount of revenue you bring into your organization to execute your mission.

Key to our Amazon education is a deep-dive analysis of the Amazon **user experience**, for it's this experience that we put under a microscope in this chapter to help our nonprofit clients and our readers fully understand how to avoid so many mistakes of donor interaction, communication, and engagement.

What Makes the Amazon User Experience Superior?

givingMD has digital staff members who have come from the commercial sector, have worked on Amazon e-commerce campaigns for Fortune 500 companies, and have considerable time clocked in raising money for nonprofit clients. As a result, our cross-over knowledge about what makes a good experience for a user, customer, consumer, or prospect has contributed to the partial list that follows.

What follows is our collective observations over the years, which have congealed into a set of beliefs and standards that we hold tightly and execute accordingly for our nonprofit clients as we help them communicate effectively to their constituent bases. We're going to examine seven key principles based on the Amazon user experience model:

1. Leverage the wisdom of the crowd to create "segments of 1," or segmentation that is so granular it focuses on each individual person and their specific online behavior, wants, and needs. In the nonprofit space, we like to call this "people-based fundraising." Creating a more personalized user experience for your target audience by leveraging the data you gather and store in your database of record will help you micro-segment and message-target your audience to increase your response and conversion rates. Just as Amazon provides its customers with unique product recommendations specific to that customer's past buying habits or current browsing needs, communicate with your donors in a way that suggests you understand why their interest is in your organization and that you know what aspects of your nonprofit's programs, opinions, policies, or resources really resonate with them.

Because unlike e-commerce and commercial transactions, people give to nonprofit organizations out of their own personal value system. This might be because of their Christian faith and they have a heart for telling others about Christ, or perhaps they grew up in a low-income family and are motivated to see the needs of the poor and the homeless met. Further, they may just be wired toward political science and community service and are interested in promoting a particular agenda. No matter the reason or the value set, donors make giving decisions based on personal affinities.[6]

Let's look at what a modern nonprofit user experience might look like based on the Amazon model:

Jane is 50 years old and married.

She's a successful pharmaceutical rep, a Christian with a heart for missions & the homeless, and unaware of your organization

While catching up with her family via email, she sees a message from your organization in her inbox and learns what they do. She doesn't take action, though.

A few days later, she's taking a fun quiz about her personality when she sees an organization's Sponsored Ad.

After reading the teaser about the NY Times article, she clicks the ad and lands on the women's shelter page.

Through **DonorSegue**, she begins receiving messaging about the women's shelter with a call to donate so your organization can reach more women.

On Mother's Day, she sees messaging about one particular mother who's life was falling to pieces before she was introduced to your organization's team and services, and she's moved to give $45.

Through DonorSegue, she begins receiving ads and emails that give her a better understanding of your organization's programs overall.

Jane later sees **DonorSegue**-based messaging designed to give a second gift, talking again to the impact she can make for people in Dallas.

In August, she makes a second gift, this time for $50 based on the giving arrays.

DonorSegue transitions her to messaging based on driving monthly donations, though she still receives fiscal year and EOY seasonal messaging.

DonorSegue brings custom messaging cadences mixed with seasonality.

See Jane's experience with Your Organization

Here's a snapshot of Ben Taylor's Amazon page that features the recommendations that Amazon is presenting him with. What has Amazon learned about Ben to help them better market to him? What do these recommendations tell you about Ben?

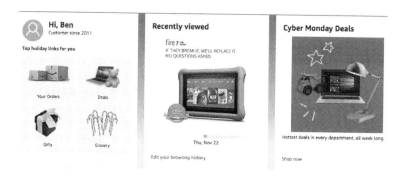

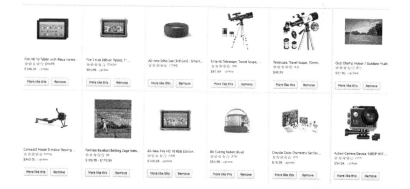

Here's where Amazon distinguishes itself among its online competitors. The Amazon team ties every product you browse, and continues to refine their profile of who you are. Looking at Ben's profile above, you'd likely conclude that he has a pretty high affinity for technology, that he has young kids, and has some level of interest in sports. Combine that with many years of purchase history, and they can predict what Ben is likely interested in for the upcoming years.

Taking it a step further, though, Amazon introduced new customer profile pieces designed to create a solid user experience and bring value to consumers. But the end game isn't a neat way to keep a wish list for a kid. They can know the stage of life you are in and every detail imaginable. That's evident with their details around your pets and your vehicle. What a great avenue for shopping for car parts. But, the reality is that tying that data back to you and focusing on larger cart items for the long haul is what is at stake for them.

2. Make it a part of your strategic marketing/fundraising plan to begin to systematically create a lot of content for your nonprofit. Become a thought leader in your missional area of expertise. Amazon has 248,000,000 pages stored in Google's index. That's 248 MILLION pages. The more pages you have on your website, the more SEO power you have indexing to search engines.

The way to consider how to accomplish this for your organization is to contemplate the power of those 248 million pages. It's not only about the incredible volume that Amazon has grown to today, but it's about the punch that each page brings. Consumers are now favoring Amazon when even *beginning their research of a given product* more than they're turning to Google. While Google has billions of pages, Google's framework makes it tough for someone to understand products as easily as they can on Amazon. Because of this, Fortune 500 brands and even small start-up brands turn to Amazon first to build their content out. And it continues to pay off.

3. Optimizing your site for lead generation. You may not win a creative award for your web design, but if users are attracted to and engaged with your site, then they're going to give. So, don't solve for the wrong problem just because you don't like the "look and feel" of your site.

When looking at Amazon's product page, nothing screams "sleek," "innovative," or is reminiscent of any award-winning design. Funny enough, our strategy lead at givingMD helped Amazon advance their product page design and won an ADDY for the work. However, the design elements are secondary to why Amazon wins.

Consumers began to love the way Amazon integrates reviews, the simple way they show product imagery, the unified layout of every single product page. At first, it was something that Amazon really pioneered. However, every other online retailer now has similar features because they became table stakes.

What's even further proof of Amazon's effectiveness is the focus brands have on Amazon's e-commerce results above and beyond their own brand sites. When was the last time you visited a consumer-packaged good brand's website? Unless you were doing market research, we're willing to bet you haven't in a while. But millions turn to their Amazon product pages every single day, and they convert. By the millions.

4. Data is power. Everything we've talked about so far in the first three points is really a lesson in futility without informed data. Data truly is power, to use a trite phrase. Understand your audience by becoming an avid data collector. Collecting website user data provides offers insight into your audience's wants, needs, and expectations. This data can also help you allocate finite digital marketing resources.

Look at the following example. We cannot claim to have created this infographic ourselves, but we are sharing this illustration with you because it is a representative sample of how Amazon uses the power of data. Look at the circled green areas and arrows. Some of the data points Amazon clearly knows about this particular customer are:

- The customer's name.
- The customer is an Amazon Prime member.
- Their browsing history and what they put in their cart and left abandoned (you can know/do this, too).
- Based on the customer's time spent on their site, what other possible products this particular customer might resonate with based on their demonstrated interests.

5. After you've gathered data on your database, use it to better refine the user experience. "Amazon is expert at tracking shopper behavioral tendencies at a granular level to better understand each segment of its ubiquitous target audience."[7]

With the help of marketing automation software, you can take a similar approach to communicate with your organization's constituency. Your annual digital communications calendar should be unique to the individuals on your database. The old model of donor communication is to send out "batch and blast" messaging to everyone on your database, and to communicate the same periodic message across all your communications channels.

And we've discovered that many nonprofits, especially small to mid-size nonprofits, still have that organizational thinking of theme-driven communications campaigns. In other words, *this is what our nonprofit wants to communicate today about what we're doing on the mission field.* Or, *we have six pillars to our programmatic mission, so we're going to communicate on each one of those six pillars over the course of the next six months, then turn around and do it again the next six months after that.*

Instead of this approach, we'd like to suggest that impactful moments are 1:1 experiences.

But how does that play itself out? We believe your fundraising is most impactful through automated, 1:1 communication for optimal long-term donor health. We do that through these three primary methodologies:

1. **Use behavior-based message modeling.** This means understanding what message drives what action, such as a first-time gift, a second gift, or an increased giving amount.

2. **Consider this illustration for a minute.**

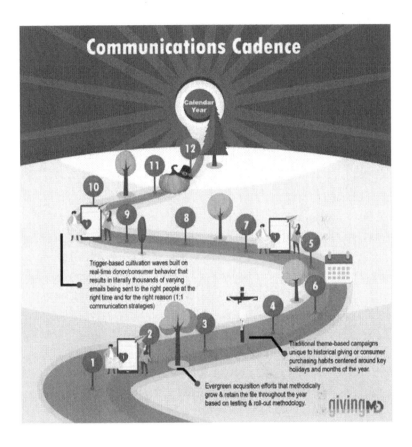

The numbers represent the months in a calendar year. The cadence of communication along the way takes on a variety of forms. Some are seasonal. If you are a faith-based ministry and fail to acknowledge Christmas, that would be an epic fail. We are not suggesting anyone would actually do that, but the point is, other than "predictable" occasions for communication such as seasonal or holiday messages, there are two other types of communication your nonprofit should consider employing:

- Trigger-based messaging across all channels. This approach means using the data above to create messaging tailored to drive those next triggers and hitting the audience across the web—through your Google Grant, through digital media, email, and dynamic site content.

- Evergreen efforts at growing your donor file that are ongoing and that grow and improve based on an ongoing testing and roll-out methodology.

3. **Campaigns driven by "next best donor action."** Outside of the seasonal table stakes you must do, such as end-of-year campaigns, our team runs dozens of "campaigns" for any given client—simultaneously— to different audiences every single week. What Jane might see on May 2 because she has given three times before will be different than what Robert sees because he has only given once and is primed to give again based on the timing between gifts. However, Susan, on that same day, will also see a very different message because she is on the file but has yet to give. This is where fundraising is going (based not entirely on big online retailers such as Amazon, but certainly influenced by them), and it should be a welcome change for organizations as well as their audiences.

Why is that? Because you can know what's important to your constituency and have more meaningful communications with your donors—and in return, your constituency will feel like you actually know and value them and the impact they have on your organization generally and your missional outcomes specifically.

6. What about email? If you've ever spent a minute browsing Amazon.com, you then know that it's only a matter of hours before you experience their **email marketing** for yourself. Every email Amazon sends is personalized using every scrap of information they have about their users: on-site behavior, past purchases, amount spent, location, age, gender, etc.[8]

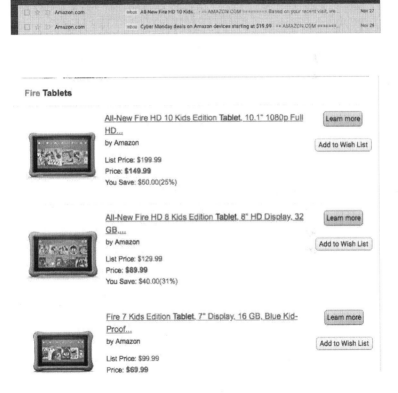

Amazon emails are the very next-best-action based campaigns you should strive to achieve. Let's take a real-world example: Ben's kids are almost on the cusp of being ready for their own tablets, but their parents refuse to buy them a phone. Digital strategists are funny about wanting their kids to be unplugged as long as possible. Just before Black Friday, Ben began researching on Amazon to understand the advantages of an Amazon Fire Tablet and the difference between the kids version and the general version. Not long after this, he started seeing emails about the tablet. Then, Amazon began hitting up Ben with an email like the one above with every Fire Tablet listed and links to buy each of them. Genius!

7. And lastly, what about the web and social advertising that seems to follow you around the internet and in your inbox after you've clicked on that pair of Nike running shoes? You're playing Candy Crush or Spades on your iPad, and all of a sudden that pair of running shoes appears at the top of your screen and you have to hit the "x" to continue your game. Frustrating, unless of course you really want or need that new pair of Nike running shoes. Your time shopping on Amazon has invaded your life and is now knocking on every door.

We can never pass up the telling of a good story, and this particular one we remember vividly, like it was yesterday. We were meeting with a new client and explaining how the retargeting and remarketing of ads works, and how we use the data and the user's behavior to identify who to serve these ads to. She had the strangest look on her face when we were done, and so we asked her, "what's wrong?" She replied, "That's really creepy. That sounds like 'big brother' to me."

As a result, our team had to take a step back and reevaluate how to explain this better. Here was our next run at describing this process. "If someone has engaged with your organization by clicking on an ad or selecting a link in an email and lands on a giving page or donation page from your organization, they have self-selected themselves. They've identified themselves to your organization as being an interested party in what you're doing and the mission you're accomplishing as an organization. You, as the nonprofit, are simply continuing the conversation they started with you. You're giving them more opportunities to engage with you, to sign a petition, give you feedback, join your social presence, get educated on the plight of the homeless, reaching unreached people groups with the Gospel, or saving young girls from being trafficked." End of the good story.

Circling back around with the prior example of the Fire Tablet browsing topic, Ben also began seeing banner ads promoting the product he had been researching. He saw them across Facebook, numerous websites, and of course, Amazon's homepage. Inevitably, Ben now has the information he needs. Will he ultimately make the purchase? And from Amazon, no less? Not so fast. We might have to save the conclusion of that story for our next book.

What if your organization didn't just focus on generalized digital media, even if you hit them across every main website? What if instead, the donor felt you were speaking to them, their nuanced interest in your mission, and what their next stage of relationship is with you? That's when you'll unleash the power that Amazon brought to e-commerce, but you'll bring it to a hurting world in need.

"We are genuinely customer-centric, we are genuinely long-term oriented, and we genuinely like to invent. Most [companies] are not those things. They are focused on the competitor, rather than the customer."
—**Jeff Bezos, Amazon Founder**

One of Amazon's core values is this customer obsession. As we've alluded to already, while Amazon's online presence isn't the most attractive website you or I have likely ever experienced, it converts site visitors into buyers at an industry-leading rate. According to a study by website traffic measurement firm Millward Brown Digital, they found that 63% of Prime members and 13% of non-members buy something during a visit to Amazon.[2] Can you imagine if your nonprofit's website experienced those kind of conversion metrics?

Bezos was convinced that word-of-mouth would generate new customers, much the same way as creating a "raving fan" from your own constituency will spread the word like wildfire about your nonprofit and its mission.

People who care about your cause share their interest with their friends by sharing your organization's content across their digital channels and through word of mouth. We've seen this with business concepts like TOMS, and when you are able to hit the root of your mission to your localized audience, your organization can gain mileage across local social reach of your constituents.

All of these elements above are how nonprofits can use Amazon's very core principles and success routes to drive their digital program forward. But as with all efforts, it's always crucial to avoid the key mistakes, even when everything seems to be in place. You must be able to focus in on your digital foundation and ensure a solid user experience every time.

Unfortunately, we see hiccups all too often in this space.

We sat down with a client once at the beginning of our relationship and listened to the Development Director tell painful stories that illustrate the fact that she believed their fundraising activities were actually communicating to donors that the organization didn't really know who they were as a person. She shared with us that a donor called the organization and she happened to be the one who took the call that day as the call was routed to the development division.

This long-time donor proceeded to tell this Development Director that she'd received an email asking for a gift for a particular program of the organization. However, not only had this donor already given a gift through the mail prior to receiving this email for the same program, but they had addressed the email to the donor's deceased spouse. The story went on and on. One mis-cue after another and the donor actually expressed these exact words to our new Development Director friend: "I just don't feel like your organization has a clue as to who I am or how long I've been supporting your cause."

That's what we'd call a negative mic drop. Exasperated, our new friend exclaimed to us, "We're just talking AT people, but not really listening to them. I want to change that! The way we have to communicate with our constituency from now on has to be legitimate, authentic, and based on accurate data!" She had no idea at the time just how much she was singing our tune.

Time and time again, we've seen situations where everything seems to be lined up for a campaign. A landing page can perform well, and emails and digital media can be all set. But is that everything? Integrating your message into your organic mix is critical for success. You have campaign messaging live and are doing a great job from an inbound perspective, but oftentimes we see organizations miss the mark directly on their websites.

One example of this is an organization that had a solid donor base and launched a backpack campaign for back to school. Digital media was impressive, retargeting those on the email file who received the message in their inbox. The landing page was top notch from a user experience perspective. However, it turns out the campaign expired on those efforts because it was created in a silo. The .org site mentioned nothing of the campaign, which obviously had a built-in time deadline. No strategy was created to direct folks from the larger organization's evergreen website to the seasonal campaign. And, unless you were on the targeted list for this campaign (in other words, you had given to the backpack appeal in the past), you never knew that this highly intriguing, timely, and universally relevant opportunity to give even existed. When you have a campaign live and all your time and efforts are focused there, it is imperative to integrate the messaging everywhere the donors see you—especially on your everyday website.

Another easy mistake to make is in not often measuring every attribute available to you for any given campaign. Every detail should be included in your review of a campaign to understand the successes and the weaknesses of a campaign. We've run into many organizations that will spend thousands of dollars on media, but not track with basic measures to understand that user's path on the site once they come in through digital media. Understanding those pieces is crucial to any long-term success of an organization.

We've all heard the phrase "a rising tide lifts all boats." While this phrase has often been attributed to President John F. Kennedy in contemporary society, it actually pre-dates President Kennedy by nearly a century. It's a phrase with origins in political, spiritual, and economic spheres, though that is important for our use of the phrase here. In a nutshell, we often focus on the positive side of that phrase, the "rising." But with rising, comes falling. In order to keep all your donations rising, you have to be mindful of the marketing, fundraising, systems, and technical issues that can often contribute to the "falling" of your best-laid plans, as the example above suggests.

Our approach to digital for our nonprofit client partners will always be similar to that of Amazon. With our background in leading brands like Coca-Cola's Amazon playbook and Kimberly-Clark's consumer and B2B brand sales on Amazon for a number of years, we understand their approach: **Data is King**.

Organizations should be measuring every attribute possible

[2] Zaroban, Stefany. "Amazon Prime Members Convert 74% of the Time." *Www.digitalcommerce360.Com*, 25 June 2015, www.digitalcommerce360.com/2015/06/25/amazon-prime-members-convert-74-time/.

[3] Rampton, John. "10 Marketing Lessons You Can Learn From Oprah, Jeff Bezos and Donald Trump." *Www.Forbes.com*, 11 Jan. 2018, www.forbes.com/sites/johnrampton/2018/01/11/10-marketing-lessons-you-can-learn-from-oprah-jeff-bezos-and-donald-trump/#5a712cb85692 .

[4] "Amazon Prime Reaches 85 Million US Members." *Www.cirpllc.com*, 6 July 2017, www.cirpllc.com/blog/2018/1/14/amazon-prime-reaches-85-million-us-members?rq=On average, US Amazon Prime members shop at Amazon.com 25 times per year. In contrast, customers without Amazon Prime shop at Amazon.com an average of 14 times per year.

[5] Baldacci, Kevin. "7 Customer Service Lessons from Amazon CEO Jeff Bezos ." *Salesforce.com*, 10 June 2013, www.salesforce.com/blog/2013/06/jeff-bezos-lessons.html.

[6] Halligan, Brian. "3 Marketing Lessons From Amazon's Web Strategy." *Hubspot.com*, 29 Aug. 2017, blog.hubspot.com/blog/tabid/6307/bid/21729/3-marketing-lessons-from-amazon-s-web-strategy.aspx.

[7] Horton, Chris. "3 Digital Marketing Lessons from Amazon.com." *Socialmediatoday.com*, 4 Jan. 2013, www.socialmediatoday.com/content/3-digital-marketing-lessons-amazoncom.

[8] Daly, Jimmy. "The Amazon Experience." *Getvero.com*, 2 Dec. 2014, www.getvero.com/resources/guides/the-amazon-experience/.

the progress they'd made on the project he funded, or anything else. It's no wonder they are losing money!

It's easy to push follow-up aside when you're busy. It's understandable that staff turnover, or changes in priorities and responsibilities, might leave gaps in your donor engagement process. But none of those things are good excuses for not intentionally setting aside time to build and maintain relationships with donors. Disregarding the relationship with donors—especially your major and planned gift donors—sends a clear signal to those people that you're really only interested in their money. And there's no better way to motivate a donor to stop giving than to make it all about their money.

The best way that I've found to be intentional about regularly engaging with donors (not asking for their money, but truly engaging relationally) is to take a full day, map out the entire communication plan (all your asks, your newsletters, event invitations, etc.), and get really clear on what the average donor's true experience is with your organization. Then step back and identify 4-6 key points throughout the year where you can go even deeper to enhance your relationship with donors through more meaningful communications. That could include personal phone calls, handwritten status updates, a detailed impact report highlighting how each specific donor's gifts were used, or even an update from the field.

MISTAKE #98

Selecting a Fundraising Agency Partner for the Wrong Reasons

By Lisa Smith

Nonprofit organizations select fundraising agency partners for many reasons. Unfortunately, I often see organizations pick their agency for all the wrong reasons. Most frequently, this mistake stems from an organization selecting the agency that is the lowest-priced option, or the one that promises results that are far beyond what could ever be possible. And even still, I see many nonprofits select agencies because a particular agency focuses on tools, tactics, and audiences that are emerging or trendy, but that might not actually effectively deliver value to the organization.

There's a better way to do this, and I want to show you what that is.

Partnering with a Fundraising Agency

I'm a big fan of fundraising agencies and not just because I've spent my career in the space. The agencies I've worked for have helped raise millions of dollars for many incredible causes. Agencies are full of energy, provide challenging and satisfying work, and are staffed with some truly smart and talented people. From my perspective it makes good sense to hire a fundraising agency, particularly if you're interested in growing your base of supporters and revenue.

Good agencies can bring volumes of proven strategies and

tactics to your program while still being incredibly innovative. Good agencies can integrate multiple services across multiple channels, seamlessly managing hundreds of details and decisions along the way. *Really* good agencies do these things and more, cost effectively and with a high level of service and integrity.

There are many things I could relay when it comes to selecting the right fundraising agency and business model for your organization. I've chosen three important topics, sharing an insider's view that I hope will help you in your selection and management process.

1. Choosing a People-Centric Partner

There are a lot of reasons to choose an agency—proven successes, flawless delivery, service excellence, and value are just a few. Underlying these outcomes are people, sometimes referred to as the talent.

There's an expression you may have heard, 'talent conquers all,' and there is no truer truth when it comes to marketing agencies. The ideas, creativity, strategies, and insights come from people—though admittedly that's evolving with the growth of AI! Still and for the near future, it's important to choose an agency where people are valued, thriving, well-resourced, and are totally engaged in their work and yours!

Here are some factors that facilitate employee engagement and loyalty, along with questions you may ask to determine if your prospective team is all fired up and ready to go.

People-Centric agencies tend toward competitive compensation packages, career-pathing, formalized training and mentoring, annual reviews, and feedback loops. Comfortable work environments and flexibility in location and hours are a bonus.

Importantly, people-centric organizations foster a sense of empowerment, inclusion, and appreciation. Questions like 'what's the average tenure of your team?' 'how often do you formally provide feedback to staff, including senior management?' and 'do you engage in employee satisfaction surveys and follow up?' may seem intrusive but can go a long way in understanding if the agency truly cares about their people.

Well-Resourced. There are many factors that impact resources and not all are about the bottom line. Sometimes companies are growing faster than they can hire, buy equipment, and upgrade systems. If you're considering hiring a rapidly growing agency, you may want to ask how they are managing the growth and how it will impact you. For example, do they intend to slow the sales pipeline until your program is well-situated? Sometimes staffing plans don't fully meet requirements, so it's important to request a comprehensive plan (including time allocation by function) as part of your RFP. Sometimes agencies run too lean—try to avoid those.

Financial and Organizational Stability. The hardest time for employees is when an agency is being flipped, is merging with another, or has lost a major piece of business and doesn't have reserves to minimize layoffs. During those events, staff are more likely to leave or be laid off, morale plummets, and focus is on internal issues versus your business. Although some information regarding a company's stability may not be accessible to you, it's important to gather basic corporate facts in your RFP process, pursue provided references, and more importantly engage your network—who may help reveal the unknowns.

2. Dynamics of Multi-Source Delivery Models

No agency can be an expert in all aspects of fundraising, making it a virtual requirement for you to engage multiple suppliers. However, over the past several years many nonprofits have unbundled products and services—particularly those related to direct response—with the goal of lowering costs while gaining new strategies, ideas, and better practices.

This approach (along with other external forces) has caused disruption in agency business, often resulting in lowered profit margins and in turn lowered levels of staffing. Proverbial 'benches' of people have disappeared, making it harder for even the most service-oriented agency to step in and help when needed.

The multi-source supplier model has also posed issues for nonprofits that (often without increased headcount) go from managing a single full-service agency to orchestrating the work of multiple suppliers—including printers, letter shops, data processors, list brokers, and more. Development teams assume the role of program manager, trafficking, negotiators, and other functions typically provided by an agency.

While I won't advocate for either single- or multi-source models, I do recommend the following if you are considering multi-sourcing your direct response or any other multi-faceted program within your organization:

Staffing. At least some of the savings yielded from direct purchasing of products and services should be invested in additional staff to ensure integration among suppliers. As noted, in a single-source model, agencies assume responsibility for integration via their account and production management functions, covering the positions financially by means of fees or agreed-upon markups. In a multi-source model the markups go away, but the need to integrate services remains—and if not staffed properly on your end, it can result in lost time and expensive mistakes.

Operating Level Agreements (OLA). An OLA creates an understanding of who—including in your organization—is doing what when there is more than one supplier involved in the process. The objective of an OLA is to define inter-dependencies, hand-offs, quality control checks, and ramifications if one of the suppliers fails to meet deadlines and other obligations. Developing an OLA amongst the suppliers helps to keep the focus on your program and needs, rather than each supplier focusing on their own deliverables.

Ongoing Communications. Even when your staff is successfully managing integration, there is benefit in creating forums to share critical information related to ongoing deliverables; evaluate and improve process; and exchange ideas, tools, and outcomes. Open lines of communication between your suppliers—sometimes even without your staff present—can expedite deliverables, resolve issues, and create a team environment where the collective energy is focused on the success of your program.

Multi-sourcing products and services only saves money when there is a plan, process, and enough staff to effectively manage and deliver integration.

3. Remember, You Own the Program, Not the Agency!

First and foremost, you the client own your fundraising program no matter how long you and your agency have been working together, how much their staff feels like an extension of your own, and even if the agency has become primary knowledge-holder due to staff issues at your organization. You own the program!

I raise the point not as a shortcoming of the nonprofit organization, but the agency's—there are many who don't provide appropriate documentation of strategies and specifications, share 'secret sauce' related to audience profiling and segmentation, and sometimes even own creative controls that can't be replicated should you sever ties. Under these circumstances, inadvertently the agency owns your program though you are a paying client.

I've managed through enough transitions to know there is no industry standard regarding documentation and knowledge across the agency/client aisle. Critical information impacting revenue and results—for example, audience criteria—can be non-existent, 'in someone's head,' or fragmented, requiring piecing facts together. This slows development and program execution, creating an unintended but potentially damaging multi-variate environment.

The remedy is easy: *Require comprehensive program documentation* and make it accessible to your current and future teams, both in-house and agency.

What does comprehensive documentation include? Enough critical information to readily replicate your fundraising program from strategy to execution *as-is*, protecting program performance . . . so new ideas and intentional change are measurable and accurate.

What are minimal requirements? Items directly related to outcomes including donors and revenue. This includes but is not limited to the following:

- **Your Donor File.** Minimally, suppressions and coding logic.

- **Audience Criteria.** This can be tricky when modeling is involved, as methodologies are product-ized and sold as a service. But creating an information trail on 'who and why,' the contact plan, and performance metrics is critical. This remains true when applying RFM.

- **Strategy/Creative Brief.** Rationale behind audience, offer, ask, timing, and testing.

- **Creative.** Access to creative files, including graphic elements and photos.

- **Personalization Specifications.** Sounds improbable, but details offer/ask to audience strategies that are critical to messaging and upgrading.

- **Results.** Better than last year? Did the test work? What are next steps?

Program documentation may seem fundamental or even a mundane topic, but it's neither when you're scrambling to understand who was mailed what and why when changing agencies!

A Last Word on Agency Partnerships

Though bound by scopes of work, service, and operation-level agreements, the fundamental contract between nonprofit and agency is trust, respect, and an uncommon commitment to grow the base of supporters and revenue. Without these elements underpinning the business agreement, your goals will not be met. With them in place you'll better navigate the difficulties, seize opportunities, grow your program, and find personal satisfaction along the way.

MISTAKES #99-#101

Treating Your Gift Catalog Like a Single Product

By Brian Tucker

I was fortunate enough to spend about six years of my career at World Vision, one of the largest global relief organizations in the world. During my tenure, our team oversaw the giving catalog program. Back in 2006, gift catalogs were just becoming a popular way for nonprofits to raise money (much to the efforts of Heifer International).

One of the benefits of working for a large NGO is that you have resources and budget to test and fail. I hope this chapter will help you avoid some of those hard-found lessons!

Now that I am a consultant, one of the biggest issues I've found with clients is that they give their gift catalog just enough effort to keep it alive, but not nearly enough to make it as profitable as it could be.

While the gift catalog was always a profitable venture at World Vision, it wasn't until the organization as a whole recognized that this was a <u>program</u>, and not simply a group of products, that it really took off.

What's the difference?

A product could also be referred to as an offer—such as drilling a well, providing emergency food, or giving vaccines to children. A program is a multi-channel effort that touches every part of the organization, from finance to marketing. It has a synergistic focus for the organization during key times of the year (such as the holiday season), and has appropriate resources dedicated towards growth.

So what? Why should my organization even have a gift catalog program?

Consider this: charitable giving in the United States has been stuck at around 2.1% of GDP for years. While the total dollars increase, that number is flat when adjusted for inflation. On the other hand, holiday shopping accounts for 3.4% of US GDP, with a projected 5% increase in spending for 2018.[1]

If you can truly create a gift-giving experience, your organization can dip into the portion of your donor's wallet by solving the age-old problem: What do you get Aunt Debbie for Christmas this year?

One of the most fulfilling parts of my career was seeing the World Vision gift catalog grow by over 300% in a five-year period. We made a lot of mistakes along the way, and I'm happy to share those with you now!

MISTAKE #99

Treat the Gift Catalog like a Direct Mail Appeal

Like it or not, your mailbox will start filling up with catalogs starting in October. While larger retailers have reduced circulation and become more strategic, there is no denying that these print catalogs are driving revenue.

The next time you get a catalog in the mail, pay special attention to the cover. A good catalog has a singular focus with a clear image featuring a top product. You can't help but notice it as you take it from your mailbox.

So why would you hide that beautiful image behind an envelope?

There are very rare exceptions, but as a general rule you should never put your catalog in an envelope. In addition to adding print costs, you are devaluing the shopping experience.

Notice I said shopping and not donation experience. A direct mail appeal requires a clear and concise call to action with a singular focus. You need the donor to do that one thing.

A catalog is different. We browse through items, set it on the coffee table and come back to it later. Some families gather together and circle the items they want to give to friends and family members, making it a teaching experience. While you still need to grab their attention, the reader might pick up and put down the catalog several times before making a purchasing decision.

MISTAKE #100

Not Doing a Detailed Product Analysis

Evaluating the effectiveness of a catalog program can be a little trickier than a traditional direct mail appeal. Instead of one offer, you have dozens (and sometimes hundreds) of products all taking up valuable real estate.

More often than not, valuable space is taken up by a product favorite of the marketing team (even though it underperforms) or by an editorial section that MUST be included.

To evaluate a catalog, you use what's called a *SQUINCH*

Analysis, which is short for *square-inch analysis*. While it primarily refers to your print catalog (which is a major driver to your online traffic), the same findings often carry over to online. If a product is performing well in print, you can bet it's probably doing well on your website!

To perform a SQUINCH, you need the following data points:

- The total costs of your print catalog (print, postage, mailing services)
- The total number of square inches in your catalog
- Product revenue, ideally by channel (print, online, and "other")

You can then take these costs to determine your total cost per square inch:

Next, you'll measure out the number of square inches that a product takes up on a page. For example, let's say your catalog page is five inches wide by 10 inches tall, which is 50 square inches. If your product takes up half a page, that's 25 square inches of catalog space.

If that product generates $10,000 in revenue, that's $400 per square inch of space. Let's say that your catalog costs $100 per square inch to print and mail, that's a 3-to-1 ROI. While that's not bad, you'll want to benchmark that product against the others and ask the following questions:

- Should I make this product smaller on the page?
- Should I move where it's at in the catalog? For example,does it deserve to be on the inside cover?
- Should I revise the product photo or description to make it more appealing?

As you can imagine, these decisions are not always cut and dry. But if you apply a solid methodology to your evaluation, you can make educated decisions that are not driven by creative (or department) biases.

MISTAKE #101

Not Optimizing Your Digital Experience

The online experience is often the most overlooked, yet it's also the most important. On average, most nonprofits are bringing in at least 65% of their catalog program revenue through their website, but they spend the least amount of time optimizing for it.

One of the reasons for this is the limitations from many of the giving platforms. If you want to get serious about catalog revenue, you might need to look for a specialized platform or potentially consider having a system custom developed for your organization. But first you need to know what to look for!

Is your cart really a cart?

When you are browsing an online shopping website, the company's entire goal is to get you to buy more than one thing. This is completely opposite of a donation form, which is designed to get you to do one thing and one thing only.

A solid catalog program gets an average of 2.25 items per transaction, which means that your donors are looking to buy multiple items. If the cart process doesn't make this easy, you are missing out on a huge portion of online revenue.

Is your website retail optimized?

An optimized website has the ability to get as many high-value products above the fold as possible, while still being visually pleasing and easy to navigate. This is usually achieved through a grid setup in a hierarchy of one hero product, 2 high-level products, then rows of 3 products in diminishing value. The product should match the description and photo of the print catalog to make it easy for the donor to find.

You'll also want to pay special attention to the product description and photos. You have a little more freedom to include more photos, videos, and stories online than in print so take advantage of it! This can be a daunting task for catalogs with hundreds of products, so focus on your top-performing products first and work your way through. Take a look at archived videos and photos from your direct mail fundraising because you might already have what you need!

Why physical gift cards are still better.

I'll leave you with one last story from my World Vision days. We were testing out a new microfinance program that had a gift card functionality built into it. For the past two years before I started working on the program, the gift cards were only digital (meaning a donor could purchase them digitally and email them to a recipient).

One day when I was in line at the checkout at my local Target store, I noticed how many fun gift card designs they had. This got me thinking that if one of America's largest retailers pushed gift cards so much, there must be a good reason!

To test this theory, we designed a special gift card that looked like a piggy bank for the microfinance product (get it?!). It even came on a neat card backer that could be hung from a retail display. When we started pushing them during the holidays, I was hoping for a 10% increase in gift card sales. Instead we ended up increasing revenue by 43% from the previous year!

We live in a digital world, but people still enjoy giving gifts to each other in person. In the end we're all just trying to facilitate a human connection and to truly make the world better, so keep that in mind before you ditch the analog parts of your catalog program.

---

[1] Saad, Lydia. "Americans Plan on Spending a Lot More This Christmas." *Gallup.com*, 16 Nov. 2015, news.gallup.com/poll/186620/americans-plan-spending-lot-christmas.aspx.

SPECIAL BONUS CONTENT

IN THE JOURNEY of writing this book we uncovered more than 101 frequent and costly mistakes that are routinely made across the nonprofit sector. For that reason, we're providing you with these additional mistakes, because avoiding these will save you even more headaches and cost across your organization.

MISTAKE #102

Focusing on Popularity Contests

By Andrew Olsen, CFRE

I can't tell you how many organizations I run across that will marshal every last internal resource, volunteer, donor, and public connection they have to vote for them in their next corporate fundraising challenge. You know what I'm talking about.

Whether it's a car company promoting a $10,000 or $30,000 social media challenge, or a local company committing to give $5,000 to the charity that gets the most likes on their Facebook page, I'm sure you've seen your fair share of nonprofits go crazy over these kind of contests and competitions. Maybe you've even had to participate in them from time to time.

Here's the thing: Those same nonprofits often have anywhere from 1,000 to 20,000 donors on their donor files. And of all those donors, anywhere from 150 to 3,000 of them likely have the capacity to give the organization a gift of $10,000 or more. What I find insane is that the same organization that will focus all of their resources for a two-week period toward winning that social media competition where success means a decent-sized one-time (non-repeatable) gift will fully balk at the idea of investing anything near that same amount of effort, time, and resources to develop relationships with high-capacity donors who, if cultivated well, could give ANNUAL gifts at that same level.

I don't get the allure of these social media competitions, but I do know why nonprofits find them easier to focus on than individual donor relationship-building. It's because participating in a social media competition is easy. There's no risk, either organizationally or personally. No one has to risk the discomfort of sitting across from a donor, asking for a gift, and hearing a "No."

MISTAKE #103

Putting Your Needs Ahead of Your Donor's Needs

By Andrew Olsen, CFRE

"Jim, if you could just make a gift today of $250,000, that would really help me hit my goal for the year and make everything so much easier for me."

How's that ask sit with you? Did you just spit your hot coffee onto the page? Let me answer the question that's in the back of your mind right now.

Yes.

That is an actual ask that was made of a donor a few years ago. One of my colleagues met with a major gift officer a few years ago to help work through a revenue challenge she was facing. During the discovery conversation, my colleague quickly pinpointed the problem in their strategy.

Instead of framing asks around programs and articulating to the donor how he could accomplish his personal philanthropic objectives through a gift to their organization, this gift officer was actually (and unfortunately) making asks exclusively focused on what she needed—specifically, to meet her personal revenue production numbers for the year!

Talk about a horrible donor experience. Nothing communicates that you see the donor as an ATM more than going to them to withdraw funds because you're behind on revenue for the year.

MISTAKE #104

Never Seeking
Outside Counsel

By Andrew Olsen, CFRE

"A fool despises good counsel, but a wise man takes it to heart."

—*Confucius*

There are many nonprofit leaders who refuse to seek outside counsel to help them navigate complex issues and situations. Some avoid it because they think "outside counsel" sounds expensive, and they can't imagine paying for something like that. But it doesn't have to be that way.

Even if you don't want to pay a consultant, you can get counsel from trusted board members, other nonprofit leaders in your local community (or even in other communities), from local university professors, or even by posting your critical questions to specific LinkedIn groups and asking members to help you think through an issue. Many successful leaders (both nonprofit and corporate) have also joined local mastermind groups where several senior-level leaders regularly gather together to share their challenges and help one another navigate whatever complex situations with which they're dealing. Sometimes these groups charge a membership fee, but plenty of free versions are available too.

In the same vein, if your organization is struggling with a major issue, or looking to launch a new program, you'd be wise to seek out others who have undertaken something similar in the past. You can save a ton of time, energy, money, and headaches by learning from someone else's mistakes (kudos for grabbing this book—it's a great start!).

The other less frequently acknowledged reason why leaders shy away from seeking outside counsel is because they feel like asking for help will make them look weak, or that people will realize they don't have all the answers. The reality couldn't be further from the truth.

Your staff, board, donors, and stakeholders will appreciate that you aren't trying to do everything on your own and that you're self-aware enough to ask for input and help in areas where you don't have the necessary level of expertise. No one can be and know everything. Pretending that you do will only highlight your lack of confidence in the mind of others—which is exactly what you're trying to avoid.

MISTAKE #105

Expecting New Major Gift Officers to Produce Revenue Immediately

By Andrew Olsen, CFRE

The rate of turnover among major gift officers in our sector is staggering. In fact, the average tenure of a gift officer for nearly as long as I've been in this industry (20 years) has consistently hovered around 18 months.

This is a terrible trend.

While there are a multitude of reasons for this pathetic tenure trend, one key issue is that CEOs and nonprofit boards often have insanely unrealistic expectations for how quickly a new gift officer can produce major gifts.

If fact, I've been called in to advise executives and boards on at least a dozen instances throughout my career, and the conversation has consistently gone something like this:

"We think we have to fire Major Gift Officer X. He's just not delivering for us. Can you help us figure out next steps?"

However, the problem with every single one of these dozen conversations is that the gift officer in question in each situation had been on staff at each of these organizations for only 3-6 months.

To be clear, I'd be one of the first to say cut ties with an employee who just isn't working out for your organization. Your work is too critical to hold onto people who can't or won't do what you need them to do to advance your mission.

That said, I also hate to see a great fundraiser get put through the wringer because an organization's leaders don't understand how long it takes to build trust-based relationships with donors and navigate the process that leads to soliciting and securing gifts.

In each of these instances, yes: the gift officers could have worked harder, faster, and smarter, I'm certain. But . . . the organizational leadership in each organization also held highly unrealistic expectations of what could be accomplished. And in a majority of these instances, this wasn't the first time the CEO or board had removed a gift officer because of an unrealistic expectation.

Expecting a new gift officer to produce revenue immediately—or even within the first six months—is dangerous, and detrimental to their success and yours. Instead, take a realistic approach that balances the need for a successful period of onboarding, training, and relationship development between your gift officer and your donors. When you recognize that a gift officer's role is to build and sustain long-term relationships with donors instead of merely producing revenue, it will allow you to reset expectations and be more realistic about how quickly new gift officers will produce revenue.

MISAKE #106

Failing to Build Your Organization's Long-Term Financial Capacity

By Andrew Olsen, CFRE

"We will never build an endowment or reserve account. Our donors give so we can help people today, not so that we can hoard their money and generate interest on it."

This is one that really confuses me.

I've met a number of nonprofit CEOs who flat-out refuse to build any kind of financial reserves because they believe doing so would violate the implied agreement with their donors that they would spend their charitable gifts to solve whatever issues the organization is working on.

The problem with this thinking is that sometimes things happen that are beyond our control, and sometimes those things require that we spend unplanned dollars to resolve them and keep our organization afloat.

Consider this: If your organization relies on government grants to deliver programs and the government shuts down for a time, you might not receive that funding when you expect and need it. If you have a cash reserve, you're more likely to weather a situation like this without a service interruption.

What if your building catches fire and requires significant repairs, or some type of natural disaster strikes in your community and impacts your facilities? How can you meet the needs of your constituents if you don't have funds socked away to spend in emergency situations?

It's prudent and responsible to build financial reserves of at least three to six months of operating expenses to make sure you can survive any challenges that come your way.

MISTAKE #107

Not Allowing a Strategy the Time it Needs to Produce Returns

By Andrew Olsen, CFRE

My team conducted a fundraising and program audit last year for a very large international nonprofit. We were surprised to uncover that in the last five years they had launched 6-8 major initiatives, only to quickly terminate each one.

In our discovery process the reason became crystal clear.

Staff members consistently told us that the organization, while having great intentions, didn't have the will to stick with a strategy if it wasn't immediately successful.

The various initiatives they launched were not immediately successful (hint: few are ever immediately successful!), and because of that, each initiative was summarily stopped before it actually had enough time to succeed.

The problem with managing an organization in this way is multifold. First, the erratic approach can wreak havoc on your staff. Your people work hard and for long hours to design and launch programs like this. Shutting them down so quickly without giving them the time to succeed is highly demoralizing to people who invest their time and energy to create them.

If any of these initiatives are public-facing (and many of these 6-8 were), the quick start/stop nature could cause your donors and other constituents to question whether your organization can be trusted.

Lastly, a constant process of starting and stopping wastes a lot of time, energy, political capital, and money, ultimately leaving you with not much to show for those investments.

MISTAKE #108

Making Decisions Based on "Gut Instinct" Instead of Data-Driven Insight

By Andrew Olsen, CFRE

As a fundraiser you'll have a lot of people offer you suggestions on how best to do your job. Well-intentioned board members, executive directors, program staffers, volunteers, and supporters will, at one time or another, probably all give you suggestions (requested or not).

Most of these suggestions are based on instinct. Unless the person making the suggestion is an experienced fundraiser herself, chances are the suggestion is based on a "gut feel." Acting on a gut feel (whether from a board member or even your own) can be devastating to your fundraising if it turns out to be wrong. And FYI, much of the time acting on instinct isn't the best course of action.

That's where insight comes into play. Insight is knowledge based on a deep understanding of your consumer (or donor) and the fundraising techniques that yield the most significant results.

When in doubt, choose insight over instinct. Here are some examples to get you thinking . . .

Mailing Frequency

Instinct: We only mail three times per year because we don't want to overload our donors. Donors hate being solicited more than that, and they'll stop giving if we ask more often.

Insight: Research and testing shows exactly the opposite is true. As long as you're doing a good job thanking donors and sharing relevant, compelling opportunities with them, increased frequency helps retain more donors and deliver more revenue. It's naive to think that donors won't continue to be solicited just because you stop asking. *They'll just not be solicited by you.* Which means they'll be more likely to give to someone else. Why? Because the number-one reason donors give is BECAUSE SOMEONE ASKED.

Social and Mobile Media

Instinct: We're shifting all of our fundraising to text messaging and Facebook. Look what Obama's campaign and the American Red Cross have been able to do on mobile and social media. We'll save a ton of money and be able to engage millions.

Insight: Your organization isn't the Obama campaign (or any other presidential campaign). The reason Facebook and mobile giving worked for Obama is because he was getting millions of dollars in paid and free TV media, and had an aggressive offline program as well. In fact, most of the Obama campaign's revenue still came from direct mail and email versus Facebook and text giving. And unless you're a major disaster-relief organization, you won't be able to compete with the American Red Cross either. Mobile giving worked for them because they had (pardon the potential pun) the perfect storm. A major natural disaster, days and days of free TV coverage, and a network of volunteers and donors built through traditional media who they could leverage in crisis. Most organizations don't have these options.

Photographs and Images

Instinct: We only want photos of happy kids. We're about positive change. Those organizations that show sad-looking, needy kids are exploiting them for financial gain.

Insight: People give to meet a need. To right a wrong. To solve a problem. If your photos and communications show only the happy "after" images, you remove the donor's natural motivation to act. You can show only happy photos—but you won't raise as much money. And that means you won't meet as much need in the community. Which is more important to you? Which is more important to those you serve?

CONCLUSION

I HOPE YOU'VE FOUND value in this extensive list of common mistakes made in our sector, as well as some of the tips and recommendations to help you avoid making them in the future. We've identified many of the most common mistakes in the nonprofit sector, but I'm sure we missed a few. What other mistakes do you see made regularly?

Feel free to connect with me or any of the other contributors to learn and share, and to continue this conversation. If you're inclined to share on social media, we'd love for you to tag us, and use the hashtag **#101NonprofitMistakes**.

Thank you for learning alongside us and for investing in your own professional development!

AUTHOR BIOGRAPHIES

IT'S MORE FUN—AND more insightful—to do things like this with other smart people instead of going it alone. And often you can learn more when you bring a diverse group of people with varied perspectives together around a complicated topic like this. That's why I brought this group of industry leaders and subject-matter experts together to share their experiences and unique points of view with you. I'm grateful for each one of them individually, and for the collective contribution they've generously made to this body of work.

Zully Avila, MBA, Nonprofit Consultant
Email: zullyavila@gmail.com
LinkedIn: www.linkedin.com/in/zullyavila

With nearly 15 years of experience in marketing and fundraising agencies like Kern, ONE HUNDRED Agency, Russ Reid, TrueSense Marketing, and Merkle, Zully Avila is a highly successful and accomplished leader in direct response marketing and fundraising strategy. She's a strategic thinker with a proven track record of building, leading, and refining complex integrated and multi-cultural marketing programs for some of the world's leading nonprofit and commercial brands.

Zully holds an MBA from Pepperdine University, The George L. Graziadio School of Business and Management, and is currently pursuing a Master's degree in International/Global Studies at Harvard University, while simultaneously consulting with several nonprofit organizations and small businesses.

Suzanne Battit, MBA, Principal/Vice President
Development Guild
Email: sbattit@developmentguild.com
LinkedIn: www.linkedin.com/in/suzanne-battit-39b772144
Website: www.developmentguild.com

For over 20 years Suzanne has committed herself to helping nonprofit organizations successfully achieve mission delivery; improving lives around the world. Suzanne's passion and diverse fundraising, marketing, and communication expertise benefits each of her clients, including: The Clayton Christensen Institute, Colby College, Fitchburg State University, Huntington Theatre, and Museum of Arts and Design. Suzanne brings a unique blend of analytic discipline and creativity that both educates and inspires her clients and her own team. Prior to joining Development Guild DDI, Suzanne served as Vice President of External Affairs and Advancement at The Greater Boston Food Bank. Her previous work also includes serving as Director of Development at Partners in Health, and as Executive Director of the Harvard College Fund. Earlier in her career, Suzanne held several leadership roles during 10 years at Putnam Investments. Suzanne earned her undergraduate degree at Colby College and a Master of Business Administration from Harvard Business School.

Aubrey Bergauer, Executive Director
California Symphony
Email: aubrey@californiasymphony.org
LinkedIn: www.linkedin.com/in/aubreybergauer
Website: www.californiasymphony.org

As Executive Director of the California Symphony, Aubrey is a graduate of Rice University with degrees in Music Performance and Business. For the last 15 years she has used music to make the world around her better, through programs that champion social justice and equality, through marketing and audience development tactics on the forefront of trends and technology, and through proving and sharing what works in the rapidly changing landscape of funding, philanthropy, and consumer behavior. Praised for her leadership and her ability to strategically and holistically examine and advance every facet of the organization, she is committed to instilling and achieving common goals and vision across what are usually siloed marketing, development, and artistic departments. Aubrey's passion is to create a transformational change in the audience, in the office, on the stage, in the community, and in the narrative for the classical music industry.

Beth Cathey, Managing Partner
givingMD
Email: bethc@givingmd.com
LinkedIn: www.linkedin.com/in/bethcathey
Website: givingmd.com

Beth's leadership roles have transcended almost every aspect of agency life—from client service, traditional media buying, list brokerage, new business development, and digital teams. Beth has excelled at the strategic development of new donor/

constituent acquisition campaigns for nonprofit organizations such as Alliance Defense Fund (now Alliance Defending Freedom), World Vision, Concerned Women for America, Prison Fellowship, National Coalition Against Pornography, The Rutherford Institute, American Bible Society, and many donor acquisition programs for rescue missions across the US. Today Beth manages a digital fundraising agency called givingMD.

Beth's entire career has been spent serving nonprofit ministries and faith-based, family-friendly for-profit organizations. Her first 20+ years of direct-response fundraising centered around best practices in direct mail fundraising and traditional media. The following 18 years have been spent transitioning that knowledge into bleeding-edge digital applications of fundraising to the world of donor engagement and online fundraising. Beth's time has been split between practicing digital in the digital advertising world with a tour of duty at Salem Web Network, and in developing, growing, and leading teams for direct-response fundraising agencies. Beth previously owned a traditional media and marketing company, working on such projects as the marketing of *The Passion of the Christ* movie; the Ronald Reagan documentary, *In the Face of Evil*; and Billy Graham's Dallas Metroplex crusade. Beth also founded a word-of-mouth marketing company called Ground Force Network.

Craig DePole, President
Newport ONE
Email: cdepole@newportone.com
LinkedIn: www.linkedin.com/in/craig-depole-223a291
Website: www.newportone.com

Craig has been raising funds for great causes for more than 20 years. He gets a lot of joy out of bringing together his right brain creativity and his left brain scientific analysis to help nonprofit organizations create a better world. He has raised millions upon millions of dollars and helped foster long-term relationships with donors through multi-channel, donor-centric, integrated fundraising strategies. Craig is a frequent speaker and author in the nonprofit industry and currently serves on the Board of Directors for the Association of Direct Response Fundraising Counsel (ADFRCO). Over the years, his work has earned dozens of awards for nonprofit direct marketing excellence from the Direct Marketing Association of Washington and the New England Direct Marketing Association. In his free time, when he is not cheering from the sideline of a soccer, lacrosse, or field hockey field, he is raising funds for his kids' school as chair of the Advancement Committee. Craig is a native Californian and lives in Maryland with his wife, three kids, and adopted dog, Vinny.

Coral Dill, Principal
Grant Writer Etc.
Email: coral.dill@gmail.com
LinkedIn: www.linkedin.com/in/grantwriteretc
Website: www.grantwriteretc.com

Coral has two passions: connecting nonprofits with the resources necessary to propel their mission into action, and grant writing in order to help them achieve this goal. In 2016, after 10 years of working in nonprofits throughout the United States and Canada, Coral founded Grant Writer Etc., a boutique consulting agency specializing in grant writing and research. Since its launch, she has consulted on over $5 million of foundation, corporate, state, and federal grants for nonprofits throughout the United States and Canada, and has been awarded grants throughout North America and Europe. She has worked with organizations of all sizes and prides herself on providing the same level of service and attention to every organization, no matter their size or budget. Her previous roles have included serving as a Development Director, Manager of Communications & Development, and Grant Writer in nonprofits in Cincinnati, Ohio and Vancouver, British Columbia.

Jessi Dobos-Marsh, Performance Mentor
BrightDot
Email: jessi@crouchandassociates.com
LinkedIn: www.linkedin.com/in/jessidobosmarsh
Website: thebrightdot.com

Jessi graduated from Ohio University with a BS degree in journalism, and from Carlow University with an MS degree in nonprofit management. She has spent nearly 20 years in nonprofit leadership, serving organizations that offer hope to those in need. After living in Athens, OH and Seattle, WA serving a variety of human services organizations, she returned to her hometown of Pittsburgh. There she spent nine years at Light of Life Rescue Mission, primarily in the role of Director of Advancement. She is currently a fundraising performance consultant with BrightDot (formerly Crouch & Associates), a national performance consulting firm that takes organizations from where they are to where they want to be.

Jenny Floria, President
Floria Consulting
Email: jenny.floria@gmail.com
LinkedIn: www.linkedin.com/in/jennyfloria1
Website: floriaconsulting.com

Jenny is President of Floria Consulting, a boutique fundraising strategy shop in the Midwest. Jenny has over 20 years of marketing and development experience, including leading annual giving at Gillette Children's Specialty Healthcare and Minneapolis Heart Institute. She is an experienced fundraiser and self-described data geek. She began her career at what is now PMX Agency, working exclusively with nonprofits to raise money through direct mail. She then worked at several non-profits—leading annual giving programs, building stewardship programs, and grilling database managers until they loved her. She is now consulting for various nonprofits, building stewardship strategic plans, writing stories for digital and print media, building social media plans, and putting her data skills to use—digging gold from donor databases across the nation.

Stacey Girdner, MBA, Managing Partner
The PRAXIS Group
Email: sgirdner@thepraxisgroup.com
Website: thepraxisgroup.com
LinkedIn: www.linkedin.com/in/thepraxisgroup

As a business owner, internal business executive, and external management consultant, Stacey has solved hundreds of unique people challenges. A consultant and facilitator in management and organization development, Stacey has more than 30 years of experience in a diversity of business settings. She is known for her work in executive coaching, leadership training, team development and offsite meeting facilitation. Stacey holds a Master of Business Administration degree from California State Polytechnic University in Pomona, California with an emphasis in organization development, and a Bachelor of Arts degree in business administration from Azusa Pacific University in Azusa, California.

Stacey has served as an adjunct faculty member of Azusa Pacific University in its School of Business and Management, and has developed innovative curriculum focusing on organizational behavior, group dynamics and conflict management, human resources management and leadership for line and mid-level managers.

Roy Jones, CFRE, Vice President
Mercy Ships
Email: getroyjones@gmail.com
LinkedIn: www.linkedin.com/in/getroyjones
Website: www.royjones.org

Roy has more than 30 years of relationship-building, major gift procurement, and fundraising experience. He co-authored the award-winning *Rainmaking: The Fundraiser's Guide To Landing Big Gifts* and is recognized professionally as one of the top relationship managers in the country. In addition to consulting professionally with some of the nation's top charities, Roy serves on the boards of several human service charities. He also founded his own foundation to promote training and philanthropy, called the Fundraising Institute Training (FIT) Foundation. FIT Fundraising assists and subsidizes training for smaller nonprofits. Roy currently serves as Vice President of Development at Mercy Ships International. His previous work includes serving as an Account Director at Russ Reid, working as the Chief Development Officer at Liberty University, and serving as Vice President of Development at U.S.A. Direct.

In addition to his work in the nonprofit sector, Roy has also worked extensively in the political campaign arena. He served as the first Director of Coalition Development at the National Republican Senatorial Committee in the 1980s, then served on the staff of President George H. W. Bush and the 1992 Bush Presidential campaign as a Coalition Building Specialist. His international political work includes a victorious presidential campaign in Guatemala, and conducting training schools on voter contact and grassroots organizing for President Lech Walensa of Poland and his political party, Solidarity. He currently serves as the national finance director for US Senator Rick Santorum's Presidential Campaign.

Jeff Kliewer, CFRE, Chief Executive Officer
ViewSpark, LLC
Email: jkliewer@viewspark.org
LinkedIn: www.linkedin.com/in/jeff-kliewer-cfre-ab9aa71
Website: viewspark.org

Jeff is a 25-year fundraising veteran and CEO of ViewSpark, LLC, a new and innovative digital donor-engagement platform designed to help bring the experiences of the field directly to donors in a meaningful way. Jeff previously held executive-level positions in development at University of Southern California, Joe Torre's Safe At Home Foundation, and Oaks Christian School. Prior to leading fundraising initiatives inside top nonprofit organizations, Jeff was Vice President of Business Development at Russ Reid (now One & All), a leading advertising agency exclusively serving nonprofits.

Megan Klingensmith, PHR, Account Manager
Newport ONE
Email: mklingensmith@newportone.com
LinkedIn: www.linkedin.com/in/megan-klingensmith-phr-ba994a36
Website: www.newportone.com

A Pacific Northwest native, Megan graduated with honors from Azusa Pacific University and holds a PHR certification from the HR Certification Institute. With a uniquely intersectional background in marketing, fundraising and human resources, Megan's been described as a Renaissance woman who doesn't fit neatly into a singular job title.

Megan's career has included work with nonprofit organizations across the US, including Feeding America Food Banks, the American Red Cross, Rescue Missions, and CARE, among others. In her human resources tenure, Megan focused on recruiting and organizational learning/development. Keenly interested in how organizational culture fosters or stifles innovation and engagement, she published and presented the paper "Building Capacity to Engage Millennials for Organizational Innovation" with the Organizational Development Network. She then became Employee 1 with an Idealab startup platform connecting workers with flex work opportunities. She's now honing her startup experience and marketing/HR background as an Account Manager at Newport ONE.

John Kozyra, Chief Philanthropy Officer
Providence St. Joseph Health, St. Mary Medical Center
Email: jkozyra@gmail.com
LinkedIn: www.linkedin.com/in/jkozyra
Website: www.stjhs.org

John came to St. Mary from CSS Fundraising. Prior to that, John was a Director for Changing Our World, where he led efforts for the Archdiocese of St. Louis to raise more than $100 million to establish an endowment to support the future of Catholic education in the Archdiocese.

He earned his Bachelor of Arts degree in psychology from Azusa Pacific University, received a certificate in digital communications from Omnicom University, and is currently working on a certificate in financial management from the University of Illinois at Urbana-Champaign. John is active in several volunteer and professional organizations, including serving on the Board of Directors for West End YMCA, and membership with the Association of Fundraising Professionals and Association for Healthcare Philanthropy.

Kathryn Landa, CFRE, Vice President
ViewSpark, LLC
Email: klanda@viewspark.org
LinkedIn: www.linkedin.com/in/kat-landa-cfre-186b9b2b
Website: viewspark.org

Kat leverages her deep fundraising background to develop the ViewSpark suite of fundraising and communication tools. She brings 16 years of integrated commercial and nonprofit marketing experience to her role, with experience spanning multiple channels/audiences including DRTV, digital, web development, radio, social media, direct mail, middle and major donor work, corporate engagement, and planned giving. Kat has managed multi-channel fundraising and awareness campaigns for World Vision, Mercy Ships, Project Hope, rescue missions in New York City, Atlanta, and a dozen other major U.S. markets, as well as 50 food banks across the country. She is committed to raising more money for nonprofits in this new era of donor-centric engagement.

Jayson Matthews, Community Impact Director
Valley of the Sun United Way
Email: jmatthews@vsuw.org
LinkedIn: www.linkedin.com/in/jaysonmatthews
Website: vsuw.org

Jayson has over a decade of experience in nonprofit management, program development, communication, and fundraising. His extensive background in human service policy analysis, planning, budgeting, advocacy, volunteer management, and philanthropy development give him a deep understanding of all aspects of the nonprofit sector.

Jayson is an experienced facilitator for community meetings, board retreats, and strategic planning, trained in the Harwood Institute Convening Model, Kotter's Change Management System, IDEO's Human-Centered Design, Results-Based Leadership and Facilitation, and Franklin Covey's 4DX. He has a passion for bringing people together to accomplish goals that make a difference in the community to generate and channel energy for the public good.

Mark McIntyre, Principal & Co-Founder
Merchant McIntyre & Associates
Email: mmcintyre@merchantmcintyre.com
LinkedIn: www.linkedin.com/in/markdmcintyre
Website: merchantmcintyre.com/index.html

Mark McIntyre is Principal and Co-Founder of Merchant McIntyre Associates, where he provides strategic oversight and manages the firm's government relations practice. Mark has three decades of federal experience, having worked on Capitol Hill, in the White House, and in the private sector. Prior to co-founding MM, Mark opened Russ Reid's DC office in 1994 and served as Senior Vice President and Director of Russ Reid's Washington, DC office.

Before leading Russ Reid DC, Mark served as the youngest Vice President in the history of Cassidy & Associates, the largest independently owned public affairs firm ever established in Washington, DC. While there, he specialized in representing colleges and universities, states and municipalities, major nonprofit organizations, and hospitals and medical centers before the Congress and the Administration. Mark previously served as Chief Speechwriter to then-Vice President Bush from 1986 through the 1988 presidential campaign, transition, and inauguration. Mark began his career with US Rep. Robert L. Livingston (retired), who became Chairman of the full House Appropriations Committee.

Brent Merchant, Principal/Co-Founder
Merchant McIntyre & Associates
Email: bmerchant@merchantmcintyre.com
LinkedIn: linkedin.com/in/brent-merchant-92292810
Website: merchantmcintyre.com

Brent helps clients achieve their federal objectives in the areas of technology, energy, transportation, housing, health care, education, social services, and international development.

Prior to becoming Principal and Co-Founder of Merchant McIntyre Associates, Brent leveraged his strong federal funding, policy, regulatory, and legislative background, as well as his wide range of expertise and relationships throughout the Executive Branch, on behalf of major nonprofit and corporate clients at Russ Reid's Washington, DC, office.

Beginning in 2009, Brent was the Government Affairs Director for LPB Energy Management, a leading energy data management firm. Brent established the federal government presence for LPB, advising company leadership on policy and legislative matters, and overseeing the development and execution of government contracts and partnerships.

From 2001 to 2008, Brent served as senior staff at the Department of Energy where he was named to the position of Deputy Chief of Staff to the Secretary of Energy. In that role, Brent advised the Secretary on policy, operational, regulatory, and legislative issues. Brent also served as Senior Advisor to the Deputy Secretary of Energy focusing on policy, project management, and operational issues throughout the Department and its National Laboratory complex.

Brent began his career working as an aide to Senator Spencer Abraham in his native Michigan.

Adam Morgan, Senior Director of Development
Phi Kappa Psi Foundation
Email: amorg005@gmail.com
LinkedIn: www.linkedin.com/in/amorgan2
Website: www.pkpfoundation.org

Adam is Senior Director of Development at Phi Kappa Psi Foundation. He has grown his career in several large, national nonprofits—including the American Cancer Society, Freedom Alliance, and The Salvation Army. While with The Salvation Army for Eastern Pennsylvania and Delaware, he led his team to raise over $5 million in his last year as the Director of Major Gifts. Adam has contributed articles about nonprofit leadership and engagement to *Planned Giving Today* magazine, and is a chapter author for the *2018 Giving USA Report of Philanthropy.* He has also helped found two small nonprofits—the Hero-Hunts Foundation, which supports veterans and their families, and Spur Impact, which provides professional development, and philanthropic opportunities for young professionals.

Andrew Olsen, CFRE, Sr. Vice President
Newport ONE
Email: aolsen@newportone.com
LinkedIn: www.linkedin.com/in/andrewolsen
Website: www.andrewolsen.net
Company Website: www.newportone.com

In his role at Newport One, Andrew provides senior-level strategic consulting for nonprofits. He and his team specialize in major gift training/coaching, direct response fundraising, development operations consulting, and strategic planning. Prior to joining Newport One, Andrew held senior-level positions at ONE HUNDRED, Russ Reid, Strategic Fundraising, and Gillette Children's Specialty Healthcare. Throughout his career Andrew has helped nonprofits raise more than $250 million to advance their strategic objectives.

Having consulted with over 500 nonprofits in his career, Andrew's client experience includes work with: CARE, Best Friends Animal Society, Save the Children, The Smile Train, St. Joseph's Indian School, International Fellowship of Christians and Jews, National Republican Congressional Committee, The Salvation Army, Christian Broadcasting Network, Children's Hospital Los Angeles, Home of Grace, Ann & Robert H. Lurie Children's Hospital of Chicago, Miller Children's Hospital, Christian Research Institute, University of Minnesota Medical Foundation, Gateway for Cancer Research, Parkinson's Institute and Clinical Center, Chosen People Ministries, Fairview Foundation, Dayspring International, University of Tennessee Medical Center, Polycystic Kidney Disease Foundation, 125 Gospel Rescue Missions, Catholic Charities, Lutheran Social Services, 75 Feeding America Food Banks, Appalachia Service Project, Goodwill Industries, Boys Town, The Society of St. Vincent de Paul, and hundreds of other organizations across the US and Canada.

Andrew is co-author of *Rainmaking: The Fundraiser's Guide to Landing Big Gifts*, and co-host of *The Rainmaker Fundraising Podcast*, available on iTunes. Andrew is also an Instructor at the University of St. Thomas Opus College of Business, where he teaches on annual fundraising strategies. He and his wife Deborah reside in the Midwest with their three daughters: Isabelle, Elisabeth, and Eilidh.

Jeremy Reis, Senior Director of Marketing
Food for the Hungry
Email: link@thatnetwork.com
LinkedIn: www.linkedin.com/in/jeremyreis
Website: nonprofitdonor.com

In addition to his work with Food for the Hungry, Jeremy serves on the Advisory Council for Christian Leadership Alliance. Formerly, Jeremy worked in consulting with Fortune 500 clients and large nonprofits. He had 13 years of technology background prior to moving full-time into nonprofit work. His aim is to help all nonprofits take advantage of technology solutions to improve donor experience and fundraising. Jeremy is author of *Raise More Money With Email,* and the upcoming book, *Magnetic Nonprofit.* He is also host of the *Nonprofit Answers Podcast,* available on iTunes. He earned his BBA from Mt. Vernon Nazarene University and his MBA from The Ohio State University. He has been married to his wife, Jennica, since 2000 and they have four girls and three boys.

Jeff Rothman, President
Rothman Talent Solutions
Email: jeff@rothmantalent.com
LinkedIn: www.linkedin.com/in/jeffrothman
Website: www.rothmantalent.com

With more than 25 years of experience in executive search, Jeff has earned a reputation as an insightful business professional with a knack for identifying, attracting, and assessing hard-to-find, game-changing talent for the data-driven marketing ecosystem. His insight is valued and trusted by employers and candidates, and his firm, Rothman Talent Solutions, has become a go-to resource for high-impact direct and digital marketing talent—the kind that can take an organization from "doing well" to "explosive growth."

Jim Shapiro, Co-Founder
The Better Fundraising Company
Email: jim@betterfundraising.com
LinkedIn: www.linkedin.com/in/jim-shapiro-a358226
Website: betterfundraising.com

Jim is the fundraising coach you always wanted, the proven Sherpa who can help you get to the top of the mountain. He has 20 years experience raising money, including serving as the VP of Development for a $100m nonprofit. He then co-founded The Better Fundraising Co. to help small-to-medium nonprofits raise more money for their causes. Jim is married and has three children, and serves his community by coaching high school football.

Lisa Smith, Senior Vice President
Newport ONE
Email: lsmith@newportone.com
LinkedIn: www.linkedin.com/in/lisa-m-smith-0616484
Website: www.newportone.com

Lisa is a renowned industry leader providing data-driven solutions for nonprofit organizations for over 25 years. Her experience involves work with regional, national, and international nonprofits in multiple sectors. She is among the original architects of donor-centric approaches to audience profiling, treatments, and messaging, mapping targeted offers to unique audiences based on information derived from constituent actions, activities, interests, demographics, and more. She has worked toward orchestrating donor journeys, capitalizing on big data and changes in technology to create increasingly targeted content and treatment strategies. Former work and consulting experience includes: The Greater Boston Food Bank, Los Angeles Regional Food Bank, American Cancer Society, CARE, Covenant House, Doctors Without Borders (MSF), Environmental Defense Fund, National Multiple Sclerosis Society, Paralyzed Veterans of America, The Smithsonian Institution, Special Olympics, and The Salvation Army Eastern Territory.

Lindsey Talerico-Hedren, Founder
Digitalish
Email: lindsey@digitalish.com
LinkedIn: www.linkedin.com/in/lindseytalerico

Lindsey is an internationally respected strategist with expertise in building digital programs for the world's largest nonprofits. Known for her unique ability to make a dull penny shine, she lives by a credo of purposeful marketing. In her first career she managed social media and celebrity relationships with World Vision USA and World Vision New Zealand, visiting more than 15 community development programs. Now, she brings together nonprofit experts across tactics executing turnkey digital programs on behalf of the world's most reputable nonprofits. Former consulting experience: CARE, Mercy Ships, Operation Smile, Catholic Alumni Partnership, The Skoll Foundation, and Women for Women International.

Lindsey is Founder and Director of Strategy at Digitalish, a boutique digital strategy and development shop. Prior to founding Digitalish, Lindsey led social media strategy at Russ Reid, and spent the early years of her career on the in-house digital team at World Vision, one of the largest global nonprofits.

**Ben Taylor, Director of Digital Strategy & Marketing
Automation**
givingMD
Email: bent@givingMD.com
LinkedIn: www.linkedin.com/in/benctaylor
Website: givingmd.com

As the VP of Digital Strategy for givingMD, Ben brings 10 years of digital experience in the nonprofit industry, driving fundraising for clients across the healthcare, political, and faith-based sectors. Mixing in his years of experience leading E-commerce programs for Fortune 100 companies like The Coca Cola Company, Kimberly Clark, and General Mills, his passion is to ensure that the brand messaging resonates with the audience to drive revenue to the next level.

His life involves Jesus at the center, and a wife and two young children. He worked to help The Village Church establish a social strategy to further expand their reach of their ministry and make a personal impact for many on those channels. His purpose in his career is to be Kingdom-focused with everything, knowing that every dollar he can bring in for ministries is a dollar stretched for the sake of the Gospel.

Brian Tucker, Senior Director
Blue North Strategies
Email: brian.tucker@bluenorth.ca
LinkedIn: www.linkedin.com/in/brianwtucker
Website: www.bluenorth.ca

Brian has more than 19 years of experience in nonprofit fundraising and marketing, and has worked for agencies such as Russ Reid, TrueSense, and DDB Seattle. He also spent more than five years on the client side working for World Vision.

His talents range from traditional direct response, gift catalog programs, digital and social media marketing, video, and content marketing.

In 2014 he started FOCUSED, a consulting firm specializing in nonprofit innovation and program development. Working with more than 15 clients in just 4 years, Brian and his partner Natalie Parker were able to develop successful and innovative solutions for both national and local nonprofit organizations. In January 2019 FOCUSED was acquired by Blue North Strategies, where Brian serves as the Senior Director of Client Services. Brian is a frequent speaker at the DMA Nonprofit Conference in New York. In his spare time, he competes in various road, cyclocross, and mountain biking events in the Pacific Northwest.

Erica Waasdorp, President
A Direct Solution
Email: erica.adirectsolution@gmail.com
LinkedIn: www.linkedin.com/in/erica-waasdorp-544b74
Website: www.adirectsolution.com

Erica founded *A Direct Solution* in December of 2003 with more than 20 years of experience in direct marketing. ADS provides part-time fundraising executive support to organizations and manages events, writes grants, and focuses on annual fund campaigns and monthly giving. Before starting her own business, Erica was Vice President of Fundraising at DMW Direct. On the client side, she was with the International Fund for Animal Welfare (IFAW) for seven years, last as Marketing Manager of Planned/Committed Giving. Prior to working at IFAW, she worked with several companies in the Netherlands, including *Reader's Digest,* Kluwer Academic Publishers, and Reed Elsevier Seminars.

Erica writes, edits, and advises various direct marketing and national and international fundraising publications. She is a Certified Master Trainer for the Association of Fundraising Professionals, and a sought-after speaker and webinar presenter. Erica is very active in her local community with many service and fundraising organizations. She has authored numerous books and resources, including *Monthly Giving—The Sleeping Giant*, the DonorPerfect Monthly Giving Starter Kit, and The Monthly Giving Marketing Kit. She created the Monthly Donor Road Map, as well as e-books *Top 7 Questions on Monthly Giving*, and *The Monthly Donor Retention Playbook*. Erica speaks four other languages besides English: Dutch, German, French, and Spanish. She is the US Ambassador to the IFC Congress, Noordwijk, the Netherlands.

Greg Warner, President
MarketSmart
Email: gregmarketsmart@gmail.com
LinkedIn: www.linkedin.com/in/gregmarketsmart
Website: imarketsmart.com

Greg Warner is CEO and Founder of MarketSmart, a revolutionary marketing software and services firm that helps nonprofits raise more for less. In 2012 Greg coined the phrase "Engagement Fundraising" to encapsulate his breakthrough fundraising formula for achieving extraordinary results. Using their own innovative strategies and technologies, MarketSmart helps fundraisers around the world zero in on the donors most ready to support their organizations and institutions with major and legacy gifts. Greg is the author of *Engagement Fundraising: How to raise more money for less in the 21st century.*

about overall site performance, and about key segments like first-time donors, repeat donors, and monthly donors.

For site performance, we recommend tracking every main content page and every blog post or video to understand volume of visitors to each page, if those pages play a part in progressing users to donation forms or content download forms, and which content drives the highest-value donors for the organization. Take the guesswork out of your marketing and fundraising efforts, and take the campaign-based report of assuming it was this campaign or that campaign. Why did they give? What was their history?

Then, once they give, understanding what you're likely to need next before giving again and at an increased amount is of paramount importance. Amazon groups segments together by the millions to know that when you buy this product, you will also likely be interested in this other product. They don't even hide their data from the user or deny that they know this about you and about what other consumers have purchased after buying the product that caught your attention. It's called "scaling the cart" and is displayed right within the product page.

Having data marry up with good, solid digital practices and design techniques is the winning combination that every organization should seek. Data doesn't only come from the digital side. Understanding every donor's interaction with direct mail, digital, telemarketing (if applicable), major donor engagements, and even volunteer history can play a significant part in driving your program to levels you've never seen before.

We wish you the best of luck and happy data gathering!

---

[1] Thomas, Lauren, and Courtney Reagan. "Watch out, Retailers. This Is Just How Big Amazon Is Becoming." *Www.cnbc.com*, 13 July 2018, www.cnbc.com/2018/07/12/amazon-to-take-almost-50-percent-of-us-e-commerce-market-by-years-end.html.